A GUIDE TO
EVERYONE'S
PERSONALITY

A GUIDE TO
EVERYONE'S
PERSONALITY

Michael Davies

Davies Personality Profile Limited

Published by Davies Personality Profile Limited,
125 Pinks Hill, Swanley, Kent, BR8 8NP, UK

First published 2010

ISBN 978-0-9562047-0-7

British Library Cataloguing in Publication Data.
A catalogue record for this book is available from the British Library.

Typeset in 11pt Book Antiqua by Troubador Publishing Ltd, Leicester, UK
Printed in Great Britain by the MPG Books Group, Bodmin and King's Lynn

Acknowledgements

This book owes a great deal to the ideas and research of Carl Jung, Raymond B Cattell and The Gallup Organization. I have been very fortunate in learning from many highly insightful biographies and autobiographies of the highest quality, many of which are listed at the end of this book in *Further reading*. My editor, Kathryn Davies, has commented in detail on every stage of this book. Her many invaluable suggestions have greatly improved every aspect of this book.

Contents

Introduction

Personal relationships take up much of our time at work. We are constantly being assessed or making judgements about people. On the basis of these judgements, we have to take vital decisions. Organisations and careers succeed or fail depending on the quality of the decisions made about people. Good decisions about people at work significantly improve performance and increase profit. Bad decisions about people at work are very expensive in time and money. Opportunities are lost and relationships at work damaged. We all need to know ourselves and understand others. We need to understand our own and other people's personalities. Fortunately, our personalities consist of recognisable characteristics. With practice and experience, these can be understood and identified.

This book provides many unique insights into everyone's personality and supplies:

- Individuals with the knowledge to take the right decisions for themselves and about other people
- Organisations with a comprehensive personality assessment system for employee recruitment, placement and promotion
- A straightforward system for the creation of highly effective organisations

It is a resource no organisation can afford to ignore. The time, effort and money spent on understanding personality will repay itself countless times in better performance, reduced costs and increased profit.

Everyone is very busy. Consequently, the ideas in this book are explained as simply as possible. The language is straightforward and non-technical. There are many diagrams and tables which emphasise the key points. The best way to understand personality is with a combination of theory, examples and practice. In this work, there are numerous examples of personality based on real people. For the most part, these examples are taken from the lives of famous historical individuals.

The chapters are intended to be read in order from the beginning. It is certainly easiest to start at Chapter 1 and read each of the following chapters in turn, because later chapters use ideas explained earlier in the book. An essential aim of this book is to show how we can apply our understanding of personality to improve significantly our decisions at work. At the end of most chapters, there are summaries and suggestions for practical exercises which may help you to remember and use the ideas. However, the use of this material is optional and your choice.

The contents of this work apply equally to the personalities of men and women. Taken as a whole, there are some differences of emphasis between men's and women's personalities, but, in this book, we are dealing with men and women as individuals and not groups. It cannot be stressed too strongly that in understanding personality we are not judging the merits of an individual's personality. One kind of personality is neither better nor worse than another. Our personalities are just different. This is a point of fundamental importance.

A note on British titles

From time to time, we study, among many others, the personality of some distinguished British citizens. Some of these individuals were awarded aristocratic or other titles, sometimes towards the end of their lives. Since this book is intended for an international audience, these titles, which are not generally granted elsewhere in the Western World, are not used. Consequently, Sir Winston Churchill (1874–1965), Britain's famous wartime Prime Minister (1940–45), is described as plain Winston Churchill and his distinguished wartime Chief of Staff is introduced as Alan Brooke (1883–1963), rather than Field Marshal Alanbrooke of Brookeborough, 1st Viscount. The reason is one of international consistency and simplicity. There is no disrespect intended, and, in any event, their great achievements speak for themselves.

CHAPTER 1

The sociability disposition

This book is about understanding ourselves and other people. We shall spend our time studying personality, which describes our nature. Our personalities reveal the ways in which we are the same or different from each other. We shall explain and illustrate both our distinctiveness and similarities. Our personality identifies our character.

We now introduce our first key concept, which is our definition of personality.

PERSONALITY is a description of a person's character which reveals both similarities and differences to other individuals.

These key concepts are repeated at the end of each chapter under 'Key Points'. They are also included in a glossary at the end of the book.

Our personalities are very complicated. In order to make progress with our understanding, we need to consider personality one step at a time. Fortunately, this approach is possible, because our personality has a structure. We start with the first part of the structure.

THE PERSONALITY DISPOSITIONS

In describing and explaining personality, it is necessary to define and use a number of new concepts. 'Personality dispositions' is one of these new concepts, although, from now on, we generally refer to 'dispositions'. They are universal features of everyone's personality. The five personality dispositions are:

- Sociability
- Emotion
- Ambition
- Curiosity
- Uncertainty

PERSONALITY DISPOSITIONS are five universal characteristics of personality and consist of sociability, emotion, ambition, curiosity and uncertainty.

We start by looking at the sociability disposition.

THE SOCIABILITY DISPOSITION

We are all sociable. To a greater or lesser extent, we all need company. Nobody can cope either physically or mentally with prolonged, complete isolation. For our own wellbeing, it is essential to have sufficient contact with other people. Our need for at least some day-to-day companionship is one of our shared features. Sociability is one of the universal characteristics of our personality and is, therefore, a disposition.

Individuals vary greatly in the amount of social contact that they need. Some people are only happy when they are with companions. They are always with others and even fear being alone. Other people are content to spend lots of time by themselves occupied with their own tasks, provided they have some day-to-day contact with colleagues, friends or family. The extent of people's sociability is an important distinguishing characteristic of their personalities.

The SOCIABILITY DISPOSITION describes the extent to which people spend their time associating with companions.

Some people are above average in their sociability, while other people are below average. In a work context, those who are above average in their sociability spend time talking with other people. They like to cooperate together in teams. They work with others to solve problems and propose solutions. Their discussions raise their productivity and that of their colleagues. Consequently, those with above average sociability seek out and enjoy the company of others.

Other people work better by themselves and are below average in their sociability. They are most productive at individual tasks and thought. They find their own solutions. Attempted contributions from others tend to confuse them. Once people with below average sociability have clarified their thoughts, they can go back to the others with their conclusions. They may even have solved the problem.

Many jobs make consistent demands. Depending on these requirements, different jobs attract people with different sorts of personalities. In most organisations, there is a front office which deals with customers and a back office which deals with production or administration. Those who have above average sociability often choose the front office. A typical example of a job for these people is that of sales staff who meet frequently with customers. In the back office, we tend to find the person with below average sociability. A typical example is of finance executives who need time alone to prepare the financial statements. When we say people in the back office work by themselves, we do not mean that they are physically isolated. Rather, their work involves mainly thinking by themselves instead of discussing matters with colleagues. To summarise, in a work context, people who have above average sociability seek opportunities which involve, for example, teamwork or meeting people. Individuals who have below average sociability choose work which enables them to work largely by themselves.

The sociability disposition is a scale which measures sociability. We can use a line to represent the sociability disposition, which increases from below average on the left hand side of the line to above average on the right hand side (see Fig. 1.1).

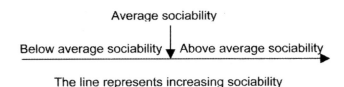

The line represents increasing sociability

Fig. 1.1 A line representing the sociability disposition

People located near the left hand end of the line spend much of their time occupied with their own thoughts. They have very low sociability. People located near the right hand end of the line spend much of their time associating with other people. They have very high sociability. People located near the middle of the line spend approximately an average amount of time occupied with their own thoughts and an average amount of time associating with others. They are more flexible in their sociability than those near the left or right end. However, individuals near the middle are less able to work for long periods either by themselves or with others. We can add the information in this paragraph to a line representing increasing sociability (see Fig. 1.2).

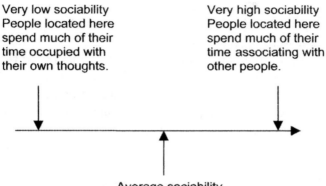

Very low sociability
People located here
spend much of their
time occupied with
their own thoughts.

Very high sociability
People located here
spend much of their
time associating with
other people.

Average sociability
People located here spend approximately
an average amount of time occupied with
their own thoughts or associating with
other people. However, these individuals
are less able to work for long periods either
by themselves or with others.

Note: as people are located further away from the left hand
end of the line, their actions become increasingly sociable.

Fig. 1.2 Locations on the sociability disposition

We now give descriptions of very high sociability and very low sociability which are taken from the lives of many individuals. These descriptions help us to identify the aspects of personality which come within this disposition. We start with very high sociability, because it is more noticeable.

Very high sociability

People with very high sociability are nearly always in the company of others whether at a committee, club, social occasion or family gathering. Nearly all their time is spent talking and chatting. It is the way they achieve results and find satisfaction. They may even seem to fear being by themselves. For example, on a long journey, they do their utmost to ensure that they do not travel alone. They start conversations with strangers.

At work, they are found cooperating in teams or talking to other people. They are most productive when working closely in the company of colleagues and associates. They are good at exchanging and generating ideas with other people. Their answer to a business problem is to set up a committee or arrange a meeting. They thrive on discussions. They enjoy meeting and working with colleagues or the public. They spend their lunch breaks in conversation. After work or at the weekend, they relax with colleagues, friends and family.

As managers, they are convinced of the value of team working. Their recollection of past achievements is very much a memory of the relationships with colleagues which made success possible. They seek business and commercial inspiration and improvements by talking and listening. If they need information or advice, they arrange to meet experts. They like to combine their business and private lives. They celebrate successes by arranging staff parties and company trips. In their private lives, they entertain often and go out frequently. They enjoy parties. They are always ready to take part in social events. Friendships are highly valued. They are often entertaining conversationalists with many interesting stories and anecdotes.

Very low sociability

People with very low sociability nearly always work by themselves. Tasks are performed as an individual, which is their way to achieve results. They do their best to avoid spending much time associating with other people. They even seem to fear social gatherings. On a long journey, they travel alone. At work, they are found in jobs which must be done individually. They are most productive when working by themselves. They enjoy working at their computer and correspond with colleagues by email. They read during their lunch break rather than spending time with colleagues. If they leave the workplace during their lunch break, they go for a walk by themselves. They dislike meetings, which they regard as largely a waste of time. If they have to meet other people, they choose a series of one-to-one meetings rather than seeing the whole team. They avoid meeting and working with the public.

As managers, they regard committees as an excuse for idle conversation which achieves very little. Their recollection of past successes is very much of individual effort. They seek inspiration by privately reflecting on their problems. If they need information, they will individually search the internet or study the literature. They very rarely mix their private and business lives. They make excuses to miss staff parties and celebrations.

In their private lives, they do not entertain, except for family, and do not go to parties. They avoid chatting with neighbours and lack gossip. They do not start conversations with strangers. Other than their family, they have no close friends. Their hobbies are typically walking with a spouse, fishing by themselves or playing computer games alone.

Very low sociability, very high sociability and average sociability are summarised in Fig. 1.3.

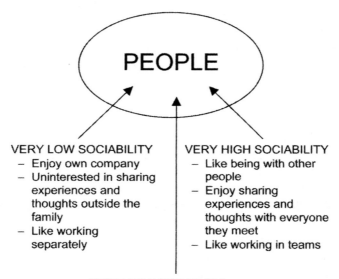

Fig. 1.3 Very low sociability, very high sociability and average sociability

CONCLUSION

People with very high sociability spend long periods of time meeting, talking and sharing their thoughts and experiences with others. Very low sociability is identified by long periods working alone on individual tasks. However, people with very low sociability are full members of society. They belong to a family, but need a great deal of time by themselves.

A successful military commander or politician is very likely to demonstrate above average sociability. Receptionists, for example, are also likely to have this characteristic. Generally speaking, university researchers and long-distance lorry drivers have below average sociability. There are always exceptions to generalisations of this kind. For example, a successful university research scientist can have above average sociability and work by discussing and arguing with colleagues.

So far, our descriptions of sociability have been rather limited. We have talked about people who are average, above average or very high in their sociability or who are below average or very low in their sociability. We will eventually need more precise concepts for our descriptions of personality. However, for the time being, we will be content with concepts like below average, very low, above average or very high. Until Chapter 15, we will not worry unduly about the exact meaning of these concepts. At that point, we will learn the concepts and their definitions which will enable us to describe personality more accurately.

We have looked at the sociability disposition by itself. We have not considered how other aspects of personality could affect sociability. In taking this approach, we are assuming people are much simpler than they really are. However, until we have completely described the structure of personality, we cannot consider people in their full complexity.

KEY POINTS

PERSONALITY is a description of a person's character which reveals both similarities and differences to other individuals. PERSONALITY DISPOSITIONS are five universal characteristics of personality and consist of sociability, emotion, ambition, curiosity and uncertainty.

The SOCIABILITY DISPOSITION describes the extent to which people spend their time associating with companions.

IMPORTANT

The following tasks are optional and at your own risk. Increased knowledge and self-knowledge can be a disturbing experience.

YOUR NOTES (OPTIONAL AT YOUR OWN RISK)

How would you describe your sociability disposition? For example, are you below average, above average or average?

What evidence are you using?
Note: evidence in the context of these questions, and the questions at the end of later chapters, can be either past facts or your expectations as regards your future conduct.

IMPORTANT

In answering the next question and later questions about other people in this and later chapters, you should ensure that the person you are describing, if alive, cannot be identified from your answer. This is necessary to avoid any legal difficulties.

Do you know anyone personally or by reputation who is below average in the sociability disposition?

What evidence are you using?

Do you know anyone personally or by reputation who is above average in the sociability disposition?

What evidence are you using?

How would you describe your manager's or other appropriate individual's sociability disposition?

What evidence are you using?

FURTHER NOTES

CHAPTER 2

The emotion disposition

We all react to what happens around us. In response to either other people or events, we experience a whole range of emotions, for example joy, sorrow, anger, happiness, fear and surprise. Individuals vary significantly in the intensity of their emotions. Some people openly display their intense pleasure, irritation, satisfaction or frustration, even over minor matters. These people may cry easily or resort to thumping the table in annoyance. If they are pleased or disappointed, their delight or anger is often plain for all to see. As managers, they motivate their teams by shows of passion and temper. They can be described as highly demonstrative, excitable and fiery.

Other people's reactions are much less visible. They can be described as calm, dispassionate, even-tempered and equable. These people rarely lose their tempers and are not very demonstrative. Even a major setback or close personal loss seems to leave them largely unmoved. From their appearance, it is sometimes very difficult to know whether triumph or disaster has affected them. As managers, they motivate their teams by deliberate, even-tempered and unflappable behaviour. They may be described as placid, cool and impassive.

As we can see, there is no shortage of words to describe

emotion. The essential point is that everyone has reactions to
other people and events, but the intensity of these reactions
varies widely. This aspect of personality is described and
measured by the emotion disposition.

**The EMOTION DISPOSITION describes the strength of
people's reactions in response to either other people
or events.**

The emotion disposition is also a scale which measures the
strength of emotion. As previously with the sociability
disposition, we can use a line to represent the emotion
disposition, which increases from below average on the left
hand side of the line to above average on the right hand side
(see Fig. 2.1).

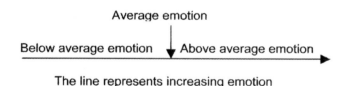

The line represents increasing emotion

Fig. 2.1 The emotion disposition

People located near the left hand end of the line respond
on most occasions in a calm manner. They have very low
emotion. People located near the right hand end of the line
respond on most occasions in a passionate manner. They have
very high emotion. People located near the middle of the line
respond in a calm or passionate manner depending on the
circumstances. They are more flexible in their reactions than
those near either end. These individuals are more likely to

vary their reactions according to their perceptions of the seriousness of the issues. The information in this paragraph can be added to a line representing increasing emotion (see Fig. 2.2).

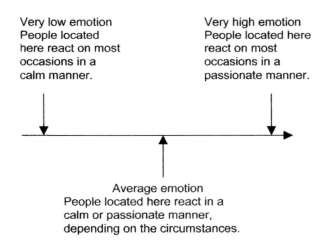

Very low emotion
People located
here react on most
occasions in a
calm manner.

Very high emotion
People located here
react on most
occasions in a
passionate manner.

Average emotion
People located here react in a
calm or passionate manner,
depending on the circumstances.

Note: as people are located further away from
the left hand end of the line, their reactions
become increasingly emotional.

Fig. 2.2 Locations on the emotion disposition

We now describe very high and very low emotion. We start with very high emotion, because it is more noticeable.

Very high emotion

People with very high emotion are deeply moved by events. They use words like 'catastrophe', 'fury', 'disaster' and 'triumph' as descriptions. Their feelings about the world range from ecstasy to grief. They are people of passionate beliefs. They are elated by outcomes they support and bitterly condemn outcomes they oppose. They cry readily. They are easily moved to elation or despair. In short, they have, compared to other people, exaggerated and extravagant reactions. Nevertheless, their very high emotion can give them great energy and dynamism.

At work, they have passionate views on the way forward. If opposed or criticised in meetings, they lose their temper and become angry. If they feel let down or betrayed, they respond with great feeling. When they are supported by others, they are very grateful. Their attitudes to colleagues range between intense liking and disliking. They have the passion to inspire or terrify others. If frustrated in their objectives, they can be perpetually angry, which, in some circumstances, can lead to violence. Their strongly expressed business opinions reveal the great intensity of their feelings.

The same pattern is visible in their private lives. Domestic difficulties lead to huge emotional outbursts. Their attitudes switch from great affection to deep anger even over minor matters. Their feelings of betrayal are expressed with passion. Again, the intensity of their feelings may lead to furious tempers or even violence to family, friends and neighbours. Their views are strongly felt and are expressed with great conviction. Their personal relationships reveal intense feelings which range from respect and admiration to loathing and enmity.

Very low emotion

People with very low emotion are largely unmoved by crises, even when their lives are threatened. They retain their composure even in times of general panic and disorder. They use unemotional words to describe events. Their views about the world are cool, calm and collected. They rarely reveal strong feelings. They are largely unmoved by the outcome of events, whether favourable or adverse. They do not often express great joy or anger.

At work, they do not stir up controversies. They are not emotionally attached to business actions. Consequently, they will review and change previous decisions. Managers with very low emotion are self-possessed at meetings and able to listen to opposing views without any displays of anger. Disputes do not become personal. They do not respond to confrontations with furious outbursts or by fierce criticism. They do not allow business differences to affect their personal relationships with other managers. They do not lose their tempers with colleagues or resort to violence. Their composed attitudes reflect their calmness.

The same pattern is seen in their private lives. Even major domestic upsets do not result in passionate outbursts. They remain even tempered and rarely provoke family and friends. They are reasonable in their attitudes and do not express passionate convictions. They do not let differences within the family or between friends turn into emotional disputes.

Very low emotion, very high emotion and average emotion are summarised in Fig. 2.3.

CONCLUSION

The wisdom of an emotional or unemotional response depends on the circumstances. We cannot say in advance which kind of reaction is preferable. For example, emotional reactions may lead to good or bad outcomes. In times of crisis, passion can inspire great deeds. Equally, excessive emotion in the form of hysteria can lead to disaster. Strong emotions may

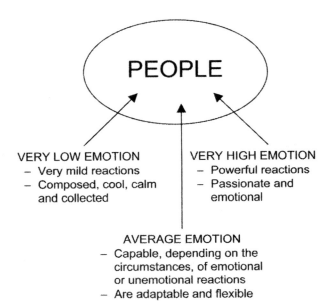

Fig. 2.3 Very low emotion, very high emotion and average emotion

make a bad situation very much worse. In some circumstances, an unemotional reaction may help a difficult situation. The calm consideration of a problem may result in a better solution. However, very low emotion also has drawbacks. It may result in an insufficient response or even inaction, which may equally lead to disaster. Both emotional and unemotional reactions have their advantages.

KEY POINTS

The EMOTION DISPOSITION describes the strength of people's reactions in response to either other people or events.

YOUR NOTES (OPTIONAL AT YOUR OWN RISK)

How would you describe your emotion disposition? For example, are you below average, above average or average?

What evidence are you using?

Do you know anyone personally or by reputation who is below average in the emotion disposition?

What evidence are you using?

Do you know anyone personally or by reputation who is above average in the emotion disposition?

What evidence are you using?

How would you describe your manager's or other appropriate individual's emotion disposition?

What evidence are you using?

FURTHER NOTES

CHAPTER 3

The ambition disposition

A striking characteristic of some people is their determination to succeed. They want to achieve something significant. They have ambitions. One common ambition is to earn more money by accepting greater responsibility at work. Without some ambition, individuals would accomplish little or nothing. However, people differ significantly in their levels of ambition. Some are driven by a sense of destiny. They believe that they are, in some sense, chosen to do great things in the world. Success is all-important to them. Nearly all of their efforts are directed at realising their goals, often concentrating on these to the exclusion of everything else. Other people have rather different objectives. They want time to spend at their ease, perhaps doing nothing at all. They are satisfied with a barely adequate performance at work. They settle for goals that are easy to attain. Even if they fail in these efforts, it is of no great consequence to them.

The AMBITION DISPOSITION describes the strength of people's determination to achieve something.

The ambition disposition is also a scale which measures the

degree of ambition. As with all the other dispositions, a line can be used to represent ambition, which increases from below average on the left hand side of the line to above average on the right hand side (see Fig. 3.1).

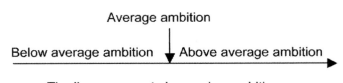

The line represents increasing ambition

Fig. 3.1 The ambition disposition

People located near the left hand end of the line have little determination to achieve their modest goals. They have very low ambition. People located near the right hand end of the line have considerable determination to achieve their substantial goals. They have very high ambition. Those located near the middle of the line have average determination to achieve their ordinary goals. The information in this paragraph can be added to a line representing increasing ambition (see Fig. 3.2).

We now describe very high and very low ambition. We start with very high ambition, because it is more noticeable.

Very high ambition

People with very high ambition put the greatest possible priority on achieving success in their chosen field. They have to be first. Their team has to win. Their performance has to be excellent. They have an overwhelming need for recognition and financial or career success. They are driven by a sense of personal destiny. They sometimes see themselves as servants

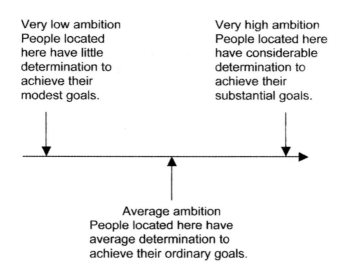

Very low ambition
People located
here have little
determination to
achieve their
modest goals.

Very high ambition
People located here
have considerable
determination to
achieve their
substantial goals.

Average ambition
People located here have
average determination to
achieve their ordinary goals.

Note: as people are located further away from the left hand
end of the line, their goals and efforts become larger.

Fig. 3.2 Locations on the ambition disposition

of providence, following divine guidance or realising the laws
of history. They believe they can make a difference and
personally save the company, country or even the world.
Above all, they want to be a person of consequence, someone
who matters. They are determined to be widely
acknowledged as having achieved something of lasting
importance.

At work, they wish to rise to the top of their organisation.
In business, their aim is to be the chairperson or chief
executive officer. In any event, they are determined to be
promoted as high as their talents can take them. Their careers
totally dominate their lives. They rarely have holidays. If they
do, they bring work with them and stay in close touch with
the office by email and phone. They are prepared to do

everything and anything which is necessary for success. Early in their careers, they take every opportunity to impress senior managers with their knowledge, abilities and wide-ranging understanding of work issues. They are prepared to take decades to achieve their goals.

Their private and family lives come second. Career commitments take precedence over family occasions. If necessary, family celebrations are postponed or abandoned. Even in their hobbies, they play to win. They will give up pastimes where they lack the talent to come first.

Very low ambition

People with very low ambition are content with their present circumstances. They do not compare themselves with others. They do not see the need to improve their situation or environment. They accept things as they are. Urgent tasks and jobs can be done tomorrow, next week or not at all. They wish to be recognised just for being themselves. They are happy to do little.

At work, they are satisfied with their existing occupation. They do just enough to keep their manager or supervisor from complaining. They work the basic week and refuse overtime unless seriously short of money. They want a quiet life and will turn down offers of promotion or more responsibility. As soon as they finish work, they do not give their job a second thought.

At home, they are content to sit and look. Household chores are repeatedly postponed unless absolutely unavoidable. As long as there is sufficient money for essentials, everything is fine. Their hobbies are for fun. It is of no consequence to them if they play badly, lose or come last in competitions.

Very low ambition, very high ambition and average ambition are summarised in Fig. 3.3.

Fig. 3.3 Very low ambition, very high ambition and average ambition

Distinguishing very low emotion from very low ambition
We need to be very careful to distinguish very low emotion from very low ambition. Ordinary language tends to confuse very low emotion with very low ambition. The incorrect conclusion is that very low emotion and very low ambition are somehow connected. For example, we talk of people having easy-going attitudes and a relaxed way of life. This description could equally well apply to people with very low emotion or to people with very low ambition. People with very low emotion appear relaxed or easy-going, because they generally react calmly. People with very low ambition appear relaxed or easy-going, because they are content with their situation.

We describe people with very low emotion and people with very low ambition with the same words, but the reasons behind the outwardly similar attitudes are very different in each case. In reality, a person with very low emotion and a relaxed way of life can have either very high or very low ambition. It is possible to combine a great determination to succeed with an easy-going way of life. People who are both very low in emotion and very high in ambition can, and do, perform outstandingly well at the highest level. They can sometimes succeed with remarkably little effort. One reason is that they are willing, and able, to delegate work to other people.

PRINCIPLE OF AUTONOMY

We have seen in the previous section that people can combine very low emotion with very low or very high ambition. This outcome is an example of the principle of autonomy. We first look at this principle in the context of the dispositions. This principle states that the five dispositions are independent of each other. Thus, the fact that people are very low in emotion tells us nothing about their level of ambition. These people could equally well be very low or very high in ambition. They could also be very low or very high in sociability. We cannot say. The principle of autonomy means that you cannot predict a person's location on one disposition from that person's location on another disposition.

> The PRINCIPLE OF AUTONOMY states that the five dispositions are independent of each other. A person's location on one disposition cannot be predicted from that person's location on another disposition.

CONCLUSION

Nothing can be achieved without ambition. However, we cannot say in advance whether an individual's very high ambition will lead to good or bad outcomes. It all depends on the circumstances. On many occasions, ambition has contributed to business success or to the wellbeing of society or individuals. Nevertheless, there are examples of where excessive ambition has brought about the collapse of a business.

KEY POINTS

The AMBITION DISPOSITION describes the strength of people's determination to achieve something.
The PRINCIPLE OF AUTONOMY states that the five dispositions are independent of each other. A person's location on one disposition cannot be predicted from that person's location on another disposition.

YOUR NOTES (OPTIONAL AT YOUR OWN RISK)

How would you describe your ambition disposition? For example, are you below average, above average or average?

What evidence are you using?

Do you know anyone personally or by reputation who is below average in the ambition disposition?

What evidence are you using?

Do you know anyone personally or by reputation who is above average in the ambition disposition?

What evidence are you using?

How would you describe your manager's or other appropriate individual's ambition disposition?

What evidence are you using?

FURTHER NOTES

CHAPTER 4

The curiosity disposition

Everybody asks questions, and we can be interested in almost anything, whether concerning ourselves or the world around us. A desire to know what we are and where we came from is shared by most people. A questioning attitude is one of our characteristics and is seen in children. Our inquisitiveness increases knowledge by asking questions which demand an answer. We are all curious.

> **The CURIOSITY DISPOSITION describes the strength of people's determination to learn and understand more by asking questions and seeking answers.**

The curiosity disposition is also a scale which measures the extent of a person's curiosity. As with all the other dispositions, we can use a line to represent the curiosity disposition, which increases from below average on the left hand side of the line to above average on the right hand side (see Fig. 4.1).

People located near the left hand end of the line ask few questions and make only small efforts to find answers. They have very low curiosity. People located near the right hand

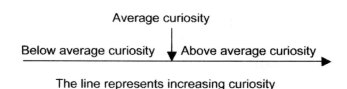

The line represents increasing curiosity

Fig. 4.1 The curiosity disposition

end of the line are very inquisitive and make great efforts to find answers. They have very high curiosity. Those located near the middle of the line are prepared to put in an approximately normal effort to satisfy their average inquisitiveness. The information in this paragraph can be added to a line representing increasing curiosity (see Fig. 4.2).

We now describe very high curiosity and very low curiosity. We start with very high curiosity, because it is more noticeable.

Very high curiosity

For people with very high curiosity, a large proportion of their decisions and actions result from asking questions and looking for answers. Their experiences provoke questions and the search for meanings, origins and causes. Their curiosity gives a goal and purpose to their lives. Their desire for answers shapes their existence; activities which are intended to discover the truth need no further justification. These people are determined to discover the answer or find the solution. The scope of the questions is without limit and can be about, for example, personal relationships, nature or technology. For the very curious, every aspect of their lives raises questions. In business, they want to know the reasons

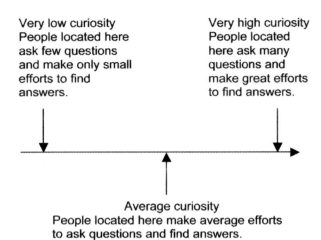

Note: as people are located further away from the left hand end of the line, their questioning and searching for answers are ever more frequent and time consuming.

Fig. 4.2 Locations on the curiosity disposition

behind the decisions that have been taken. They wonder how competitors, global markets and technological change will affect them, their colleagues or the business. In their private lives, they seek to understand their social situations and the actions of themselves and others.

Very low curiosity

People with very low curiosity ask very few questions about their companions, society or the world. They do not waste time and effort on speculation about how a situation arose or may change in the future. They do not wonder how things were formed or made. In their view, the understanding of causes and origins makes no significant contribution to decisions and actions. Everything is accepted as it is. As far as they are concerned, events just happen. At work, they reveal little questioning about how changing circumstances may affect them, their colleagues or the business. Their concern is to solve problems and to sort out difficulties undisturbed by the need to ask questions and find answers.

Very low curiosity, very high curiosity and average curiosity are summarised in Fig. 4.3.

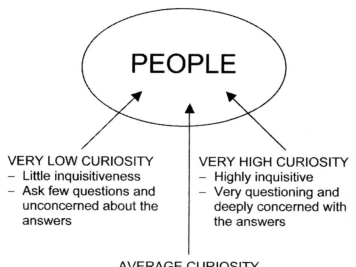

Fig. 4.3 Very low curiosity, very high curiosity and average curiosity

CONCLUSION

People with very high curiosity continually ask questions and seek answers. A very high curiosity disposition has an important impact on an individual's personality and can shape a person's life. From the business point of view, people with above average curiosity have the potential to ask many valuable questions. If these questions lead to increased knowledge, the effect on businesses can be far reaching. However, if the questioning is unproductive, a great deal of time and effort may be wasted. People with very low curiosity can use their time and efforts constructively instead of asking questions which may not contribute to solving the problem.

KEY POINTS

The CURIOSITY DISPOSITION describes the strength of people's determination to learn and understand more by asking questions and seeking answers.

YOUR NOTES (OPTIONAL AT YOUR OWN RISK)

How would you describe your curiosity disposition? For example, are you below average, above average or average?

What evidence are you using?

Do you know anyone personally or by reputation who is below average in the curiosity disposition?

What evidence are you using?

Do you know anyone personally or by reputation who is above average in the curiosity disposition?

What evidence are you using?

How would you describe your manager's or other appropriate individual's curiosity disposition?

What evidence are you using?

FURTHER NOTES

CHAPTER 5

The uncertainty disposition

People enjoy the thrills of competitions, sporting events and elections as well as the tension found in literature and films, for example in crime stories. The thrills and tension, and therefore the enjoyment, lie in the unpredictability of the outcome (which individual or team will win or whether the hero or villain will triumph). Much of the pleasure in entertainment, whether as a participant or spectator, lies in the tension created by the unpredictability of the result. Many entertainers rely on uncertainty to create tension and suspense in their audiences' minds. The entertainment's uncertain outcome maintains the audience's interest to the end. Few people find much enjoyment in watching a quiz or sporting event where the result is already known or almost certain. Any interest in watching a recorded sporting event with a known outcome is small compared to the anticipation of a live competition's result.

People vary significantly in the enjoyment they derive from the tension of competitions or of similar events with uncertain outcomes. Some find little pleasure in the tension generated by uncertainty. These people have hardly any interest in the tension of competitions either as participants or spectators. On the other hand, some lives are shaped by the great enjoyment they derive from the tension of unpredictable outcomes.

> The UNCERTAINTY DISPOSITION **describes the intensity of people's enjoyment which derives from the tension of unpredictable outcomes.**

The uncertainty disposition is also a scale which measures the amount of enjoyment people find in the tension experienced from unpredictable outcomes. We can use a line to represent the uncertainty disposition, which increases from below average on the left hand side of the line to above average on the right hand side (see Fig. 5.1).

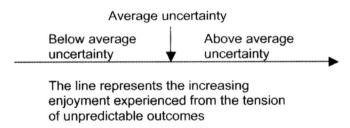

Fig. 5.1 The uncertainty disposition

People located near the left hand end of the line derive little pleasure from the tension of unpredictable outcomes. They have very low uncertainty. People located near the right hand end of the line derive great pleasure from the tension of unpredictable outcomes. They have very high uncertainty. Those located near the middle of the line derive average pleasure from the tension of unpredictable outcomes. The information in this paragraph can be added to a line representing increasing uncertainty (see Fig. 5.2).

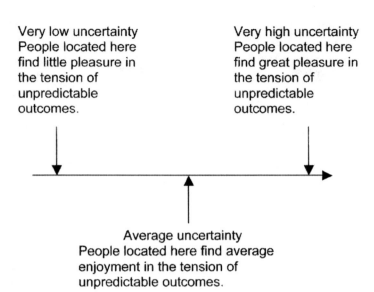

Very low uncertainty
People located here
find little pleasure in
the tension of
unpredictable
outcomes.

Very high uncertainty
People located here
find great pleasure in
the tension of
unpredictable
outcomes.

Average uncertainty
People located here find average
enjoyment in the tension of
unpredictable outcomes.

Note: as people are located further away from the left hand
end of the line, they find greater enjoyment from the tension
of unpredictable outcomes.

Fig. 5.2 Locations on the uncertainty disposition

We now describe very high uncertainty and very low
uncertainty. We start with very high uncertainty, because it is
more noticeable.

Very high uncertainty
People with very high uncertainty deliberately seek out
situations with unpredictable outcomes. Their pastimes are
hazardous sports, for example rock climbing, potholing, sky
diving and winter expeditions into desolate mountain
regions. The great attraction of hazardous pastimes for these

individuals lies in the thrill of their lives depending on some uncertain outcome. They willingly expose themselves to unpredictable dangers. Their keenest memories are of the greatest dangers they have met. They find competitions hugely stimulating, particularly those which have a close finish. For these people, the thrill of the anticipation is markedly increased by adding to the significance of the occasion. This can be achieved, for example, by creating the chance for a potentially large financial gain. Gambling is a common way of increasing the tension, and people with very high uncertainty often gamble.

They seek work which has perils and dangers. A natural choice is a career in the military or emergency services, where they volunteer for the most dangerous missions. Other attractive jobs are in politics, with the uncertainty of elections and of the striving for political office. Another possible choice is in the financial sector, where fortunes can be made or lost gambling on unpredictable market movements.

Very low uncertainty
People with very low uncertainty find little pleasure in the tension of uncertain outcomes. They believe that unnecessarily seeking danger and peril is foolish and pointless. As far as practical, they eliminate all hazards. Safety is reassuring and comfortable. Whether a sporting result is uncertain right up to the finish adds little enjoyment to the occasion.

In their work, they also avoid peril and danger. They are happiest in a safe environment, for example working in a reliable, well-established retail company. As business owners, they do not gamble the future of the business on unpredictable outcomes. In their private lives, they equally avoid uncertainty. They refuse to endanger life or suffer injury to experience thrills. They do not even consider spending money on gambling. Their hobbies, for example gardening, are safe.

Very low uncertainty, very high uncertainty and average uncertainty are summarised in Fig. 5.3.

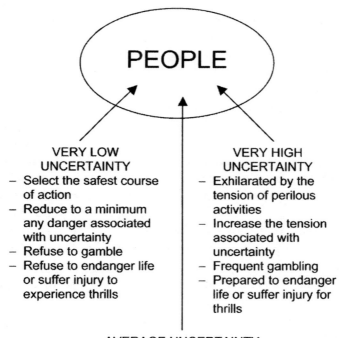

PEOPLE

VERY LOW UNCERTAINTY
- Select the safest course of action
- Reduce to a minimum any danger associated with uncertainty
- Refuse to gamble
- Refuse to endanger life or suffer injury to experience thrills

VERY HIGH UNCERTAINTY
- Exhilarated by the tension of perilous activities
- Increase the tension associated with uncertainty
- Frequent gambling
- Prepared to endanger life or suffer injury for thrills

AVERAGE UNCERTAINTY
- Seek some tension, for example as a spectator of sporting competitions
- Increase the thrill of uncertainty through slightly hazardous activities
- Some gambling
- Prepared to experience very minor injuries to increase excitement

Fig. 5.3 Very low uncertainty, very high uncertainty and average uncertainty

CONCLUSION

A very high uncertainty disposition motivates remarkable actions. The desire for thrills which is derived from very high uncertainty drives explorers and competitive sports people to the summit of achievement. It leads to ground-breaking triumphs of all kinds. Equally, the search for thrills may result in death or crippling injury. For example, the thrill of jumping off cliffs into water that is too shallow regularly causes death or lasting serious injuries to the participants.

We have now looked at the five dispositions. Our sociability is common to us all. We are all, to a greater or lesser extent, part of a community. Emotion stirs everyone into action, but some people are much more passionate than others. Ambition is another source of our actions. Ambitious individuals are determined to achieve something with their lives. Their ambition drives the others forward. Curiosity stimulates our thoughts, raising questions in our minds. Curious people do not stop until they find the answers. The enjoyment of the tension associated with uncertainty also guides our choices. People who like uncertainty seek thrills from unpredictable situations. They are not deterred by perils from pushing back the boundaries of our experience.

Our sociability, emotion, ambition, curiosity and uncertainty are universal characteristics of our personality. Since we are all curious to a degree, the question immediately arises why is sociability, emotion, ambition, curiosity and uncertainty universal to all our personalities and highly variable between individuals? The universality and variability of our dispositions must tell us something very significant about ourselves. We look at this difficult question later.

A DIAGRAM TO REPRESENT AN INDIVIDUAL'S DISPOSITIONS

We can represent an individual's dispositions by a diagram. The font size of the disposition and the thickness of the arrow on the diagram describe each disposition. The larger the font size and thicker the arrow, the higher is the disposition (see Fig. 5.4).

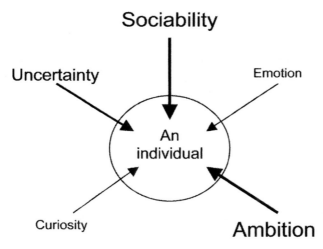

Fig. 5.4 Illustrates an individual whose personality has two very high dispositions (sociability and ambition), two very low dispositions (emotion and curiosity) and one average disposition (uncertainty)

KEY POINTS

The UNCERTAINTY DISPOSITION describes the intensity of people's enjoyment which derives from the tension of unpredictable outcomes.

YOUR NOTES (OPTIONAL AT YOUR OWN RISK)

How would you describe your uncertainty disposition? For example, are you below average, above average or average?

What evidence are you using?

Do you know anyone personally or by reputation who is below average in the uncertainty disposition?

What evidence are you using?

Do you know anyone personally or by reputation who is above average in the uncertainty disposition?

What evidence are you using?

How would you describe your manager's or other appropriate individual's uncertainty disposition?

What evidence are you using?

FURTHER NOTES

CHAPTER 6

The ways of thinking dimension

So far, we have examined the five dispositions, which are sociability, emotion, ambition, curiosity and uncertainty. Each disposition consists of one characteristic which all people have to a greater or lesser extent. For example, some people may be above average in the sociability disposition, while others may be below average in the sociability disposition. We now look at a new concept, which is called the 'personality dimensions', although we generally refer to 'dimensions'.

THE PERSONALITY DIMENSIONS

There are five personality dimensions, which are found in everyone's personality. The five dimensions are the:

- Ways of thinking
- Ways of interacting
- Ways of relating
- Social interests
- Attitudes to the future

The nature of a dimension can best be illustrated by the attitudes to the future dimension. There are two fundamentally conflicting attitudes to the future. These are either an optimistic attitude (expecting a good outcome) or a pessimistic attitude (expecting a bad outcome). Optimism and pessimism are the two conflicting attitudes or aspects within the attitudes to the future dimension. These attitudes or aspects are conflicting because you cannot at the same instant of time be both optimistic and pessimistic about the same future events.

PERSONALITY DIMENSIONS are descriptions of those parts of personality which consist of two conflicting aspects.

We can now see why each of the dimensions has a plural name. Unlike the dispositions, there are two aspects, for example optimism and pessimism, within each dimension. People have these two aspects to a greater or lesser extent. The rule is that the more people have of one aspect within a dimension, the less they have of the other. This necessarily makes dimensions more complicated than dispositions. The name for the two conflicting aspects within a dimension is 'personality traits', although we generally refer to 'traits'. The two conflicting traits within the attitudes to the future dimension are called optimistic and pessimistic.

PERSONALITY TRAITS are the two conflicting aspects within each personality dimension.

The following points can be made about the two traits in each dimension:

- The traits conflict with each other, for example

optimistic and pessimistic.
- People differ in their amounts of each trait, for example some people are mostly optimistic, while others are mostly pessimistic.
- The more people have of one trait, the less they have of the other trait.

When the traits within a dimension have a more or less equal influence, they are described as 'broadly equal' traits. For example, some individuals have optimistic and pessimistic traits which have a more or less equal influence.

> BROADLY EQUAL TRAITS within a dimension have approximately the same influence on an individual's personality.

Alternatively, one trait may have a greater influence than the other. A person may be more optimistic than pessimistic or more pessimistic than optimistic. The more influential trait is known as the 'primary' trait of the dimension.

> A PRIMARY TRAIT of a dimension is the trait of that dimension which has the greater influence on an individual's personality.

The less influential trait of a dimension is known as the 'secondary' trait.

> A SECONDARY TRAIT of a dimension is the trait of that dimension which has the lesser influence on an individual's personality.

Within each dimension, everyone who is not broadly equal in

their traits has both a primary and a secondary trait. However, in some cases, the secondary trait is weak. We come back to the attitudes to the future dimension (optimistic and pessimistic) in Chapter 10. We start with the ways of thinking dimension, which has an important effect on shaping an individual's personality.

THE WAYS OF THINKING DIMENSION

Thinking is our defining feature. We act on the basis of our thoughts. At work, home or play, we use our reasoning ability. The ways of thinking dimension describes how we, as individuals, solve problems and make decisions.

The WAYS OF THINKING DIMENSION describes how individuals solve problems and make decisions.

In the ways of thinking dimension, there are two different methods for solving problems and making decisions. These two methods are the two conflicting traits in the ways of thinking dimension. These two conflicting traits are the facts trait and the possibilities trait.

The facts trait

We can use information in order to make decisions. This is thinking by using the facts trait. When people think in this way, they take their decisions after studying the facts. They discover the significant detail before making a decision which is based on a careful consideration of this evidence. An example of thinking by using the facts trait is a finance executive who takes business decisions solely on the basis of financial information.

The FACTS TRAIT describes solving problems and making decisions by using information.

The possibilities trait

We can also make decisions by imagining and assessing alternative outcomes. This is thinking by using the possibilities trait. When people think in this way, they use their imagination to find the possible answers. They consider the likely alternative outcomes before choosing a course of action. An example of thinking by using the possibilities trait is a marketing executive who introduces new products and services by imagining and assessing customers' anticipated reactions.

The POSSIBILITIES TRAIT describes solving problems and making decisions by imagining and assessing alternative outcomes.

The facts and possibilities traits

The facts and possibilities traits conflict, because it is impossible to use both traits at the same instant of time. We cannot at the same instant of time assess information and imagine alternative outcomes.

Representing the ways of thinking dimension by a diagram

Since dimensions consist of two traits, we have to represent

IMPORTANT

For reasons of simplicity, we shall in the remainder of the book use the expression 'at the same time' to mean 'at the same instant of time'.

each dimension as a rectangle. Our first rectangle represents the ways of thinking dimension. The varying proportions of the facts trait and possibilities trait which can be found in people are represented by the space within the rectangle (see Fig. 6.1).

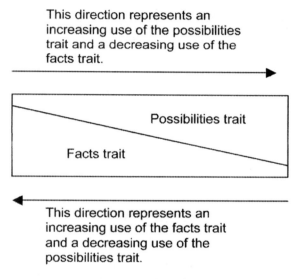

This direction represents an increasing use of the possibilities trait and a decreasing use of the facts trait.

Possibilities trait

Facts trait

This direction represents an increasing use of the facts trait and a decreasing use of the possibilities trait.

Fig. 6.1 The ways of thinking dimension

We need to represent individuals on the ways of thinking rectangle. We do this by adding vertical lines on the rectangle at specific places. As an illustration, we represent three individuals (A, B and C) on the ways of thinking rectangle (see Fig. 6.2).

The three dotted lines in Fig. 6.2 represent the three individuals (A, B and C). The dotted lines indicate visually the approximate contribution of each trait to an individual's

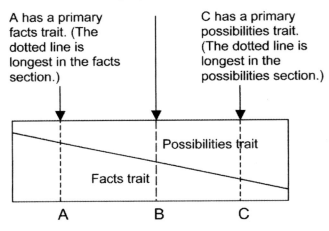

Fig. 6.2 Representing three individuals (A, B and C)
on the ways of thinking dimension

personality. For example, the dotted line that represents A is longest in the facts section. This reveals a primary facts trait, while the possibilities trait is secondary. The dotted line that represents B is equal in the facts and possibilities sections, revealing broadly equal traits. The dotted line that represents C is longest in the possibilities section. This reveals a primary possibilities trait, while the facts trait is secondary.

People located near the left hand side of the ways of thinking rectangle mostly solve problems and make decisions by using information. In this case, they have a very pronounced facts trait. People located near the right hand side of the ways of thinking rectangle mostly solve problems and make decisions by imagining and assessing alternative outcomes. In this case, they have a very pronounced possibilities trait. Those located near the middle of the rectangle are equally able to solve problems and make decisions by using information or by imagining and assessing alternative outcomes. In this case, the traits within this dimension are broadly equal. People located near the middle of the rectangle are more flexible in their ways of thinking than people from near either end. However, these more flexible individuals are less able to solve problems or make decisions by mostly using information or by mostly imagining and assessing alternative outcomes (see Fig. 6.3).

We now describe a very pronounced facts trait and a very pronounced possibilities trait. In these cases, the secondary trait is weak. These descriptions help us to identify the aspects of personality which come within this dimension and illustrate the complexity and variety in our ways of thinking.

Very pronounced facts trait

For people with a very pronounced facts trait, information is very important. Decisions have to be based on a careful consideration of the facts. For example, people with a very pronounced facts trait could not conceive of making an important decision without establishing all the relevant information. They would not consider marrying someone without collecting and analysing all the relevant details about their proposed spouse. Their decision on a future spouse has to be grounded in fact. Thus, their choice of a spouse depends on carefully considering the person's age, appearance, personality, interests, ambitions, outlook, family and cultural background and so on. If all these aspects are sufficiently

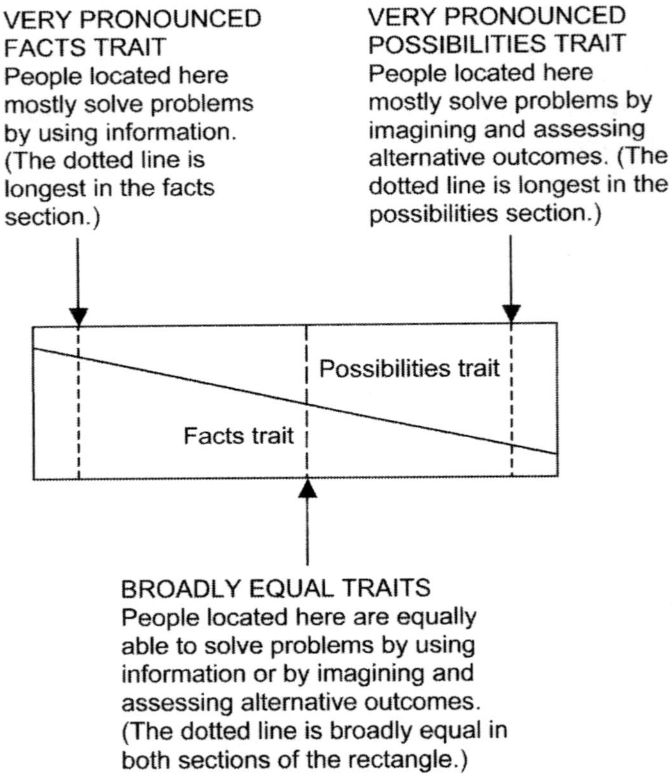

VERY PRONOUNCED
FACTS TRAIT
People located here
mostly solve problems
by using information.
(The dotted line is
longest in the facts
section.)

VERY PRONOUNCED
POSSIBILITIES TRAIT
People located here
mostly solve problems by
imagining and assessing
alternative outcomes. (The
dotted line is longest in the
possibilities section.)

Possibilities trait

Facts trait

BROADLY EQUAL TRAITS
People located here are equally
able to solve problems by using
information or by imagining and
assessing alternative outcomes.
(The dotted line is broadly equal in
both sections of the rectangle.)

Note: as people are located further away from the
central dotted line, their reasoning by one way of
thinking becomes more frequent and their
reasoning by the alternative way of thinking
becomes less frequent.

Fig. 6.3 Locations on the ways of thinking dimension

compatible (and they are also in love!), they will go ahead
with the marriage.

If challenged by friends and family to justify their
choice, individuals with a very pronounced facts trait

respond with appropriate facts. Their choice of spouse is rational and logical, because the individual is physically attractive, of the right age, has a compatible personality, shares the same hobbies, wants the same number of children and also has similar social, religious and political views. Moreover, the prospective spouse comes from a well-matched social and economic background. Both families can be expected to be comfortable with each other. In the view of a person with a very pronounced facts trait, facts are a much more reliable guide to action than any sudden insights.

When faced with difficult decisions, people with a very pronounced facts trait carefully assess all the factual arguments for and against each of the alternatives. For example, if they are considering changing their job, they may produce a list (see Table 6.1).

Table 6.1 Business facts relevant to changing job

FOR (PERSONAL OPPORTUNITIES)	AGAINST (BUSINESS SITUATION OF THE COMPANY)
1. More interesting work	1. The business is losing market share
2. More money	2. Products need updating
3. Opportunities for involvement in strategic decision making	3. Risk of strong foreign competition
4. Supply appropriate experience for move into senior management	4. New management yet to prove its worth

On the basis of the importance and number of facts in the 'For' and 'Against' columns, the decision is made. Sometimes, the list is shortened by cancelling out from each side factual arguments which are considered of approximately equal force.

Business people who have a very pronounced facts trait are straightforward to identify. They insist that the effective use of information is crucial to business success. They often place great emphasis on financial facts and figures. They demand detailed plans and statistics. They want to know precisely which parts of the business and which products are profitable. They insist that new business proposals are fully supported by detailed factual research, which they study with very great care. They want all the details on markets, customers, competitors and technology.

Scientists who have a very pronounced facts trait also have characteristic views. They assure colleagues that science consists of facts. They are convinced that if the facts of science are systematically ordered in the right way, then the general laws of nature will become obvious. In their view, scientific truth is to be found by concentrating on the patterns and regularities in facts. They place considerable emphasis on experiments to discover and test theories. In their opinion, facts drive science forward.

Very pronounced possibilities trait

People with a very pronounced possibilities trait solve problems and make decisions by forming a mental picture of possible alternative outcomes and their consequences. In their personal affairs, they imagine what their thoughts and feelings would be if certain events were to happen. For example, they may, on the basis of their previous experience, visualise a future life together with a potential spouse. They picture themselves and their proposed spouse as a married couple meeting together the challenges of marriage. On the basis of these insights, they make their choices. By these means, they decide if a particular person is a suitable spouse.

Problems are solved by freely speculating on what the answer could be. The solution is often found suddenly, when the answer forces its way uninvited into the mind. Their conscious thoughts may be elsewhere on other matters when the inspiration seizes them. People with a very pronounced possibilities trait have learned that these good ideas really do just come from nowhere. They know their inner vision can be trusted. Their insights are worth exploring.

Business people who have a very pronounced possibilities trait imagine the alternative ways forward. In their view, this mental picture can, if soundly based on experience, be turned into a new commercial reality. They can find creative solutions which are better than today's practices and assumptions. In science and technology, those scientists and inventors with a very pronounced possibilities trait can go far beyond present knowledge. A scientist who has a very pronounced possibilities trait can make fundamental breakthroughs by imagining what reality would be like if certain seemingly impossible things were true. An inventor with a very pronounced possibilities trait can put new materials and original devices together in ways that no one just assessing information would have thought possible.

Artists who have a very pronounced possibilities trait are convinced by their creative imagination. For them, their artistic solutions are valid, even if based solely on their inner visions. They know the dreams of the artist are real and meaningful. They are certain that their artistic insights do not betray them. They know when their ideas will work whether, for example, on film, in the theatre, on canvas or in literature. Justifications, reasons and explanations are pointless and unnecessary.

Very pronounced facts, very pronounced possibilities and broadly equal traits are summarised in Fig. 6.4.

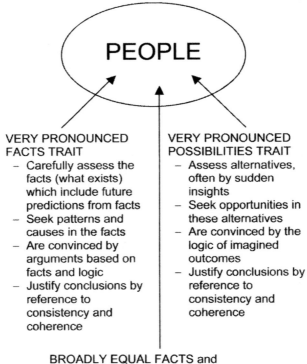

PEOPLE

VERY PRONOUNCED
FACTS TRAIT
  – Carefully assess the
    facts (what exists)
    which include future
    predictions from facts
  – Seek patterns and
    causes in the facts
  – Are convinced by
    arguments based on
    facts and logic
  – Justify conclusions by
    reference to
    consistency and
    coherence

VERY PRONOUNCED
POSSIBILITIES TRAIT
  – Assess alternatives,
    often by sudden
    insights
  – Seek opportunities in
    these alternatives
  – Are convinced by the
    logic of imagined
    outcomes
  – Justify conclusions by
    reference to
    consistency and
    coherence

BROADLY EQUAL FACTS and
POSSIBILITIES TRAITS
  – Can solve problems and make
    decisions using either the facts trait or
    possibilities trait
  – Are adaptable and flexible but are less
    able to solve problems by mostly using
    the facts trait or possibilities trait

Fig. 6.4 Very pronounced facts, very pronounced
possibilities and broadly equal traits

A DIAGRAM TO REPRESENT INDIVIDUALS

We can also use a diagram to represent an individual's ways of thinking. The font size of the facts and possibilities traits and the thickness of the arrows on the diagram reveal the strength of each trait. Accordingly, the larger the font and arrow size of one trait compared to the other, the more influential is that trait (see Figs. 6.5 and 6.6).

CONCLUSION

A primary facts trait or a primary possibilities trait is often apparent from a person's reasoning, especially the way in which an argument is presented. The key signs of a primary facts trait are arguments derived from a detailed, logical consideration of known information. Serious efforts are made to ensure that any conclusions are consistent with these facts.

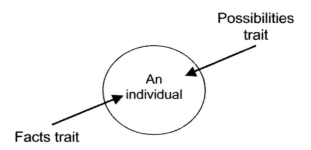

Fig. 6.5 Illustrates an individual whose personality demonstrates both the facts and possibilities traits in broadly equal proportions (the font sizes of each trait are equal). This individual is flexible and can use both traits in carrying out tasks.

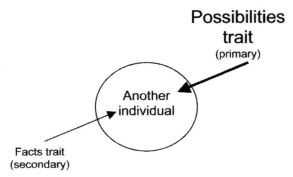

Fig. 6.6 Illustrates an individual whose personality reveals a primary trait (possibilities). The secondary trait (facts) is only slightly revealed. The primary trait enables this individual to perform certain tasks really effectively. The tasks would demand an ability to imagine and assess alternative outcomes, for example managing the marketing department in a dynamic, market-led business.

On the other hand, the key signs of a primary possibilities trait are arguments derived from imagined outcomes. Typically, the arguments start with a conclusion or answer, which is then justified by referring to previous experience. People with primary facts or primary possibilities traits can succeed in the same careers, for example in business, the creative arts, science and technology. Although we have only considered the ways of thinking dimension, we are beginning to appreciate the complexity of personality. The differing proportions of the facts and possibilities traits within individuals lead to a very large number of personalities.

KEY POINTS

PERSONALITY DIMENSIONS are descriptions of those parts of personality which consist of two conflicting aspects.

PERSONALITY TRAITS are the two conflicting aspects within each personality dimension.

BROADLY EQUAL TRAITS within a dimension have approximately the same influence on an individual's personality.

A PRIMARY TRAIT of a dimension is the trait of that dimension which has the greater influence on an individual's personality.

A SECONDARY TRAIT of a dimension is the trait of that dimension which has the lesser influence on an individual's personality.

The WAYS OF THINKING DIMENSION describes how individuals solve problems and make decisions.

The FACTS TRAIT describes solving problems and making decisions by using information.

The POSSIBILITIES TRAIT describes solving problems and making decisions by imagining and assessing alternative outcomes.

YOUR NOTES (OPTIONAL AT YOUR OWN RISK)

How would you describe your ways of thinking dimension? For example, do you have a primary facts trait, a primary possibilities trait or are you broadly equal in both traits?

What evidence are you using?

Do you know anyone personally or by reputation who has a primary facts trait?

What evidence are you using?

Do you know anyone personally or by reputation who has a primary possibilities trait?

What evidence are you using?

How would you describe your manager's or other appropriate individual's ways of thinking dimension?

What evidence are you using?

FURTHER NOTES

CHAPTER 7

The ways of interacting dimension

Present-day industrial society is highly complex. Nearly everyone is a member of one or more communities, for example a family, club, business and nation. We use the word communities to include all these types of organisations.

COMMUNITIES are any kind of organisation to which people belong.

Communities' values and objectives shape individuals, but individuals' values and objectives also shape their communities. Everyone interacts with their communities, but people can have conflicting attitudes towards their communities. For example, some people mostly put their communities' objectives and values first. They are largely guided in their behaviour by their communities' needs. Other people have a different kind of association with their communities. They are guided much more by their own objectives and values. As a consequence, these individuals take much less notice of their communities' objectives and values and place considerable emphasis on their own objectives and values.

The ways of interacting dimension identifies the differing importance attached by individuals to their communities.

The WAYS OF INTERACTING DIMENSION **describes people's attitudes towards their communities**.

There are two alternative attitudes to communities within the ways of interacting dimension. People can give priority to the objectives and values of their communities. This is called the group trait. Examples of a primary group trait are found among professional members of the armed services. They take great pride in their units and are loyal to their country and colleagues. They can be trusted to obey orders and do their duty.

The GROUP TRAIT **describes a person's interaction with communities which is based on the communities' objectives and values.**

The conflicting trait is the independent trait. People with a primary independent trait give priority to their own objectives and values. Examples of the independent trait are individuals who put their careers before the needs of their organisations.

The INDEPENDENT TRAIT **describes a person's interaction with communities which is based on that person's own objectives and values.**

You cannot be guided at the same time by your communities' objectives and values (the group trait) and your personal objectives and values (the independent trait). These two approaches are the conflicting traits within the ways of interacting dimension. As before, it helps to see the ways of interacting dimension as a rectangle. Again, the varying proportions of the group and independent traits which can be found within individuals are represented by the space within the rectangle (see Fig. 7.1).

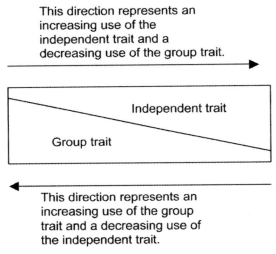

Fig. 7.1 The ways of interacting dimension

People located near the left hand side of the rectangle mostly interact with their communities on the basis of their communities' objectives. The group trait is primary, while the independent trait is secondary. People located near the right hand side of the rectangle mostly interact with their communities on the basis of their own objectives and values. The independent trait is primary, while the group trait is secondary. Those located near the middle of the rectangle interact in a group or independent manner, depending on the circumstances. They are broadly equal in their traits within this dimension and are more flexible in their ways of interacting with communities than people from near either end. As an illustration, the locations of a very pronounced group trait, a very pronounced independent trait and broadly equal traits are added to the ways of interacting rectangle (see Fig. 7.2).

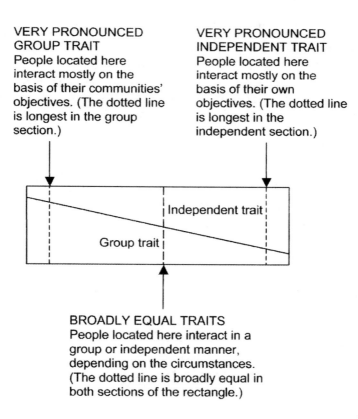

VERY PRONOUNCED GROUP TRAIT
People located here interact mostly on the basis of their communities' objectives. (The dotted line is longest in the group section.)

VERY PRONOUNCED INDEPENDENT TRAIT
People located here interact mostly on the basis of their own objectives. (The dotted line is longest in the independent section.)

Independent trait

Group trait

BROADLY EQUAL TRAITS
People located here interact in a group or independent manner, depending on the circumstances. (The dotted line is broadly equal in both sections of the rectangle.)

Note: as people are located further away from the central dotted line, their actions in one way of interacting become more frequent and their actions in the alternative way of interacting become less frequent.

Fig. 7.2 Locations on the ways of interacting dimension

We describe a very pronounced group trait and a very pronounced independent trait.

Very pronounced group trait

People with a very pronounced group trait take their identities from their communities. For them, communities are real and have a separate existence. They are happiest when furthering community objectives. They are very proud of the communities to which they belong. They believe them to be, in many ways, special, even unique. For them, the community comes first, and people should be prepared to make sacrifices on its behalf. The communities' interests come before personal interests.

Individuals who have a very pronounced group trait insist that community rules should be respected and obeyed. They support community projects and social cohesion. They are prepared to do their duty, even if the task is exceptionally unpleasant or threatens their lives. They can be trusted to further community goals and perform their community obligations reliably and conscientiously. They refuse to let down their communities or act in a way that reflects badly on their communities. They do nothing to harm their communities. They expect and demand that a community acts in that community's interests.

IMPORTANT

A very pronounced group trait can lead to either individual work or working with others. People with a very pronounced group trait who work as individuals will still be furthering group objectives in their decisions and actions. Whether people work as individuals or with others is not connected with the ways of interacting but depends on whether their sociability disposition is below average (individual working) or above average (working with others).

Very pronounced independent trait

People with a very pronounced independent trait find their identity in their own personal aims and objectives. They are self-reliant in their beliefs, opinions and priorities. They personally want to initiate action and be the source of ideas. They are happiest when furthering their own objectives. They support a community, if their own personal aims are the same as the community. They progress their own projects and are interested in social cohesion when it promotes their own goals. They may enlist the help of colleagues, friends and family to further their own purposes.

Individuals who have a very pronounced independent trait are committed to their own ideas. If it is necessary, they are prepared to disregard or even break community rules in order to pursue their own interests. They will, if possible, leave any community which significantly hinders or opposes their personal objectives. Their aims and beliefs come first, and they consider that people should be prepared to listen to their opinions. Authority exercised over them is resented and, if possible, ignored. In a hierarchy, they take little notice of the chain of command. As individuals, they demand the liberty and freedom to act according to their own personal convictions. They assert the right to disobey any orders with which they strongly disagree.

Very pronounced group, very pronounced independent and broadly equal traits are summarised in Fig. 7.3.

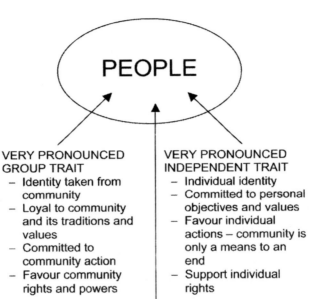

**VERY PRONOUNCED
GROUP TRAIT**
  - Identity taken from
    community
  - Loyal to community
    and its traditions and
    values
  - Committed to
    community action
  - Favour community
    rights and powers

**VERY PRONOUNCED
INDEPENDENT TRAIT**
  - Individual identity
  - Committed to personal
    objectives and values
  - Favour individual
    actions – community is
    only a means to an
    end
  - Support individual
    rights

**BROADLY EQUAL GROUP and
INDEPENDENT TRAITS**
  - Have both community and individual
    identity
  - Interact in a group or independent
    manner, depending on the
    circumstances
  - Are adaptable and flexible

Fig. 7.3 Very pronounced group, very pronounced
independent and broadly equal traits

IMPORTANT

A very pronounced independent trait can lead to either individual work or working with others. People with a very pronounced independent trait who work with others will still be furthering their own objectives in their decisions and actions. Whether people work as individuals or with others is not connected with the ways of interacting but depends on whether their sociability disposition is below average (individual working) or above average (working with others).

Distinguishing the sociability disposition from the ways of interacting dimension

As has been indicated by the previous 'Important' text boxes, the sociability disposition and the ways of interacting dimension must be carefully distinguished from each other. People who have a very high sociability disposition may identify with community objectives and values or they may pursue their own objectives and values. People who have a very low sociability disposition may pursue their own objectives and values or they may support community objectives and values. A comparison of a very high sociability disposition and a very pronounced group trait is summarised in Table 7.1. A comparison of a very low sociability disposition and a very pronounced independent trait is summarised in Table 7.2.

Table 7.1 The difference between a very high sociability disposition and a very pronounced group trait

DISPOSITION / TRAIT	PERSONALITY	ACTIONS
Very high sociability	Spend their time associating with other people	Work with others in teams
Very pronounced group	Identify very strongly with community objectives and values	Actions further community objectives and values

Table 7.2 The difference between a very low sociability disposition and a very pronounced independent trait

DISPOSITION / TRAIT	PERSONALITY	ACTIONS
Very low sociability	Spend their time by themselves	Work and think on their own
Very pronounced independent	Guided by own objectives and values	Actions further own objectives and values

A DIAGRAM TO REPRESENT INDIVIDUALS

We can also use a diagram to represent an individual's ways of interacting (see Figs. 7.4 and 7.5).

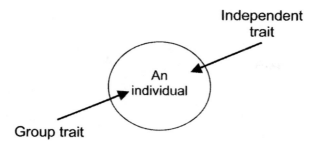

Fig. 7.4 Illustrates an individual whose personality demonstrates both the group and independent traits in broadly equal proportions. This individual is flexible and can use both traits in their dealings with communities.

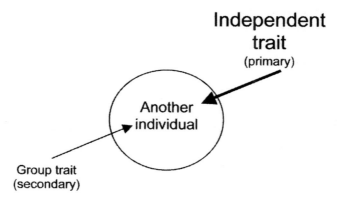

Fig. 7.5 Illustrates an individual whose personality reveals a primary trait (independent). The secondary trait (group) is only slightly revealed. The primary trait enables this individual to perform certain tasks really effectively. In this example, the tasks would demand an ability to follow one's own objectives and values.

PRINCIPLE OF AUTONOMY

We first met the principle of autonomy in Chapter 3. At that point, it only applied to dispositions. In regard to dispositions, the principle of autonomy states that the location of people on one disposition is independent of their location on any other disposition. However, the principle of autonomy also applies to dimensions. In other words, a person's location on any one dimension is independent of that individual's location on any other dimension. Consequently, we cannot predict the location of people on one dimension from their location on any other dimension. For example, people with a primary group trait are no more or less likely to have either a primary facts trait or a primary possibilities trait.

> The PRINCIPLE OF AUTONOMY applies to dimensions. People's location on one dimension cannot be predicted from their location on any other dimension. People's location on any one dimension is independent of their location on any other dimension.

Moreover, the principle of autonomy also extends to the relationships between dispositions and dimensions. A person's location on any disposition is also independent of that individual's location on any dimension and vice versa. This significantly increases the number of possible personalities.

> The PRINCIPLE OF AUTONOMY also applies to dispositions and dimensions. For example, people's location on any disposition is also independent of their location on any dimension and vice versa.

CONCLUSION

Primary group and independent traits are often apparent from people's attitudes to their communities. A key issue is one of loyalty. If people are loyal to, for example, a nation or a commercial enterprise, they have a primary group trait. Loyalty to an organisation consists of putting the organisation's objectives and values first. Personal considerations and values are secondary. A person with a primary group trait is concerned that the organisation's aims are met. In business, managers who are committed to their employer's corporate culture and vision demonstrate their primary group trait. They respect and admire the company's past and tradition. Their self-image comes from their membership of the company.

If people are committed to their individual objectives and values, they have a primary independent trait. Commitment to their own objectives and values means putting their priorities before the demands of their communities. Community obligations are less important. Individuals with a primary independent trait want their beliefs and values to prevail. In business, managers who emphasise their own objectives and values demonstrate a primary independent trait. For them, the company is a means to an end. As employees, they will change companies and seek outside opportunities at their own convenience.

There is a real danger of making incorrect judgements about the ways of interacting traits. Some people may conclude that individuals with a primary group trait are morally superior to those with a primary independent trait. They may argue that people with a primary group trait are loyal, whereas those with a primary independent trait lack loyalty. It is true that people with a very pronounced independent trait have little commitment to communities.

From this point of view, they may appear disloyal and untrustworthy. From another point of view, they are committed to their personal objectives and values. They can take the necessary but unpopular action to challenge, for example, serious mistakes being made by their community or the excessive power of their community over an individual. They can prevent great evils.

KEY POINTS

COMMUNITIES are any kind of organisation to which people belong.

The WAYS OF INTERACTING DIMENSION describes people's attitudes towards their communities.

The GROUP TRAIT describes a person's interaction with communities which is based on the communities' objectives and values.

The INDEPENDENT TRAIT describes a person's interaction with communities which is based on that person's own objectives and values.

The PRINCIPLE OF AUTONOMY:

- Applies to dimensions. People's location on one dimension cannot be predicted from their location on any other dimension. People's location on any one dimension is independent of their location on any other dimension.
- Also applies to dispositions and dimensions. For example, people's location on any disposition is also independent of their location on any dimension and vice versa.

YOUR NOTES (OPTIONAL AT YOUR OWN RISK)

How would you describe your ways of interacting dimension? For example, do you have a primary group trait, a primary independent trait or are you broadly equal in both traits?

What evidence are you using?

Do you know anyone personally or by reputation who has a primary group trait?

What evidence are you using?

Do you know anyone personally or by reputation who has a primary independent trait?

What evidence are you using?

How would you describe your manager's or other appropriate individual's ways of interacting dimension?

What evidence are you using?

FURTHER NOTES

CHAPTER 8

The ways of relating dimension

Everyone has relationships with other individuals. However, we can have very different attitudes with regard to our relationships with other individuals. For some, their own needs and feelings largely determine their attitudes and conduct in their personal relationships. Their own needs and feelings have priority over those of their companions. Other people take a very different view. Their perception of their companions' needs and feelings largely guides their attitudes and conduct. In their case, they give priority in their personal relationships to other people's needs and feelings rather than to their own.

The ways of relating dimension describes how people associate as individuals.

The WAYS OF RELATING DIMENSION describes people's priorities with regard to their dealings with other individuals.

There are two conflicting ways of relating. We call these two ways of relating the own-feelings trait and the others'-feelings trait. The own-feelings trait describes the priority given by individuals to their own needs and feelings in their personal relationships. The key issue for people with a primary own-feelings trait is how they feel about the issues and actions which relate to other individuals. They are less concerned about other people's feelings than their own. An example of a primary own-feelings trait in the workplace is when a senior executive bluntly criticises employees for their mistakes. The executive with a primary own-feelings trait accepts the distress these criticisms may cause to employees.

The OWN-FEELINGS TRAIT describes a person's relationship with other individuals in which that person's own needs and feelings take priority.

The others'-feelings trait describes the priority given by individuals to their perception of other people's needs and feelings in their personal relationships. The key issue for people with a primary others'-feelings trait is how those individuals affected by their actions and decisions will feel and respond. An example of a primary others'-feelings trait in the workplace is when an executive refuses to criticise employees for mistakes. The executive with a primary others'-feelings trait is concerned about the distress the comments may cause to employees.

The OTHERS'-FEELINGS TRAIT describes a person's relationships with other individuals in which that person's perceptions of other individuals' needs and feelings take priority.

In your relationships with another individual or individuals, you cannot at the same time give priority to your own feelings and give priority to your perception of their feelings. The own-feelings trait conflicts with the others'-feelings trait. It helps to show the ways of relating dimension as a rectangle (see Fig. 8.1).

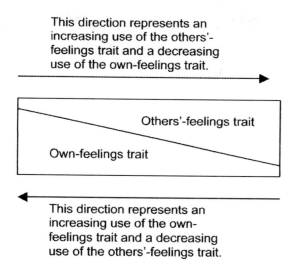

This direction represents an increasing use of the others'-feelings trait and a decreasing use of the own-feelings trait.

Others'-feelings trait

Own-feelings trait

This direction represents an increasing use of the own-feelings trait and a decreasing use of the others'-feelings trait.

Fig. 8.1 The ways of relating dimension

People located near the left hand side of the rectangle mostly relate to another person or persons by giving priority to their own feelings. The own-feelings trait is primary, while the others'-feelings trait is secondary. People located near the right hand side of the rectangle mostly relate to another person or persons by giving priority to their perception of other people's feelings. The others'-feelings trait is primary, while the own-feelings trait is secondary. Those located near the middle of the rectangle relate to another person or persons in either an own-feelings or others'-feelings manner, depending on the situation. They are broadly equal in their traits within this dimension and are more flexible in their ways of relating than people from near either end. As an illustration, the locations of a very pronounced own-feelings trait, a very pronounced others'-feelings trait and broadly equal traits are added to the ways of relating rectangle (see Fig. 8.2).

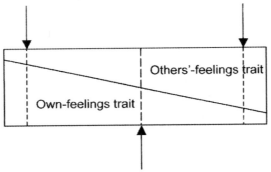

VERY PRONOUNCED
OWN-FEELINGS
TRAIT
People located here
relate to individuals
mostly on the basis of
their own feelings.

VERY PRONOUNCED
OTHERS'-FEELINGS
TRAIT
People located here relate
to individuals mostly on the
basis of their perception of
other people's feelings.

Others'-feelings trait

Own-feelings trait

BROADLY EQUAL TRAITS
People located here relate to
individuals more or less equally in
an own-feelings manner or in an
others'-feelings manner.

Note: as people are located further away from the
dotted central line, their behaviour in one way of
relating becomes more frequent and their
behaviour in the alternative way of relating
becomes less frequent.

Fig. 8.2 Locations on the ways of relating dimension

In order to understand the own-feelings and others'-feelings traits more completely, we describe a very pronounced own-feelings trait and a very pronounced others'-feelings trait.

Very pronounced own-feelings trait

People who have a very pronounced own-feelings trait talk at other people rather than with them. They discuss issues which are of interest to themselves. Their conversation is one-way, and there is no real exchange of opinions or feelings. They are chiefly aware of themselves and their concerns. The feelings experienced by other people are largely hidden from them. They have very little idea about the effects that their comments have on other people's feelings. They find other people's responses unpredictable. For this reason, they are capable of spectacular misjudgements of other people's reactions or moods. For example, as parents, they may have almost no idea of their children's real feelings about them.

People with a very pronounced own-feelings trait are impolite. They are often blunt in their comments. They are indiscreet, do not keep secrets and freely pass on personal information which they were told in confidence. Consequently, they can be very hurtful to others in their words and deeds without ever realising the fact. In their personal relationships, the truth must be told. They do not try to hide their opinions about other people. They see little reason to consider the needs and feelings of other individuals.

Since they are largely unable to empathise, they are often uncertain about the motives of companions. They frequently doubt the loyalty of friends. They are easily deceived when young. If this has happened, they are, as adults, often suspicious of those around them. For this reason, they may believe individuals can only cooperate on the basis of common interests. Their humour often upsets people, because it disregards others' feelings. They play practical jokes and are unaware of the distress caused to the victims.

Very pronounced others'-feelings trait

People who have a very pronounced others'-feelings trait are very sensitive to the needs and desires of companions. Accordingly, they largely lack feelings of self-pity. They are exceptionally tactful and know exactly what to say whatever the situation. Their charming, kind and sympathetic attitude and manner warms the hearts of those around them. For this reason, they can attract great personal loyalty. They thrive on praise, admiration and encouragement. At work, they are most anxious for colleagues to approve their actions.

They like giving pleasure to friends. For example, they often find excuses for giving praise. They have a close interest in the affairs of others. They respect personal confidences and secrets. They are genuinely and deeply upset at seeing companions' suffering or pain. The reaction of an audience to their work is all-important to them. Criticism dismays them, and their fear of criticism means that they do not break the rules. They will go to great lengths to prevent adverse comment from companions. They do not want to hurt the feelings of family and friends.

Since their actions are significantly influenced by those around them, they may seriously neglect their own interests. They may allow their lives to be ruined by other people. For example, they find it exceptionally difficult to upset friends and colleagues. Consequently, they are unable to condemn or criticise in their personal relationships. They may put up with a highly unsatisfactory companion in preference to ending the relationship because of their desire to avoid personal unpleasantness. They find the sadness of goodbyes too painful and may just leave a note rather than saying farewell in person.

Very pronounced own-feelings, very pronounced others'-feelings and broadly equal traits are summarised in Fig. 8.3.

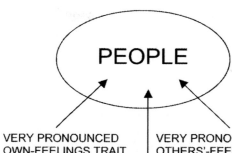

VERY PRONOUNCED OWN-FEELINGS TRAIT
- Mostly aware of own needs and feelings
- Individual relationships guided and influenced by their own requirements
- Prepared to take tough and difficult decisions about others
- Honest, plain-speaking and blunt
- Unresponsive to praise and criticism from other individuals

VERY PRONOUNCED OTHERS'-FEELINGS TRAIT
- Mostly aware of others' needs and feelings
- Individual relationships guided and influenced by the requirements of others
- Unwilling to criticise or distress companions
- Sympathetic and tactful
- Highly responsive to praise and criticism from other individuals

BROADLY EQUAL OWN-FEELINGS and OTHERS'-FEELINGS TRAITS
- Capable of relating, depending on the circumstances, in an own-feelings or others'-feelings manner
- Are adaptable and flexible

Fig. 8.3 Very pronounced own-feelings, very pronounced others'-feelings and broadly equal traits

A below average sociability disposition and a primary others'-feelings trait

Individuals with a below average sociability disposition and a primary others'-feelings trait can be uncomfortable in the company of other people and concerned about the feelings of those people towards them. One outcome is that individuals with a below average sociability disposition and a primary others'-feelings trait can experience shyness, especially when young.

The ways of relating dimension and sex differences

There is a great deal of evidence that, on average, more women than men have a primary others'-feelings trait. Conversely, on average, more men than women have a primary own-feelings trait. Consequently, as a general rule, women tend to be more interested than men in matters which involve people's feelings, for example women are over-represented in 'caring' professions. Equally, men tend to be more interested than women in matters which do not involve people's feelings, for example men are over-represented in engineering and other 'practical' professions. The fact that more women than men have a primary others'-feelings trait may be due to women's role in motherhood and child-rearing. Nevertheless, there are some women who have a very pronounced own-feelings trait and some men who have a very pronounced others'-feelings trait.

A DIAGRAM TO REPRESENT INDIVIDUALS

We can also use a diagram to represent an individual's ways of relating (see Figs. 8.4 and 8.5).

CONCLUSION

At work, a primary own-feelings trait and a primary others'-feelings trait are often apparent from people's relationships with each other. The decisive aspect is the extent to which

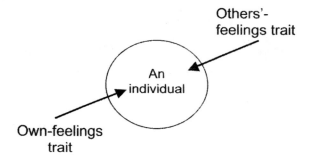

Fig. 8.4 Illustrates an individual whose personality demonstrates both the own-feelings and others'-feelings traits in broadly equal proportions. This individual is flexible and can use both traits in their dealings with other individuals.

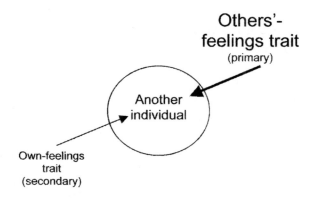

Fig. 8.5 Illustrates an individual whose personality reveals a primary trait (others'-feelings). The secondary trait (own-feelings) is only slightly revealed. The primary trait enables this individual to perform certain tasks really effectively. In this example, the tasks would demand an ability to take account of the feelings of others.

people take account of the feelings of those around them. Executives with a primary own-feelings trait take decisions without worrying unduly about the effects their actions have on the feelings of others. They are forthright and outspoken. They are largely unconcerned about their managers' or staff's feelings about them. Employees are dismissed for poor performance. Unpleasant truths are confronted and, if necessary, tough decisions are taken. The important issue is performance.

People with a primary others'-feelings trait are concerned about the effect their actions have on other people's feelings. At work, they are sensitive to the feelings towards them of both their managers and their staff. Since they are highly responsive to praise from other people, they praise their staff whatever their real opinions. Executives with a primary others'-feelings trait are tactful and considerate. They even thank staff whose performance is unsatisfactory. All motivation is positive. Staff are criticised or dismissed with extreme reluctance. Managers with a primary others'-feelings trait find difficulty in personally dismissing incompetent staff and ask colleagues with a primary own-feelings trait to carry out the task for them. Executives with a primary others'-feelings trait believe that a company with a happy, highly-motivated workforce will beat any competition.

This is yet another aspect of personality where there is a real danger of making incorrect judgements. People with a primary own-feelings trait put their own feelings first and disregard the feelings of companions. From this point of view, they may appear uncaring. From another point of view, they are honest and can take the decisions in their treatment of colleagues which are necessary for efficiency and success. Their actions may avoid disaster. People with a primary others'-feelings trait are sympathetic and tactful. They bring comfort and kindness to the lives of their colleagues.

However, their inability to take essential, but unpleasant decisions with regard to other individuals may result in disaster for the organisation, themselves or others.

KEY POINTS

The WAYS OF RELATING DIMENSION describes people's priorities with regard to their dealings with other individuals.
The OWN-FEELINGS TRAIT describes a person's relationship with other individuals in which that person's own needs and feelings take priority.
The OTHERS'-FEELINGS TRAIT describes a person's relationships with other individuals in which that person's perceptions of other individuals' needs and feelings take priority.

YOUR NOTES (OPTIONAL AT YOUR OWN RISK)

How would you describe your ways of relating dimension? For example, do you have a primary own-feelings trait, a primary others'-feelings trait or are you broadly equal in both traits?

What evidence are you using?

Do you know anyone personally or by reputation who has a primary own-feelings trait?

What evidence are you using?

Do you know anyone personally or by reputation who has a primary others'-feelings trait?

What evidence are you using?

How would you describe your manager's or other appropriate individual's ways of relating dimension?

What evidence are you using?

FURTHER NOTES

CHAPTER 9

The social interests dimension

The social interests dimension describes the scope of an individual's concerns about society. People are interested in very different aspects of society. Some people are largely involved with events and issues that affect society as a whole. Other individuals mostly pay attention to those aspects of society that affect them directly. You cannot at the same time be mostly concerned about society as a whole and mostly concerned about events and issues in society that affect you directly. These two conflicting attitudes make up the social interests dimension.

> **The SOCIAL INTERESTS DIMENSION describes the scope of an individual's concerns about society.**

Some people are more concerned about major famines, wars and political crises in foreign countries than incidents in their own locality. For these people, the social and political issues which affect their country and the world at large are of the first importance. They have opinions on many, if not all, present-day social controversies. They are interested in politics. These people have a primary wide-interests trait within the social interests dimension.

The WIDE-INTERESTS TRAIT describes a person's interest in events and issues which affect society as a whole.

Some people are more concerned with local affairs than the sometimes much more dramatic events in society as a whole or in the world at large. Political and social issues are important to them if they affect their day-to-day lives or those of their immediate companions. These people have a primary narrow-interests trait within the social interests dimension.

The NARROW-INTERESTS TRAIT describes a person's interest in events and issues which affect them directly.

National politicians, who from the choice of their career are clearly interested in issues that tend to affect everyone, are examples of people with a primary wide-interests trait. Artists who take little notice of the world outside their art are examples of people with a primary narrow-interests trait. We follow previous practice and represent the social interests dimension as a rectangle. The varying proportions of the wide-interests trait and the narrow-interests trait which can be found in people are represented by the space within the rectangle (see Fig. 9.1).

People located near the left hand side of the rectangle mostly respond to events and issues which affect society as a whole. The wide-interests trait is primary, while the narrow-interests trait is secondary. People located near the right hand side of the rectangle mostly respond to events and issues in society which affect them directly. The narrow-interests trait is primary, while the wide-interests trait is secondary. Those located near the middle of the rectangle respond, depending on the circumstances, to events and issues which affect society

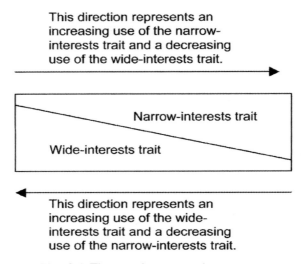

Fig. 9.1 The social interests dimension

as a whole or which affect them directly. They are broadly equal in their traits within this dimension and are more flexible in their social interests than people from near either end of the rectangle. Their flexibility means that they are more likely to respond to a greater variety of issues. As an illustration, the locations of a very pronounced wide-interests trait, a very pronounced narrow-interests trait and broadly equal traits are added to the social interests rectangle (see Fig. 9.2).

In order to understand these wide-interests and narrow-interests traits more completely, we describe a very pronounced wide-interests trait and a very pronounced narrow-interests trait.

Very pronounced wide-interests trait
People who have a very pronounced wide-interests trait are

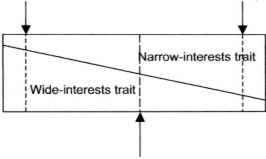

VERY PRONOUNCED
WIDE-INTERESTS TRAIT
People located here
mostly respond to events
and issues which affect
society as a whole. (The
dotted line is longest in the
wide-interests section.)

VERY PRONOUNCED
NARROW-INTERESTS
TRAIT
People located here mostly
respond to events and
issues in society which affect
them directly. (The dotted
line is longest in the narrow-
interests section.)

Narrow-interests trait

Wide-interests trait

BROADLY EQUAL TRAITS
People located here respond more
or less equally to events and
issues which either affect society
as a whole or affect them directly.
(The dotted line is broadly equal in
both sections of the rectangle.)

Note: as people are located further away from the
central dotted line, their response to the one type of
social interests becomes more frequent and their
response to the other type of social interests
becomes less frequent.

Fig. 9.2 Locations on the social interests dimension

deeply interested in national and international politics and
social controversies. They constantly read, think or talk about
the state of society and the world. Public affairs dominate their

conversation. They closely follow national and international news and current affairs. They take every opportunity to keep up to date with what is happening in society and the world at large. They reveal an interest in national pressure groups and political parties. They have social and political opinions about society as a whole. Directly or indirectly, they take sides in national controversies. Political victories or defeats are significant to them. Their role models are outstanding individuals, who have, or had, similar social or political convictions. The affairs of the wider society are their first priority. They comment on public issues. They express their views about society in words or action. In analysing any issue, the wider social or political aspects are very important. They are very concerned about the broader society.

Very pronounced narrow-interests trait

People who have a very pronounced narrow-interests trait pay great attention to their immediate circumstances. Their communities contain only a few individuals, who are united by close social ties. They are interested in the events happening around them in which they are directly involved. They are very concerned about the lives of their immediate companions, whose circumstances matter greatly to them. The illness of a close companion is much more important to them than any controversy in society as a whole. They personalise social issues into relationships between individual people. Accordingly, they think of global problems, for example poverty, famine, disease and natural disasters, in terms of how individual parents or children are affected.

Their main media interest is in news items which directly affect them or their companions. They support local events or charities. The great political issues, world revolutions and crises of their time mean very little to them. They are far more concerned with immediate matters than national political triumphs or defeats. They show little interest in how their actions affect society as a whole. They play no active part in national life. They ignore national politics and political parties. If in business, their aims and objectives only extend to the success of their own venture. The wider social consequences of their business actions are mostly irrelevant to them. If they are creative artists, their work contains almost no political or social messages.

Very pronounced wide-interests, very pronounced narrow-interests and broadly equal traits are summarised in Fig. 9.3.

Distinguishing the sociability disposition from the social interests dimension

The sociability disposition and the social interests dimension must be carefully distinguished from each other. People who have a very high sociability disposition may have a primary wide-interests trait or a primary narrow-interests trait. People who have a combination of a very high sociability disposition and a very pronounced narrow-interests trait have a small number of very close companions, with whom they spend much of their time. People who have a very low sociability disposition may have a primary narrow-interests trait or a primary wide-interests trait. People who have a combination of a very low sociability disposition and a very pronounced wide-interests trait can still influence society at large. They are able to do this when working alone by, for example, writing books and articles. A comparison of a very high sociability disposition and a very pronounced wide-interests trait is summarised in Table 9.1. A comparison of a very low sociability disposition and a very pronounced narrow-interests trait is summarised in Table 9.2.

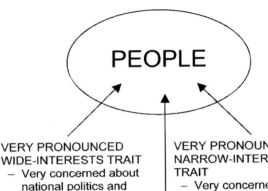

VERY PRONOUNCED
WIDE-INTERESTS TRAIT
- Very concerned about
  national politics and
  controversies, which they
  take very seriously
- Keen interest in national
  and international news
  and current affairs
- Concerned about
  matters which affect
  society as a whole (even
  without a direct personal
  interest)

VERY PRONOUNCED
NARROW-INTERESTS
TRAIT
- Very concerned about
  immediate
  circumstances
- Interested in matters
  which directly affect
  them, their few close
  companions and
  business interests

BROADLY EQUAL WIDE-INTERESTS and NARROW-
INTERESTS TRAITS
- Interested in matters which affect either society at
  large or their close companions and their business
  interests, depending on the circumstances
- Interested in global news and current affairs or in
  very local issues, depending on the circumstances
- Are adaptable and flexible

Fig. 9.3 Very pronounced wide-interests, very pronounced
narrow-interests and broadly equal traits

Distinguishing the ways of interacting dimension from the social interests dimension

The ways of interacting dimension must also be carefully
distinguished from the social interests dimension. People who

Table 9.1 The difference between a very high sociability disposition and a very pronounced wide-interests trait

DISPOSITION / TRAIT	PERSONALITY	ACTIONS
Very high sociability	Spend their time associating with other people	Work with others in teams
Very pronounced wide-interests	Interested in matters that affect society generally and the world as a whole	Respond to national and international events and politics

Table 9.2 The difference between a very low sociability disposition and a very pronounced narrow-interests trait

DISPOSITION / TRAIT	PERSONALITY	ACTIONS
Very low sociability	Spend their time by themselves	Work and think on their own
Very pronounced narrow-interests	Interested in events and issues which affect them directly	Respond to local issues and immediate companions

have a very pronounced group trait may have a primary wide-interests trait or a primary narrow-interests trait. People who have a combination of a very pronounced group trait and a very pronounced narrow-interests trait are very loyal to their local community. People who have a very pronounced independent trait may have a primary narrow-interests trait or a primary wide-interests trait. People who have a combination of a very pronounced independent trait and a very pronounced wide-interests trait contribute to national and international controversies and politics on the basis of their own aims and objectives. A comparison of a very pronounced group trait and a very pronounced wide-interests trait is summarised in Table 9.3. A comparison of a very pronounced independent trait and a very pronounced narrow-interests trait is summarised in Table 9.4.

A DIAGRAM TO REPRESENT INDIVIDUALS

We can use a diagram to represent an individual's social interests (see Figs. 9.4 and 9.5).

Table 9.3 The difference between a very pronounced group trait and a very pronounced wide-interests trait

TRAIT	PERSONALITY	ACTIONS
Very pronounced group	Identify very strongly with community objectives and values	Actions further community objectives and values
Very pronounced wide-interests	Interested in matters that affect society generally and the world as a whole	Respond to national and international events and politics

Table 9.4 The difference between a very pronounced independent trait and a very pronounced narrow-interests trait

TRAIT	PERSONALITY	ACTIONS
Very pronounced independent	Guided by own objectives and values	Actions further own objectives and values
Very pronounced narrow-interests	Interested in events and issues which affect them directly	Respond to local issues and immediate companions

CONCLUSION

The wide-interests trait and narrow-interests trait are straightforward to identify from people's actions and opinions. People who have a primary wide-interests trait are concerned about, and have views on, society as a whole. However, people with a primary wide-interests trait affect society in many different ways. For example, people with low sociability, a primary independent trait and a primary wide-interests trait work alone and argue for their own aims and objectives in their comments on national and international issues. People who show little interest in society at large have a primary narrow-interests trait. They are often much less visible in society. If they rise to social prominence, it is generally on the basis of some particular talent, for example as a scientist or entertainer.

We have again greatly increased the number of possible personalities. So far, we have explored four dimensions by which individuals can differ. What cannot be denied is that there are a puzzlingly large variety of personalities. As a

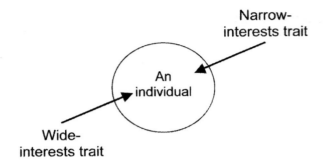

Fig. 9.4 Illustrates an individual whose personality reveals both the wide-interests and narrow-interests traits in broadly equal proportions. This individual is flexible and can use both traits in their responses to society.

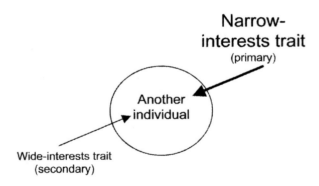

Fig. 9.5 Illustrates an individual whose personality reveals a primary trait (narrow-interests). The secondary trait (wide-interests) is only slightly revealed. The primary trait enables this individual to perform certain tasks really effectively. In this example, the tasks would demand an ability to take a close interest in immediate companions.

result, individuals seem capable of dealing with all kinds of different situations, problems and decisions. The variety of our personalities demands an explanation.

KEY POINTS

The SOCIAL INTERESTS DIMENSION describes the scope of an individual's concerns about society.

The WIDE-INTERESTS TRAIT describes a person's interest in events and issues which affect society as a whole.

The NARROW-INTERESTS TRAIT describes a person's interest in events and issues which affect them directly.

YOUR NOTES (OPTIONAL AT YOUR OWN RISK)

How would you describe your social interests dimension? For example, do you have a primary wide-interests trait, a primary narrow-interests trait or are you broadly equal in both traits?

What evidence are you using?

Do you know anyone personally or by reputation who has a primary wide-interests trait?

What evidence are you using?

Do you know anyone personally or by reputation who has a primary narrow-interests trait?

What evidence are you using?

How would you describe your manager's or other appropriate individual's social interests dimension?

What evidence are you using?

FURTHER NOTES

CHAPTER 10

The attitudes to the future dimension

No one knows the future. We have to deal with a future which is unknown. The attitudes to the future dimension describes our very different attitudes towards this unknown future. These very different expectations as regards the future have important effects on our personalities.

The ATTITUDES TO THE FUTURE DIMENSION describes an individual's expectations with regard to forthcoming events.

Some people have a cheerful view of the future. They anticipate that most things will turn out for the best. They assume their business targets will be achieved. They emphasise the opportunities. In their opinion, it is likely that their hopes and expectations will be realised. These people have a primary optimistic trait.

The OPTIMISTIC TRAIT describes the attitudes of a person who expects good outcomes.

Other people regard the future with concern. They anticipate and emphasise problems and difficulties. In their opinion, it is unlikely that their business targets will be achieved. It is probable that their hopes and expectations will be disappointed. These people have a primary pessimistic trait.

The PESSIMISTIC TRAIT describes the attitudes of a person who expects bad outcomes.

In short, people with a primary optimistic trait generally anticipate good outcomes, while people with a primary pessimistic trait generally anticipate bad outcomes. The attitudes to the future dimension describes these aspects of personality. A typical example of a person with a primary optimistic trait is an investor who has a general expectation of making immediate profits. Salespeople with a primary optimistic trait are cheerful about the future. They assume, irrespective of past disappointments, that the next customer will place a profitable order. A typical example of a person with a primary pessimistic trait is an investor who has a general expectation of making immediate losses. Finance executives with a primary pessimistic trait believe that the sales targets, however carefully prepared, are unlikely to be achieved.

You cannot at the same time base your actions on an optimistic and pessimistic view of the future. These attitudes result in conflicting expectations. As before, it helps to see the attitudes to the future dimension as a rectangle. The varying proportions of the optimistic trait and pessimistic trait which can be found in people are represented by the space within the rectangle (see Fig. 10.1).

People located near the left hand side of the rectangle mostly expect good outcomes. The optimistic trait is primary,

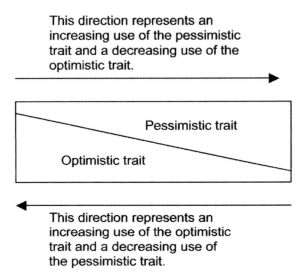

This direction represents an
increasing use of the pessimistic
trait and a decreasing use of the
optimistic trait.

Pessimistic trait

Optimistic trait

This direction represents an
increasing use of the optimistic
trait and a decreasing use of
the pessimistic trait.

Fig. 10.1 The attitudes to the future dimension

while the pessimistic trait is secondary. People located near the right hand side of the rectangle mostly expect bad outcomes. The pessimistic trait is primary, while the optimistic trait is secondary. Those located near the middle of the rectangle expect good or bad outcomes, depending on the circumstances. They are broadly equal in their traits within this dimension and are more flexible in their attitudes to the future than people from near either end. As an illustration, the locations of a very pronounced optimistic trait, a very pronounced pessimistic trait and broadly equal traits are added to the attitudes to the future rectangle (see Fig. 10.2).

We describe a very pronounced optimistic trait and a very pronounced pessimistic trait. For the purposes of comparison, we also describe broadly equal optimistic and pessimistic traits, when expectations depend on the circumstances.

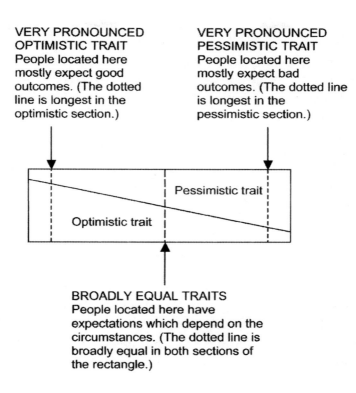

VERY PRONOUNCED
OPTIMISTIC TRAIT
People located here
mostly expect good
outcomes. (The dotted
line is longest in the
optimistic section.)

VERY PRONOUNCED
PESSIMISTIC TRAIT
People located here
mostly expect bad
outcomes. (The dotted line
is longest in the
pessimistic section.)

Pessimistic trait

Optimistic trait

BROADLY EQUAL TRAITS
People located here have
expectations which depend on the
circumstances. (The dotted line is
broadly equal in both sections of
the rectangle.)

Note: as people are located further away from the
central dotted line, their expectations based on one
attitude to the future become stronger and their
expectations based on the alternative attitude to
the future become weaker.

Fig. 10.2 Locations on the attitudes to the future dimension

Very pronounced optimistic trait

People with a very pronounced optimistic trait are certain that
they were born lucky. They take confident decisions based on bold
assumptions. They have a high opinion of their own abilities and
the quality of their work. Their future business, artistic or political

success is inevitable. One day, they will be wealthy, powerful or famous. They are convinced that their hopes will be realised. Everything will work out just fine. The future will be richer, freer and happier. Every problem can be overcome. They anticipate neither failure nor rejection. They know they will recover quickly from illness. They are not disheartened by setbacks. If one idea fails, they will try another. Disappointments are easily overcome. Their optimism is unaffected by mistakes and disasters. They are not discouraged by failure. They remain cheerful and hopeful even when things look their worst. Everything will work out for the best. Their final triumph is guaranteed.

Very pronounced pessimistic trait

People with a very pronounced pessimistic trait continually worry about the future. Everything is becoming worse. Society, the economy and the environment are deteriorating. Everything was better in the past. Present-day success, prosperity, happiness and health will not last. The trends in society are disastrous. People are incapable of learning from experience or changing their beliefs or attitudes. The world is bound to be devastated by, for example, economic collapse, a giant meteor, a deadly plague, disastrous climate change or a nuclear catastrophe. The world's problems are completely insoluble. They doubt the quality of their own work. They expect criticism and rejection. They readily anticipate failure, personal poverty and financial ruin. Their car and household machinery are certain to break down at the most inconvenient moment.

Broadly equal optimistic and pessimistic traits

People with broadly equal optimistic and pessimistic traits do not accept that the future is inevitably good or bad. They consider the various possible future outcomes and try to

establish which one is the most likely. They do not assume a
period of good luck or bad luck will continue indefinitely. They
accept that there will be both happier and sadder times. People
can, and do sometimes, learn from their mistakes and change
their beliefs and attitudes. Humankind is neither doomed nor
certain of success.

Very pronounced optimistic, very pronounced pessimistic
and broadly equal traits are summarised in Fig. 10.3.

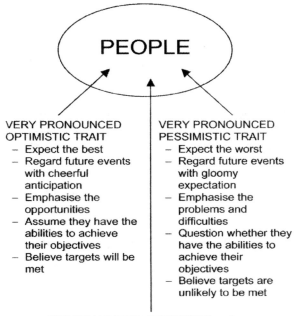

Fig. 10.3 Very pronounced optimistic, very pronounced
pessimistic and broadly equal traits

A DIAGRAM TO REPRESENT INDIVIDUALS

We can use a diagram to represent an individual's attitudes to
the future (see Figs. 10.4 and 10.5).

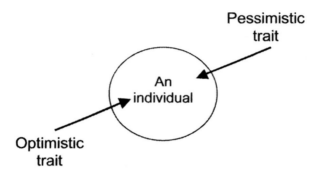

Fig. 10.4 Illustrates an individual whose personality demonstrates both
the optimistic and pessimistic traits in broadly equal proportions. This individual is flexible and can use both traits in their attitudes to the future.

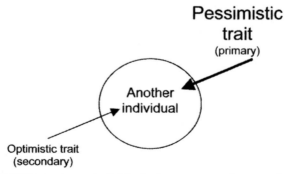

Fig. 10.5 Illustrates an individual whose personality reveals a primary trait (pessimistic). The secondary trait (optimistic) is slightly revealed. The primary trait enables this individual to perform certain
tasks really effectively. In this example, the tasks would demand an
ability to identify the risks and dangers in a situation.

CONCLUSION

People with a primary optimistic trait tend to be rather visible. They remain, despite repeated setbacks, hopeful about future opportunities. For them, their targets can be achieved. In times of crisis, they can supply hope. Equally, they can encourage others down a truly disastrous path. People with a primary pessimistic trait are also straightforward to identify. They worry. They see problems and pitfalls. The future is regarded with concern. Of course, at times, they may be right, but their advice tends to lead to inaction.

Nevertheless, an individual with either a primary optimistic trait or a primary pessimistic trait can find a useful role in, for example, business. Only a person with a primary optimistic trait can cope with a career, perhaps in sales, which involves rejection or failure. A person with a primary pessimistic trait is discouraged by the disappointments. Projects or activities which involve high risks can benefit from the presence of a person with a primary pessimistic trait. At the very least, all the risks are brought to everyone's attention. A person with a primary pessimistic trait can sometimes prevent business or personal disaster by timely warnings.

In Chapters 6 to 10, we have introduced the five personality dimensions. Each dimension consists of two conflicting traits, making ten traits in total. The dimensions and traits are summarised in Table 10.1. There is much to learn about people's personalities from their location on each of these five dimensions. As an illustration, we can create two imaginary people (A and B). In each dimension, we give A and B conflicting, very pronounced traits. One possible combination of conflicting traits is listed for A and B in Table 10.2. We assume that A and B are men.

From the information in Table 10.2, we know that A is imaginative and makes decisions by assessing alternative

Table 10.1 The five dimensions and ten traits

DIMENSIONS	TRAITS
Ways of thinking	Facts and possibilities
Ways of interacting	Group and independent
Ways of relating	Own-feelings and others'-feelings
Social interests	Wide-interests and narrow-interests
Attitudes to the future	Optimistic and pessimistic

Table 10.2 A's and B's very pronounced conflicting traits

DIMENSIONS	A'S VERY PRONOUNCED TRAITS	B'S VERY PRONOUNCED TRAITS
Ways of thinking	Possibilities	Facts
Ways of interacting	Independent	Group
Ways of relating	Own-feelings	Others'-feelings
Social interests	Wide-interests	Narrow-interests
Attitudes to the future	Optimistic	Pessimistic

outcomes. He is interested in his own aims and objectives. He is blunt and self-centred. A's abiding concerns are national politics and society at large. A is buoyant and cheerful about the future. On the other hand, B makes decisions based on a careful review of the facts. B is a loyal member of his communities and is tactful and considerate. His abiding concerns are his immediate circumstances and companions. B is worried and views the future with apprehension. We can see at once that A and B have very different personalities (see Table 10.3). It seems unlikely, to say the least, that A and B would ever find much in common or become close friends. In later chapters, we will meet two real people who had similar traits.

In fact, there are thirty-two possible combinations of very pronounced traits. In other words, we could have had thirty-two examples of people with different very pronounced trait combinations. The resulting variety that can be found in these personalities is truly astonishing.

KEY POINTS

The ATTITUDES TO THE FUTURE DIMENSION describes an individual's expectations with regard to forthcoming events.

Table 10.3 A comparison of A's and B's personalities with regard to their traits

A'S PERSONALITY	B'S PERSONALITY
Assesses alternative outcomes	Assesses information
Puts his own objectives first	Puts his communities' objectives first
Blunt and self-centred	Tactful and considerate
Interested in society at large	Interested in his immediate circumstances
Buoyant and cheerful	Worried and apprehensive

The OPTIMISTIC TRAIT describes the attitudes of a person who expects good outcomes.

The PESSIMISTIC TRAIT describes the attitudes of a person who expects bad outcomes.

YOUR NOTES (OPTIONAL AT YOUR OWN RISK)

How would you describe your attitudes to the future dimension? For example, do you have a primary optimistic trait, a primary pessimistic trait or are you broadly equal in both traits?

What evidence are you using?

Do you know anyone personally or by reputation who has a primary optimistic trait?

What evidence are you using?

Do you know anyone personally or by reputation who has a primary pessimistic trait?

What evidence are you using?

Do you know anyone personally or by reputation who is broadly equal in the optimistic and pessimistic traits?

What evidence are you using?

How would you describe your manager's or other appropriate individual's attitudes to the future dimension?

What evidence are you using?

Which two people do you know personally or by reputation who differ most in the five dimensions?

What evidence are you using?

Describe how these two people differ in each of the five dimensions.

What evidence are you using?

FURTHER NOTES

CHAPTER 11
Social attitudes

In Chapter 1, we noted that people's personalities are very complicated. For this reason, we have so far introduced each of the dispositions and dimensions in turn. We now start exploring the complexity of personality. In this and the next chapter, we look at how various dispositions and dimensions influence each other. We begin by exploring how the ways of interacting dimension (the group and independent traits) and the ways of relating dimension (the own-feelings and others'-feelings traits) affect individuals' personalities.

The ways of interacting describes people's attitudes to their communities. This dimension tells us the extent to which people give priority either to their communities' aims and objectives (the group trait) or to their own aims and objectives (the independent trait). On the other hand, the ways of relating describes people's attitudes to each other as individuals. This dimension tells us whether people in their individual dealings with each other give priority either to their own feelings (the own-feelings trait) or to their perception of other people's feelings (the others'-feelings trait). We call the interplay between these two dimensions people's 'social attitudes'.

SOCIAL ATTITUDES describe the combined effect of a person's ways of interacting dimension and ways of relating dimension.

However, before examining these issues, we require a concept which describes two or more personality dimensions collectively. Two or more dimensions considered together are called a 'personality bundle', although we generally refer to a 'bundle'. For example, the ways of interacting dimension and the ways of relating dimension, when considered together, are a bundle of two dimensions.

A PERSONALITY BUNDLE is two or more personality dimensions considered together.

The four traits within the ways of interacting and ways of relating bundle are:

- Group
- Independent
- Own-feelings
- Others'-feelings

These traits describe how people associate with communities and individuals. People's social attitudes differ significantly depending on which of these four traits are primary, secondary or broadly equal. We can explore only some of the main issues which arise out of the ways of interacting and ways of relating bundle. We also restrict our attention to individuals who have two primary traits within this bundle. These two primary traits can only be combined in four ways. It is useful to describe two or more traits from different dimensions when combined together as a 'personality trait combination', although we generally refer to a 'trait combination' or even 'combination'.

A PERSONALITY TRAIT COMBINATION is two or more traits from different dimensions considered together.

The personality trait combinations of primary traits within the ways of interacting and ways of relating bundle are:

- Group and own-feelings
- Group and others'-feelings
- Independent and own-feelings
- Independent and others'-feelings

However, individuals with one of these four combinations still have the secondary trait within each dimension, even though these secondary traits have a lesser influence on their social attitudes. In order to ensure that the resulting social attitudes arising from these four combinations are very distinctive, we discuss the situation where the two primary traits from the ways of interacting and ways of relating bundle are very pronounced.

We now use three diagrams to confirm the identity of the four combinations of two very pronounced traits within the ways of interacting and ways of relating bundle. In order to prepare these diagrams, it is necessary to adjust an earlier diagram from Chapter 8. We make the adjustment by rotating clockwise into the vertical position the ways of relating rectangle in Fig. 8.1 (see Fig. 11.1). By these means, we can show both the ways of interacting and ways of relating rectangles on the same diagram (see Fig. 11.2).

The diagram in Fig. 11.2 brings together the ways of interacting and ways of relating dimensions as a bundle. We now add to Fig. 11.2 the location of the four combinations of two very pronounced traits which occur within the ways of interacting and the ways of relating bundle. We also add arrows and dotted lines to produce the completed diagram of

Fig. 11.1 The ways of relating rectangle from Chapter 8, Fig. 8.1 rotated clockwise into the vertical position

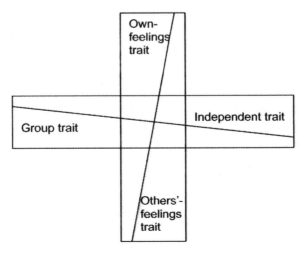

Fig. 11.2 The ways of interacting and ways of relating bundle

this bundle. The length of the dotted line in each combination of two very pronounced traits indicates broadly the contribution from the two very pronounced traits to an individual's social attitudes (see Fig. 11.3).

We now describe the social attitudes arising from each very pronounced trait combination. A person pursuing a particular career illustrates each very pronounced trait

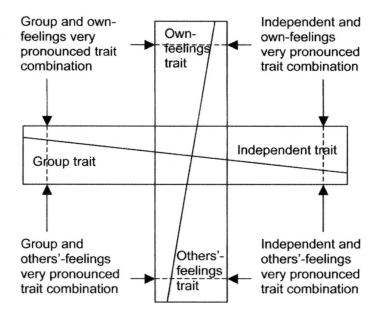

The length of the dotted line in each of the traits indicates broadly the contribution of each of the traits to an individual's social attitudes.

Fig. 11.3 Location of the four combinations of two very pronounced traits from the ways of interacting and ways of relating bundle with the arrows and dotted lines shown

combination. Many other careers could equally well have been chosen. Moreover, people with many different social attitudes succeed in the careers actually selected.

Group and own-feelings very pronounced trait combination

This combination describes individuals who are very loyal to their communities (the group trait) yet give strong priority to their own needs and feelings (the own-feelings trait). These two very pronounced traits give rise to identifiable social attitudes. Individuals with these traits are committed to their communities yet can offer their own forthright contributions to community decisions. When they have made their own frank suggestions, they are still prepared to accept community decisions. This is the case even if a community decision is inconsistent with their advice.

The example is of some military commanders. Their pride in their military units illustrates their very pronounced group trait. They are loyal and do not betray their country. They are prepared to do their duty and obey their orders. They volunteer for unpleasant tasks or dangerous missions. Their very pronounced own-feelings trait is revealed by their blunt remarks to people in their command. Their relationships with colleagues are difficult, because they misjudge other officers' moods and reactions. However, as commanders, they are prepared to take the tough decisions about the people in their unit that are sometimes necessary in war.

Group and others'-feelings very pronounced trait combination

This combination describes individuals who are both very

loyal to the community (the group trait) and very responsive to the feelings and needs of other community members (the others'-feelings trait). They help everyone to work together in harmony to achieve community aims. This very pronounced trait combination may seem a more compatible combination than the preceding group and own-feelings very pronounced trait combination. However, a very difficult problem arises for people with the group and others'-feelings very pronounced trait combination when a large minority refuses to accept a community decision. People with this trait combination may be unable to act, because it is impossible to reconcile loyalty to the community with respect for the feelings of others. For example, a company management may disagree on the future strategic direction. A large minority of the management may strongly oppose the majority opinion. Members of the management with a very pronounced group and others'-feelings trait combination find themselves unable to take sides. They cannot be loyal to the company and respect the feelings of the opponents.

The career illustration is of some teachers. Their very pronounced group trait is reflected in their pride in their school or college. They are loyal to its traditions and institutions. They play their part in school and college activities. They are conscientious in carrying out their duties. Their very pronounced others'-feelings trait means that they are sympathetic to students. They are concerned about the disappointment of students who fail to understand the lessons. They are very tactful in their teaching and do their best to avoid giving offence. They show genuine interest in the comments and work of their students. They are polite and considerate when talking to parents or guardians.

Independent and own-feelings very pronounced trait combination

This combination describes individuals who are committed to their own aims and objectives (the independent trait) and give strong priority to their own needs and feelings (the own-feelings trait). At first sight, people with this very pronounced trait combination may appear to have social attitudes which conflict with community membership. However, as has been stressed earlier in discussing the sociability disposition, one of our fundamental universal characteristics is our sociability. No individual can survive either mentally or physically in complete isolation. Even people with a very pronounced independent trait are active members in some community. People with the very pronounced independent and own-feelings trait combination may be able to bring some very different views to the attention of their community. For example, some scientists have this trait combination. They are able to challenge existing scientific ideas because they lack both loyalty to traditional schools of thought (the independent trait) and sensitivity to their colleagues' feelings (the own-feelings trait). In times of crisis, politicians with this trait combination are able to offer important contributions. They can force their community to admit making serious mistakes (the independent trait), while, at the same time, bluntly criticising the poor performance of some community members (the own-feelings trait). The risk for those with this combination is that they may make errors through a lack of shared understanding or knowledge that comes from closer social involvement. Their frank, uncompromising manner may also be unacceptable to part of their audience and counterproductive in its effect.

We use some business people to illustrate this trait combination. As a result of their very pronounced independent trait, these executives put their own careers before the interests of the company. If they fail to achieve an expected promotion, they may leave the company. They have no time for company traditions or practices with which they disagree. If they consider it necessary, they disobey instructions and ignore rules and regulations. Their very pronounced own-feelings trait is revealed in their honesty and blunt manner. They frankly criticise employees whose performance is unsatisfactory. They are prepared to dismiss those whose performance remains unsatisfactory. They openly disagree with other managers. They may misjudge the mood of a meeting or committee. They may be reluctant to trust anyone. They play practical jokes and are unaware that the victims feel foolish.

Independent and others'-feelings very pronounced trait combination

This combination describes individuals who are committed to their own aims and objectives (the independent trait) but are very responsive to the feelings and needs of other people (the others'-feelings trait). Individuals with this trait combination are able to protest against a mistaken community consensus. In some cases, they may argue that the needs of individuals should be put before those of the community. They are prepared to disagree with community actions which contradict their values or upset some community members. Their concern is with any conflict between community decisions and their own values (the independent trait), and the effect these decisions have on individuals (the others'-feelings trait). However, in some circumstances, members with the very pronounced independent trait risk underestimating the need for social solidarity.

The example is of some artists. Their very pronounced independent trait is revealed in their lack of respect for authority. They ignore the rules of institutions to which they belong. In extreme cases, they may even support the abolition of all government. At college, they do not attend classes. They do not belong to, or try to create, any artistic school. They are interested in their own work and disregard the ideas of fellow artists. Their very pronounced others'-feelings trait is revealed in their great concern with their friends' or acquaintances' opinions of their work. They are kind, generous and think nothing of making gifts of their art. They avoid causing offence with their art. They are aware when their actions upset other people and readily apologise. They are embarrassed when they realise they have made tactless or hurtful remarks.

The social attitudes associated with each combination of very pronounced traits are summarised briefly in Table 11.1. The contents of Table 11.1 are also illustrated in Fig. 11.4. Some of the key points from the four examples are summarised in Fig. 11.5.

Table 11.1 Ways of interacting and ways of relating very pronounced trait combinations and associated social attitudes

VERY PRONOUNCED TRAIT COMBINATIONS	*ASSOCIATED SOCIAL ATTITUDES*
Group and own-feelings	Closely identify with a community from the standpoint of their own needs and feelings
Group and others'-feelings	Closely identify with a community from the standpoint of their perceived understanding of others' needs and feelings
Independent and own-feelings	Pursue largely their own objectives from the standpoint of their own needs and feelings
Independent and others'-feelings	Pursue largely their own objectives from the standpoint of their perceived understanding of others' needs and feelings

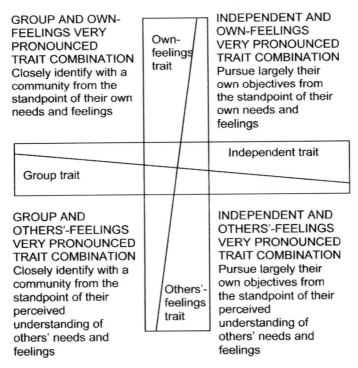

GROUP AND OWN-FEELINGS VERY PRONOUNCED TRAIT COMBINATION
Closely identify with a community from the standpoint of their own needs and feelings

Own-feelings trait

INDEPENDENT AND OWN-FEELINGS VERY PRONOUNCED TRAIT COMBINATION
Pursue largely their own objectives from the standpoint of their own needs and feelings

Group trait

Independent trait

GROUP AND OTHERS'-FEELINGS VERY PRONOUNCED TRAIT COMBINATION
Closely identify with a community from the standpoint of their perceived understanding of others' needs and feelings

Others'-feelings trait

INDEPENDENT AND OTHERS'-FEELINGS VERY PRONOUNCED TRAIT COMBINATION
Pursue largely their own objectives from the standpoint of their perceived understanding of others' needs and feelings

Fig. 11.4 Social attitudes associated with the four very pronounced trait combinations of the ways of interacting and the ways of relating bundle

GROUP and OWN-FEELINGS VERY PRONOUNCED TRAIT COMBINATION	INDEPENDENT and OWN-FEELINGS VERY PRONOUNCED TRAIT COMBINATION
- Proud of, and loyal to, their communities - Do their duty - Prepared to undertake thankless and unpleasant tasks on behalf of their communities - Able to bring unwelcome news to the attention of others - Honest and blunt - May misjudge other people's attitudes	- Prepared to criticise their communities - Prepared to oppose authority - Ignore rules and regulations - May underestimate the need for group solidarity - Able to bring unwelcome news to others' attention - Honest and blunt - May misjudge other people's attitudes
GROUP and OTHERS'-FEELINGS VERY PRONOUNCED TRAIT COMBINATION	INDEPENDENT and OTHERS'-FEELINGS VERY PRONOUNCED TRAIT COMBINATION
- Proud of, and loyal to, their communities, do their duty - Prepared to undertake thankless and unpleasant tasks on behalf of their communities - Tactful and considerate - Concerned about opinions of others - Unable to cope with serious internal community conflicts - Able to promote an inclusive harmony	- Prepared to criticise their communities - Prepared to oppose authority - Ignore rules and regulations - May underestimate the need for group solidarity - Tactful and considerate - Concerned about opinions of others - Able to argue in favour of others' needs

Fig. 11.5 Social attitudes of the four very pronounced trait combinations within the ways of interacting and the ways of relating bundle

A DIAGRAM TO REPRESENT INDIVIDUALS

We can use a diagram to represent an individual's ways of interacting and ways of relating bundle. As before, the font size of each trait and the thickness of the arrow on the diagram reveal the strength of each trait. Accordingly, the larger the font size and thicker the arrow of one trait compared to the other, the more influential is that trait (see Figs. 11.6 and 11.7).

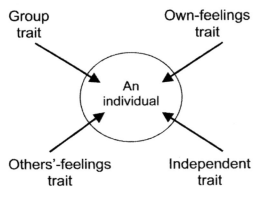

Fig. 11.6 Illustrates an individual whose social attitudes reveal all four traits within the ways of interacting and ways of relating bundle (group, independent, own-feelings and others'-feelings) in broadly equal proportions (the font and arrow size of the traits are equal). This person has no primary or secondary traits. People like this are flexible in their social attitudes and can use all four traits equally in their associations with their communities and with individuals.

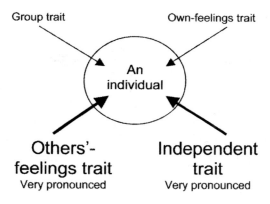

Fig. 11.7 Illustrates an individual whose social attitudes reveal two very pronounced traits (independent and others'-feelings). The secondary traits (group and own-feelings) are only slightly revealed. The two primary traits enable this person to perform certain tasks really effectively. In this example, the tasks would demand a high ability to follow one's own objectives and values in a situation where dealing with the feelings of other individuals is central to its successful completion.

CONCLUSION

The interplay between two dimensions adds considerably to the complexity of our personalities. For example, people's social attitudes depend on the nature of their primary and secondary traits in the ways of interacting and the ways of relating bundle. The variety and complexity of our social attitudes is a valuable and important resource to any organisation. The value arising from our very different social attitudes is illustrated by the four career examples. Military commanders who have a group and own-feelings very pronounced trait combination are very loyal yet can take the tough decisions about people which are needed in wartime.

Teachers who have a group and others'-feelings very pronounced trait combination are loyal to their institution and considerate to students and colleagues. Their actions increase social harmony. Business executives who have an independent and own-feelings very pronounced trait combination reject outdated company traditions and bluntly tell others the essential truth that they must improve their performance. Finally, artists who have an independent and others'-feelings very pronounced trait combination follow their own creative vision but with the intention of pleasing their audience.

In order to make the best use of people's social attitudes we need to assess accurately the traits within the ways of interacting and ways of relating dimensions. We examine assessment in more detail in Chapters 15, 16, 17 and 19. However, we first need to explore our most important lifestyles in Chapter 12. Then, in Chapters 13 and 14, we will learn about the remaining parts of our personality structure.

KEY POINTS

SOCIAL ATTITUDES describe the combined effect of a person's ways of interacting dimension and ways of relating dimension.

A PERSONALITY BUNDLE is two or more personality dimensions considered together.

A PERSONALITY TRAIT COMBINATION is two or more traits from different dimensions considered together.

YOUR NOTES (OPTIONAL AT YOUR OWN RISK)

How would you describe your social attitudes (your trait combination within the ways of interacting and ways of relating bundle)? For example, which traits are primary, secondary or broadly equal?

What evidence are you using?

Do you know anyone personally or by reputation who has a group and own-feelings primary trait combination?

What evidence are you using?

Do you know anyone personally or by reputation who has a group and others'-feelings primary trait combination?

What evidence are you using?

Do you know anyone personally or by reputation who has an independent and own-feelings primary trait combination?

What evidence are you using?

Do you know anyone personally or by reputation who has an independent and others'-feelings primary trait combination?

What evidence are you using?

How would you describe your manager's or other appropriate individual's social attitudes (their trait combination within the ways of interacting and ways of relating bundle)?

What evidence are you using?

FURTHER NOTES

CHAPTER 12

Lifestyles

In Chapter 11, we started to look at the complexity of people's personalities. We examined how very pronounced traits in the ways of interacting and the ways of relating dimensions come together to shape the social attitudes of an individual. We continue to explore the complexity of personality by considering a disposition and a dimension. We examine the effect of the sociability disposition on the ways of thinking dimension. Specifically, we look at how a very high or very low sociability disposition influences a very pronounced facts trait or very pronounced possibilities trait.

In many cases, behaviour by itself is a very uncertain guide to people's personalities. Similar behaviour can have its origins in very different personalities. Consequently, we have to be very cautious about drawing conclusions concerning people's personalities based solely on the observation of their behaviour. In order to understand people's personalities, it is generally necessary to spend significant time listening and talking to them. We need to know a great deal about them. Nevertheless, if a disposition is very high or very low or a trait is very pronounced, some associated behaviour does give largely reliable information about personality. Moreover, this behaviour is revealed in many situations and is, therefore, straightforward to observe. Consequently, there is often much evidence with which to identify very high or very low dispositions and very pronounced traits.

In this chapter, we are interested in behaviour which:

- Occurs noticeably and often in a wide variety of situations
- Is associated with a specific disposition or trait
- Reveals reliable information about an individual's personality

We call these aspects of behaviour a 'lifestyle'. Lifestyles are some people's usual ways of going about their day-to-day tasks and pastimes.

LIFESTYLES are some people's usual ways of behaving which also reveal their personality.

We now examine the lifestyles which arise from a very high or very low sociability disposition and very pronounced traits within the ways of thinking dimension. People with very high sociability have a lifestyle derived from their frequent social contact with their friends and acquaintances. Consequently, if we notice that a person is always in the company of other people and talking with them, we can assume a very high sociability disposition.

A VERY HIGH SOCIABILITY LIFESTYLE is one of working and relaxing with others through social contact.

The everyday lifestyle associated with people with very low sociability is one of working and relaxing as individuals. This is a very different lifestyle from people with very high sociability. Consequently, if we observe that a person nearly always spends their time occupied with their own thoughts, we can assume a very low sociability disposition.

A VERY LOW SOCIABILITY LIFESTYLE is one of working and relaxing by oneself.

The next lifestyles arise from the ways of thinking dimension. The reason is that lifestyles also flow from the way people think and take decisions. Although the connection is less obvious than with the sociability disposition, the very pronounced facts and very pronounced possibilities traits are each associated with distinct lifestyles. The lifestyle of a person with a very pronounced facts trait is very ordered and routine, while the lifestyle of a person with a very pronounced possibilities trait is full of spontaneity and variety. The differences in people's ways of thinking lifestyles follow from the nature of their thinking process.

People with a very pronounced facts trait arrive at their decisions by reasoning using known information. Finding and assessing facts takes time. Equally, accurate reasoning using facts needs careful thought and attention to detail. It cannot be done instantaneously or even quickly. In other words, people with a very pronounced facts trait have to be deliberate in their actions. They can only have the time necessary for their careful thinking, if their lifestyles contain a high degree of planning and routine. There has to be plenty of time between starting to solve a problem and finding and applying the solution.

A VERY PRONOUNCED FACTS LIFESTYLE is very planned and routine.

People with a very pronounced possibilities trait arrive at

their decisions by imagining and assessing alternative outcomes. Their ideas often come suddenly and fully formed into their minds. The origin and justification of their thinking is found in their previous experience. Their insights are immediate. Once they have established the reasonableness of their ideas using their previous experience, any decision can be acted on immediately. There is no necessity for a significant period of time between beginning to solve a problem and finding and applying a solution. People with a very pronounced possibilities trait can only take advantage of their immediate decisions, if their lifestyles contain a significant amount of freedom and spontaneity.

A VERY PRONOUNCED POSSIBILITIES LIFESTYLE is very spontaneous and varied.

Consequently, people with a very pronounced facts trait and people with a very pronounced possibilities trait have conflicting lifestyles. The lifestyle of people with a very pronounced facts trait is very planned and routine, while the lifestyle of people with a very pronounced possibilities trait is very spontaneous and varied.

Very high sociability lifestyles have a significant effect on very pronounced facts and very pronounced possibilities lifestyles. People with very high sociability lifestyles spend a great deal of time in the company of other people. Inevitably, the continued presence of other people has a noticeable influence. For those who also have very pronounced facts lifestyles, this association with other people may limit their ability to plan ahead. From time to time, they may be required to act more spontaneously than they would on their own. For those who also have very pronounced possibilities lifestyles, this association with other people may limit their freedom to act spontaneously. They may be required to take part in some routine activity and planning.

People who have very low sociability lifestyles spend a great deal of time on their own and are much less influenced by the needs of companions. Consequently, those who also have very pronounced facts lifestyles are able to plan their routine lives to suit themselves. Those who also have very pronounced possibilities lifestyles are able to respond to events spontaneously, unrestricted by the demands of others.

The effect of very high or very low sociability lifestyles on very pronounced facts or very pronounced possibilities lifestyles are summarised in Table 12.1. In Fig. 12.1, the locations of these lifestyles are identified on a diagram. In Fig. 12.2, the descriptions of the associated lifestyles are added to Fig. 12.1.

Table 12.1 The effect of very high or very low sociability lifestyles on very pronounced facts or very pronounced possibilities lifestyles

LIFESTYLES	BEHAVIOUR
Very low sociability and very pronounced facts	Highly routine, planned lifestyle
Very high sociability and very pronounced facts	Companions' requirements may restrict the routine, planned lifestyle, creating the necessity for some more spontaneous activity
Very high sociability and very pronounced possibilities	Companions' requirements may restrict the varied, spontaneous lifestyle, creating the necessity for some more planned activity
Very low sociability and very pronounced possibilities	Highly varied, spontaneous lifestyle

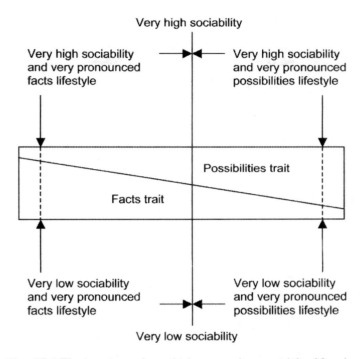

Fig. 12.1 The locations of very high or very low sociability lifestyles and very pronounced facts or very pronounced possibilities lifestyles

Any conclusions about personality using individual lifestyles must be made with care. It may be necessary to take account of other aspects of personality and the specific situations of individuals, particularly their work and home lives. For example, industrial society is governed by timetables, which inevitably force on some people a more routine lifestyle than might otherwise be the case. In these circumstances, people with a very pronounced possibilities trait who have a very low sociability disposition may have

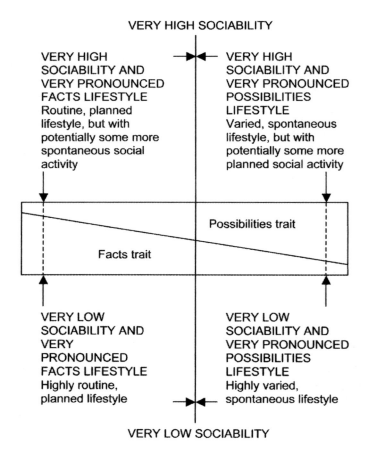

Fig. 12.2 The locations and descriptions of very high or very low sociability lifestyles and very pronounced facts or very pronounced possibilities lifestyles

some routine in their lifestyles, if they work, for example, within timetabled environments. Consequently, a very pronounced possibilities lifestyle may be impossible for these people.

Nevertheless, where people have a choice, those with a very pronounced facts trait choose employment which is ordered and predictable, for example administrators who perform their tasks to weekly, monthly and annual timetables. Equally, people with a very pronounced possibilities trait seek opportunities which involve the unexpected and to which an immediate response is required, for example those journalists who have to go out each day to find news stories.

The different lifestyles which are associated with a very high or very low sociability disposition and very pronounced traits within the ways of thinking dimension are illustrated by four examples. Each illustration describes a person following a particular career. Many other careers could equally well have been chosen. Moreover, many different personalities succeed in the careers actually chosen in these examples.

Very high sociability and very pronounced facts lifestyle

In this example, we describe some administrators. Their frequent personal contact with other managers illustrates their very high sociability. They enjoy meetings and committees. When not talking in person, they are on the phone. They spend their lunch hours and early evenings chatting with colleagues. They enjoy socialising and attending company functions. They are prepared to deal with staff problems when they occur. Nevertheless, their routine ways of working reflect their very pronounced facts traits. They are punctual. At meetings, they keep to the agenda and aim to start and finish on time. The department has a formal organisation. Extensive use is made of organisational charts and rule books. Future work is planned in detail. The annual plan is the most important yearly activity.

Very low sociability and very pronounced
facts lifestyle

We describe some teachers. Their quiet lives reflect their very low sociability lifestyle. Lunchtimes are spent by themselves, perhaps marking, using the internet or going for solitary walks. They rarely talk to students outside lessons. Conversations with colleagues are generally short and very largely about work. There is very little sharing of social gossip or family news. They do not mix with colleagues outside work. Their carefully planned, orderly way of teaching reveals their very pronounced facts lifestyle. Each lesson has a detailed plan and timetable. There is little departure from this prepared programme. Teaching starts and finishes on time. They place a strong emphasis on students remembering facts and reasoning correctly. The same material, updated as necessary, is taught year after year.

Very high sociability and very pronounced
possibilities lifestyle

We describe some news reporters. The need to find news stories leads to frequent contact with other people. They largely spend their working lives talking to people and enjoy socialising with their contacts and colleagues. News reporters have to take advantage of any opportunities as soon as they occur. Meetings can be held with little warning. In any event, they start late and overrun. There is no agenda. Decisions are made immediately. These journalists are happiest when reporting on unexpected crises. They enjoy novelty but soon lose interest when a story becomes routine. Unforeseen opportunities arouse their greatest enthusiasm. Each day is different. Order is maintained, perhaps, by list-making, although, from time to time, the lists may be lost.

Very low sociability and very pronounced possibilities lifestyle

We describe some creative writers. Their lack of friends reveals their very low sociability lifestyle. They do not mix socially with their fellow writers, even when they are not working. They are absorbed in their own private imagination. In this sense, they are self-sufficient. Social contact outside the family is difficult for them, because they lack gossip. They rarely stay very long in one place. Decisions are made immediately. Projects are started with no idea where they will lead. Inner feelings are very important. Reasons are unnecessary. Facts are ignored. Their work schedules are irregular and unpredictable. No one can guess their future actions or direction.

The lifestyles arising from a very high or very low sociability disposition and very pronounced traits within the ways of thinking dimension are summarised in Fig. 12.3. The descriptions of lifestyles in Fig. 12.3 are simplified. For example, they assume that people's actual lifestyles are free from other external constraints and that people do not adjust their lifestyles in line with their experience. They also ignore other aspects of personality which can have a significant influence on lifestyles. We explore some of these issues later.

Distinguishing a very pronounced possibilities lifestyle from a lifestyle arising from a very high uncertainty disposition

The lifestyles of people with a very pronounced possibilities trait need to be carefully distinguished from the lifestyles of people with a very high uncertainty disposition. A very pronounced possibilities lifestyle is one of variety and spontaneity. A very high uncertainty lifestyle is one of tense

VERY HIGH SOCIABILITY and VERY PRONOUNCED FACTS LIFESTYLE
In the company of others:
  – Lead ordered social lives as far as is practical
  – Unexpected is unsettling
  – Plan future in detail as far as is practical
  – Act after careful reflection on the facts as far as is practical
	VERY HIGH SOCIABILITY and VERY PRONOUNCED POSSIBILITIES LIFESTYLE
	In the company of others:
	  – Seek variety in their social lives as far as is practical
	  – Enjoy change
	  – Do not plan for the future as far as is practical
	  – Act immediately as far as is practical

VERY LOW SOCIABILITY and VERY PRONOUNCED FACTS LIFESTYLE
As individuals:
  – Lead very ordered lives
  – Unexpected is unsettling
  – Plan future in great detail
  – Act after very careful reflection on the facts
	VERY LOW SOCIABILITY and VERY PRONOUNCED POSSIBILITIES LIFESTYLE
	As individuals:
	  – Highly spontaneous in their lives
	  – Enjoy change
	  – Do not plan for the future
	  – Act immediately

Fig. 12.3 Lifestyles arising from a very high or very low sociability disposition and very pronounced traits within the ways of thinking dimension

situations arising from unpredictable outcomes. In some circumstances, these two lifestyles may be confused because the spontaneity may be a reaction to an unpredictable outcome. However, although a very pronounced possibilities lifestyle is full of constant variety and spontaneity, it is not one of thrills arising from the uncertainty of unpredictable outcomes.

People can have a very pronounced possibilities trait and a very low uncertainty disposition. The lifestyle of these people is one of variety but contains no significant tension from unpredictable outcomes. Rather, they are opposed to risk taking and avoid all dangerous situations. Furthermore, a lifestyle derived from a very high uncertainty disposition can be found in a person with a very pronounced facts lifestyle. In these circumstances, the tension of unpredictable outcomes is experienced in a planned and organised manner, for example when taking part in a sporting competition. Consequently, there is no necessary connection between a very pronounced possibilities lifestyle and a very high uncertainty lifestyle. This is yet another example of the principle of autonomy. The differing lifestyles which are associated with a very pronounced possibilities trait and with a very high uncertainty disposition are compared in Table 12.2.

Table 12.2 A comparison of the lifestyles associated with a very pronounced possibilities trait and a very high uncertainty disposition

TRAIT/ DISPOSITION	PERSONALITY	LIFESTYLE
Very pronounced possibilities trait	Imagine and assess alternative outcomes	Lead a spontaneous life based on immediate decisions
Very high uncertainty disposition	Excited by the tension associated with unpredictable outcomes	Lead a life in which there are many tense situations associated with unpredictable outcomes

CONCLUSION

The effect of the sociability disposition on the ways of thinking dimension adds yet more complexity to people's personalities. Lifestyles vary significantly depending on individuals' locations on the sociability disposition and the nature of their primary and secondary traits in the ways of thinking dimension. This further variety and complexity in our personalities increases the resources available to any organisation. We can begin to hope that whatever lifestyle is needed to perform a particular task, there will be someone who has an appropriate personality.

The variety of lifestyle resources available to us is clearly seen in the four career examples. Administrators who have a very high sociability and very pronounced facts lifestyle enjoy associating with many people while managing the routine of their department. Teachers with a very low sociability and a very pronounced facts lifestyle like their individual routine within their school or college. News reporters who have a very high sociability and a very pronounced possibilities lifestyle look forward to the variety of meeting many different people each day. Creative writers with a very low sociability and a very pronounced possibilities lifestyle spend long periods exploring the variety of their thoughts, during which they develop their imaginative insights.

People's lifestyles, which are generally reliable guides to aspects of their personalities, are often clearly seen in their actions. The key signs of a very pronounced facts (planned) lifestyle are order and regularity. The future has to be reasonably certain. Daily routines bring confidence and security. On the other hand, spontaneity and variety identify the very pronounced possibilities lifestyle. New situations generate immediate interest and bring about quick action.

However, in all cases, lifestyles may be strongly influenced by work, home lives and other aspects of personality.

KEY POINTS

LIFESTYLES are some people's usual ways of behaving which also reveal their personality.

A VERY HIGH SOCIABILITY LIFESTYLE is one of working and relaxing with others through social contact.

A VERY LOW SOCIABILITY LIFESTYLE is one of working and relaxing by oneself.

A VERY PRONOUNCED FACTS LIFESTYLE is very planned and routine.

A VERY PRONOUNCED POSSIBILITIES LIFESTYLE is very spontaneous and varied.

An individual's lifestyle may be affected significantly by, for example, the requirements of work and home life.

YOUR NOTES (OPTIONAL AT YOUR OWN RISK)

How would you describe your lifestyle arising from the sociability disposition? For example, is your lifestyle one of largely working with others, largely working by yourself or some combination of working with others and working by yourself?

What evidence are you using?

How would you describe your lifestyle arising from the ways of thinking dimension? For example, is your lifestyle largely planned (routine), largely spontaneous (varied) or some combination of planned and spontaneous?

What evidence are you using?

Does your lifestyle arising from your sociability disposition affect your lifestyle arising from your ways of thinking dimension?

What evidence are you using?

Do your work and home life affect your lifestyle arising from your sociability disposition or your lifestyle arising from your ways of thinking dimension?

What evidence are you using?

Do you know anyone personally or by reputation who has a very high sociability and very pronounced facts lifestyle?

What evidence are you using?

Do you know anyone personally or by reputation who has a very low sociability and very pronounced facts lifestyle?

What evidence are you using?

Do you know anyone personally or by reputation who has a very high sociability and very pronounced possibilities lifestyle?

What evidence are you using?

Do you know anyone personally or by reputation who has a very low sociability and very pronounced possibilities lifestyle?

What evidence are you using?

How would you describe your manager's or other appropriate individual's lifestyle arising from their sociability disposition and ways of thinking dimension?

What evidence are you using?

Describe some circumstances which may have a significant effect on an individual's lifestyle arising from their sociability disposition or ways of thinking dimension.

FURTHER NOTES

CHAPTER 13

The social roles

The dispositions and dimensions apply to everyone. Consequently, the five dispositions and the five dimensions are part of everyone's personality. However, there are aspects of personality which are not universal. These personality characteristics are found in some people but not others. For example, one person may communicate effectively, while another is an efficient organiser. Yet another person may have both of these characteristics, while someone else may lack these characteristics but have others. Personality characteristics of this kind are called the 'social roles', which some people, but not others, possess. The social roles are the resources to perform certain tasks. In other words, some individuals have the ability to undertake one or more social roles.

> SOCIAL ROLES **are specific functions undertaken by those community members who have the relevant resources.**

The seven social roles are:

- Communicators
- Cost-benefit calculators

- Educators
- Innovators
- Lifelong learners
- Organisers
- Accumulators

We look at each one of these social roles and examine their contribution to personality. There are different levels of social role performance. A person who has very large resources in a social role is 'very high' in that social role. Our examples are of individuals who are very high in each social role in order to illustrate the nature of the social role.

COMMUNICATORS

Communicators produce all manner of material, for example words, art and music. Their means of communicating are, among other things, personal contact, books, newspapers, television and films. The content of communications includes, for example, storytelling, mythology and news. Consequently, actors, novelists, music composers and journalists are all communicators. Humour, emotion, images and sound often add to the impact made by the content. An illustration is the way communicators often use jokes to enrich and reinforce storytelling.

> COMMUNICATORS **express or transmit information,**
> **ideas or emotion to individuals and communities.**

Business executives who are very high in the communicator social role know how to emphasise the key issues. They rely on frequent repetition and different media to put across the essential messages. Storytelling is often the most important way of identifying and emphasising the really important lessons and themes. Diagrams and charts are also widely used. Direct personal contact with the most influential audiences is often a vital part of their communication.

A very high communicator social role is of great value to politicians. Inspiring speeches are frequently an important means of political advancement. Voters are often impressed by skilful presentations. Memorable words or images can remain long in the electorate's mind. The written word is often as effective, and sometimes more so, than the spoken word. People can be roused to great enthusiasm by the clever use of language. Politicians who can expertly use humour and ridicule against opponents and critics are much feared by their rivals for power.

Distinguishing a very high communicator social role from a very high sociability disposition

A very high communicator social role and a very high sociability disposition need to be distinguished with care, because the same evidence can suggest both. A person with a very high communicator social role is very good at expressing or transmitting information, ideas or emotion to individuals and communities. A person with very high sociability enjoys the company of others. Accordingly, spending time with other people can be common to both the social role and the disposition. However, there is no necessary connection between the communicator social role and the nature of a person's sociability disposition (a further example of the principle of autonomy). For example, some actors, artists and writers communicate very effectively even though they spend little time with other people. The personality and actions of people with a very high communicator social role and of

people with a very high sociability disposition are compared
in Table 13.1.

Table 13.1 A comparison of a very high communicator social role
and a very high sociability disposition

SOCIAL ROLE / DISPOSITION	PERSONALITY	ACTIONS
Very high communicator social role	Very effectively express or transmit information, ideas or emotion to individuals and communities	Communicate, for example, stories, mythology and news by words, art or music
Very high sociability disposition	Spend much of their time associating with companions	Work and relax with other people

COST-BENEFIT CALCULATORS

The cost-benefit calculator social role is of great importance
to decision making. Most decisions or actions result in
benefits and costs. Good decisions depend on correctly
assessing these benefits and costs. We have to give a very
wide meaning to benefits and costs. Benefits include
enjoyment, good health and financial prosperity. Costs
include unhappiness, poor health and poverty. People with
a very high cost-benefit calculator social role are very good
at assessing the benefits and costs of their decisions and
actions.

COST-BENEFIT CALCULATORS **assess whether the benefit achieved from a future course of action is worth the cost.**

At work, we frequently make cost-benefit decisions. They are among the most important. For example, businesses need to make decisions that are likely to be profitable. They have to compare the economic costs with the economic benefits. In business, a proposed action is only profitable if the benefits exceed its costs. Governments are not required to make profits, but public money still has to be spent wisely to achieve the best possible results. Politicians who spend the people's taxes have to ensure that the benefits are maximised and any costs are minimised. In military action, the armed forces have to be organised to achieve the best possible results with the resources available. These cost-benefit calculations are essential to good governmental or military decisions.

People with a very high cost-benefit calculator social role take sensible actions in their private and work life. Their personal decisions result in outcomes which, when viewed in the long term, are good for them. They are able to avoid or stop activities which, in the long term, are bad for them. In a business context, you can often identify them by their great talent for arithmetic. They understand what figures mean. Successful business people often have a very high cost-benefit calculator social role.

Successful investors depend greatly on their very high cost-benefit calculator social role. They have a tremendous ability to understand and use financial information. They can quickly identify profitable investment opportunities. Executives in commercial enterprises who are very high in the cost-benefit calculator social role often find ways to reduce costs or increase sales. They are able to discover profitable markets, which they identify from the growth prospects and lack of competition. They quickly and accurately assess alternative business strategies and select the ones which maximise market share and profit. They understand, seemingly without being taught, the need for businesses to grow, increase productivity and achieve economies of scale.

Individuals who are very high in the cost-benefit calculator social role refrain from excessive gambling, even if they are very high in the uncertainty disposition. They realise that the harm done by excessive gambling far exceeds any benefit in terms of gambling thrills. They understand that excessive gambling leads to personal and financial ruin, the disastrous consequences of which far exceed any immediate pleasure experienced.

EDUCATORS

Educators teach the knowledge and skills which improve other individuals', mostly children's and adolescents', understanding and performance. There are two kinds of educator:

- Educators of everyone, who want all their students to achieve the necessary basic standard
- Educators of the talented, who want their gifted students to reach the highest standard

Naturally enough, educators are found in the teaching professions.

> EDUCATORS **assist people in gaining the knowledge and skills which improve their understanding and performance.**

Teachers who are very high in the educator social role know how to make their subject interesting and relevant.

They involve their students in the learning process. They introduce topics clearly, starting with the simpler aspects and then carefully progressing to the more complicated issues. They make good use of stories and anecdotes. They supply informative diagrams and charts. Student activities are interesting, and student assessment is instructive and rewarding. These teachers fully understand that student achievement is based on continuous success. In schools or colleges, teachers who are educators of everyone want all their students to achieve the essential basic standard. They do not pay special attention to gifted students. On the other hand, educators of the talented concentrate their efforts on the few students who can attain excellence.

Education is an important task for management in any private or government organisation. Business executives who are very high in the educator social role can make a major contribution to their businesses' growth and profit. Their teaching can transform employees' knowledge and attitudes. In business, educators can help colleagues accept the need for change. Individual employees are able to learn new practical skills and techniques from educator managers.

INNOVATORS

Innovators look for original solutions to problems. Innovation can apply to almost any aspect of life, for example scientific theories, technology, social organisation and the marketing of products and services. Innovators seek opportunities where new ideas are welcome, for example that of a development engineer in a high technology company.

INNOVATORS solve problems or make decisions through the application of original ideas.

Innovators are prepared to change or review some of their opinions and beliefs and are open to new ideas. In dynamic business situations with plenty of new opportunities, innovators may be expected to do well. Some people's personalities are greatly influenced by their very high innovator social role, particularly when it is combined with a very high curiosity disposition.

Scientists who have a very high innovator social role and a very pronounced facts trait study all the relevant information in detail. They perform original experiments to establish new facts. They look for new ideas which make sense of the facts. If they find an interesting new explanation, they test the idea against the facts. Their very pronounced facts lifestyles enable them to work on the same problem for years on end. Scientists who have a very high innovator social role and a very pronounced possibilities trait speculate freely in the search for new ideas. They imagine what a world would be like if their speculations based on their new ideas were true. They then test this imagined world against the real world to discover if their new ideas are true. Their very pronounced possibilities lifestyles mean they are easily bored and need to work on several projects at the same time.

Inventors who have a very high innovator social role and a very pronounced facts trait carry out detailed research. Their new inventions are based upon systematic experiments. As a consequence of their very pronounced facts lifestyles, they are prepared to spend years patiently developing their inventions. Inventors who have a very high innovator social role and a very pronounced possibilities trait familiarise themselves with all the practical aspects of a problem. More often than not, new ideas appear suddenly and fully formed in their minds. With their very pronounced possibilities lifestyles, they become bored quickly and soon move on to new projects.

Distinguishing a very high innovator social role from a very high curiosity disposition

A very high innovator social role and a very high curiosity disposition, while sometimes forming a very productive partnership, need to be distinguished with care. People with a very high innovator social role find and apply original solutions. People with a very high curiosity disposition continually ask questions and look for answers. In some situations, the same questioning behaviour can be evidence for both a very high innovator social role and a very high curiosity disposition. However, although very high innovators solve problems with new ideas, they do not necessarily continually question and look for answers. It is possible to find an original way of dealing with a task without showing much curiosity about the task itself. People with a very high curiosity disposition are very questioning but may not seek to answer those questions by finding and applying new ideas. For example, it is possible to be highly curious about nature or society even though any answers accepted or found lack originality. Some highly curious people are completely satisfied with explanations based entirely on existing knowledge. The personalities and actions are compared in Table 13.2.

LIFELONG LEARNERS

Lifelong learners continue to acquire additional skills and knowledge throughout most of their lifetimes.

LIFELONG LEARNERS **acquire additional skills and knowledge on a continuing basis.**

Table 13.2 A comparison of a very high innovator social role and a very high curiosity disposition

SOCIAL ROLE / DISPOSITION	PERSONALITY	ACTIONS
Very high innovator social role	Apply original ideas	Look for new ideas in making decisions and solving problems
Very high curiosity disposition	Ask questions and seek answers	Try to understand the people and world around them, can be entirely satisfied with applying existing knowledge

CREATIVITY AND ORIGINALITY

In describing personality, we need to distinguish between a creative person and an original person. In order to achieve this distinction, creativity and originality are defined as follows:

CREATIVITY is the application of existing knowledge or practice in a new context.

ORIGINALITY is the discovery or invention of something new.

When we use the words with these meanings, a creative person is not original and, therefore, does not have the innovator social role.

We illustrate this social role by people who keep mastering new skills and knowledge for a large part of their lives. People who have a very high lifelong learner social role may start their career in business. They then may move on to scientific research. In the meantime, they may become highly regarded authors. Later still, they may have a political or diplomatic career. The same is true of their hobbies. Later in life, they may take up oil painting or dancing.

ORGANISERS

Organisers have the natural dignity and authority to coordinate the work of others. They are able to manage other people, who willingly accept their guidance.

> ORGANISERS, with their natural dignity and authority, bring about cooperation between individuals and between communities.

Business executives with a very high organiser social role inspire confidence because of their managerial competence and self-belief. They are supportive and encouraging. They make sure that everyone understands that their efforts are important and appreciated. They consult, listen, take advice and achieve a consensus. They delegate effectively and appropriately and ensure that people have sufficient abilities, experience, training, resources and time to achieve their tasks. Business executives with a very high organiser social role know the talents of colleagues and have good insights into their personalities. They identify those people who work best together and give the right tasks to the right people. They set sensible targets and fairly review performance. Their well-mannered, democratic style motivates everyone. They are highly effective at coordinating each part of the business to achieve growth in sales and profits.

Leadership and the organiser social role

Leadership supplies a sense of direction or purpose to a community. The resulting aims and objectives can be, for example, moral, intellectual or practical. The organiser social role is distinguished from that of leadership in that the organiser's aims and objectives are provided by the leadership within the organisation or community. In business, leadership is sometimes taken to include the organiser social role. In this book, leadership refers solely to the function of direction and has no necessary connection with the organiser social role.

Distinguishing a very high organiser social role and a very high sociability disposition

The same evidence can suggest both a very high organiser social role and a very high sociability disposition, which, therefore, need to be distinguished with care. A person with a very high organiser social role has the natural dignity and authority to enable people to work together. A person with very high sociability enjoys the company of others. A very high organiser social role and a very high sociability disposition both involve spending time with other people. However, there is no necessary connection between the organiser social role and the nature of a person's sociability disposition (the principle of autonomy). For example, some senior executives with a very high organiser social role manage a business very effectively even though they have a below average sociability disposition. Generally, these executives work by themselves and only meet with employees to organise tasks. The relevant personality and actions of people with a very high organiser social role and of people with a very high sociability disposition are compared in Table 13.3.

Table 13.3 A comparison of a very high organiser social role and a very high sociability disposition

SOCIAL ROLE / DISPOSITION	PERSONALITY	ACTIONS
Very high organiser social role	With their natural dignity and authority, they bring about successful cooperation between people	Coordinate relationships between communities and manage individuals
Very high sociability disposition	Spend much of their time associating with companions	Work and relax with other people

ACCUMULATORS

Accumulators actively collect and retain experiences. Many collections of experiences have no practical value and are often a pastime. Some people may travel extensively to accumulate experiences, while others may read widely. The kinds of experiences and the way in which people collect them are often a consequence of other personality characteristics. For example, people with a very high ambition disposition may have a collection which demonstrates their financial success. A person with a primary facts trait may accumulate information or things, for example stamps, antiques, wine and coins. In this case, the accumulation of experiences is carefully planned, even for years in advance.

ACCUMULATORS **collect and retain experiences.**

People who have a very high accumulator social role find great pleasure in adding to their experiences. They are delighted to add something new. Experiences are their own justification and are greatly valued.

Distinguishing a very high accumulator social role and a very high curiosity disposition

A very high accumulator social role and a very high curiosity disposition need to be distinguished with care. The same activity (adding to experience) can be evidence for both personality characteristics. However, the social role of accumulator involves collecting and retaining experiences (sometimes represented by things). A very high curiosity disposition consists of questioning, problem solving and understanding, whether based on existing knowledge or new insights. The accumulator social role is not associated with any attempt to ask questions about, understand or explain what is experienced. The relevant personality and actions of people with a very high accumulator social role and of people with a very high curiosity disposition are compared in Table 13.4.

Distinguishing a very high accumulator social role and a very pronounced possibilities trait

A very high accumulator social role and a very pronounced possibilities trait also need to be distinguished with care. Similar behaviour (seeking new experiences and seeking variety) can be evidence for both personality characteristics. The social role of accumulator involves collecting and retaining experiences (sometimes represented by things). People with a very pronounced possibilities trait seek variety and spontaneity. However, people who have a very

Table 13.4 A comparison of a very high accumulator social role and a very high curiosity disposition

SOCIAL ROLE / DISPOSITION	PERSONALITY	ACTIONS
Very high accumulator social role	Collect and retain experiences	Seek out new experiences
Very high curiosity disposition	Ask questions and seek answers	Try to understand the people and world around them

pronounced possibilities trait without a very high accumulator social role do not attempt to retain the experiences which arise from their varied lifestyles. The personality and actions of people with a very high accumulator social role and of people with a very pronounced possibilities trait are compared in Table 13.5.

PRINCIPLE OF AUTONOMY

The principle of autonomy also applies to the social roles. Accordingly, there is no necessary connection between dispositions, dimensions and social roles. People's social roles cannot be predicted from their dispositions, dimensions or other social roles.

The PRINCIPLE OF AUTONOMY applies to dispositions, dimensions and social roles. There is no consistent, predictable relationship connecting dispositions,

Table 13.5 A comparison of a very high accumulator social role and a very pronounced possibilities trait

SOCIAL ROLE / TRAIT	PERSONALITY	ACTIONS
Very high accumulator social role	Collect and retain experiences	Seek out new experiences
Very pronounced possibilities trait	Imagine and assess alternative outcomes	Lead a varied and spontaneous life

dimensions and social roles to each other. In other words, the dispositions, dimensions and social roles are all independent of each other.

A DIAGRAM TO REPRESENT AN INDIVIDUAL'S SOCIAL ROLES

We can represent an individual's social roles by a diagram. The font size of the social roles and the thickness of the arrows on the diagram reveal the resource in each social role. Accordingly, the larger the font size and thicker the arrow, the higher is the resource in that social role (see Fig. 13.1).

CONCLUSION

People's social role or roles are an important aspect of their personality. The possession of significant resources in several

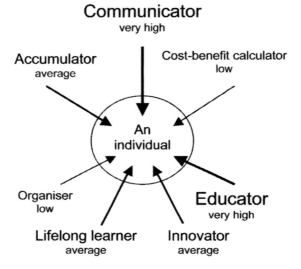

Fig. 13.1 Illustrates an individual whose personality has two very high social roles (communicator and educator), two low social roles (cost-benefit calculator and organiser) and three average social roles (innovator, lifelong learner and accumulator)

social roles adds noticeably to the complexity of an individual's personality. A person who has these social roles can fulfil considerably more social functions than a person who lacks any social roles. People's success in a career often depends on finding an opportunity which uses their social role or roles. The seven social roles are yet another important addition to the variety of our personalities. However, people who are very high in a social role may perform that social role either badly or unwisely. People may also have a very high social role but, because of their other personality characteristics or situation, may lack the interest or opportunity to develop that social role.

There is convincing evidence that some people can

perform at least six social roles competently, while some of the six are performed to the very highest standard. For example, their outstanding communication skills are amply demonstrated in writings of an exceptional quality. The same people are also good cost-benefit calculators and financially very successful in business. These individuals are excellent at educating colleagues in business skills. They can also be important innovators in their work, as well as mastering new skills until late in life. Finally, as organisers, these people can be highly successful in managing companies or departments. This extraordinary range of social roles can be found in just one individual. In this case, the only social role that does not feature is that of accumulator.

The social role of accumulator is rather puzzling. Why should some people have such a social role? In what sense is it a social role? What is its value to communities? Any explanation of personality has to account for a great deal. In particular, why do dispositions, dimensions and social roles exist? We look at this and related issues in Chapter 18.

KEY POINTS

SOCIAL ROLES are specific functions undertaken by those community members who have the relevant resources.
The seven social roles are:

- COMMUNICATORS express or transmit information, ideas or emotion to individuals and communities.
- COST-BENEFIT CALCULATORS assess whether the benefit achieved from a future course of action is worth the cost.
- EDUCATORS assist people in gaining the knowledge and

skills which improve their understanding and performance.

- INNOVATORS solve problems or make decisions through the application of original ideas.
- LIFELONG LEARNERS acquire additional skills and knowledge on a continuing basis.
- ORGANISERS, with their natural dignity and authority, bring about cooperation between individuals and between communities.
- ACCUMULATORS collect and retain experiences.

CREATIVITY is the application of existing knowledge or practice in a new context.

ORIGINALITY is the discovery or invention of something new.

The PRINCIPLE OF AUTONOMY applies to dispositions, dimensions and social roles. There is no consistent, predictable relationship connecting dispositions, dimensions and social roles to each other. In other words, the dispositions, dimensions and social roles are all independent of each other.

YOUR NOTES (OPTIONAL AT YOUR OWN RISK)

How would you describe your social roles, if any?

What evidence are you using?

Do you personally or by reputation know people who have one or more social roles? Identify the social role(s) of each person.

What evidence are you using?

How would you describe your manager's or other appropriate individual's social roles, if any?

What evidence are you using?

FURTHER NOTES

CHAPTER 14

The intelligence span

Intelligence describes people's ability to solve problems and take decisions. People vary in their capacity to solve problems and take decisions. Some people solve very difficult problems and take very good decisions in complex situations. Other people can only solve very simple problems and only take good decisions in very straightforward situations. We need a measure of people's intelligence, which we call the 'intelligence span'.

> The INTELLIGENCE SPAN is a measure of people's ability to solve problems and take decisions.

In Chapter 1, personality is defined as 'a description of a person's character which reveals both similarities and differences to other individuals'. Intelligence differs significantly between individuals and is a relevant factor in distinguishing one person from another. Consequently, our intelligence certainly contributes to our character and makes us the people we are. Therefore, we include intelligence in our guide to personality.

The intelligence span is a scale which measures decision-making ability. As with the dispositions, we can use a line to represent the intelligence span, which increases from below average on the left hand side of the line to above average on the right hand side (see Fig. 14.1).

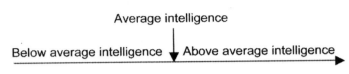

Average intelligence

Below average intelligence ↓ Above average intelligence

The line represents increasing intelligence

Fig. 14.1 The intelligence span

People located near the left hand end of the line can only solve very simple problems. They have very low intelligence. People located near the right hand end of the line can solve very difficult problems. They have very high intelligence. People located near the middle of the line can solve problems of average difficulty. The information in this paragraph can be added to a line representing increasing intelligence (see Fig. 14.2).

We now describe very high and very low intelligence. We start with very high intelligence.

Very high intelligence

People with very high intelligence quickly solve complex problems which involve difficult or abstract concepts. People with very high intelligence and a very pronounced facts trait are excellent at finding patterns in facts. They quickly decide which facts are relevant or irrelevant to a problem and draw the correct conclusions from these facts. They do very well in school examinations or tests which measure reasoning using the facts trait, for example examinations or tests which require remembering and reasoning with facts. However, they

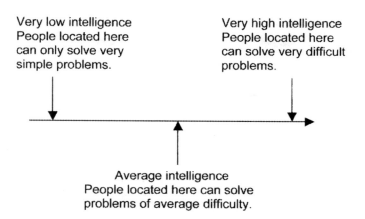

Fig. 14.2 Locations on the intelligence span

perform less well in tests which use their imagination. People with very high intelligence and a very pronounced possibilities trait are excellent at solving problems by imagining and assessing alternative outcomes. They can quickly decide if the imagined outcomes are consistent with their previous experience. They do well in school examinations or tests which require the use of imagination. However, they perform less well in tests which involve remembering facts and reasoning with facts.

Very low intelligence

People with very low intelligence can only slowly solve very simple problems.

Very low intelligence, very high intelligence and average intelligence are summarised in Fig. 14.3.

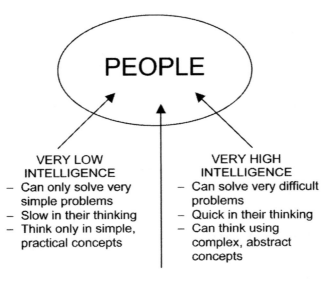

Fig. 14.3 Very low intelligence, very high intelligence and average intelligence

PRINCIPLE OF AUTONOMY

The principle of autonomy also applies to the intelligence span. Accordingly, there is no necessary connection between any of the dispositions, dimensions, social roles and the intelligence span.

The PRINCIPLE OF AUTONOMY applies to dispositions, dimensions, social roles and the intelligence span. There is no consistent, predictable relationship

connecting dispositions, dimensions, social roles and the intelligence span to each other. In other words, the dispositions, dimensions, social roles and the intelligence span are all independent of each other.

CONCLUSION

Above average intelligence increases the contribution individuals can make and widens their opportunities. People with above average intelligence are an important resource to any organisation. However, these people are unproductive in tasks which do not use their intelligence, because they are soon bored. People with below average intelligence can be very productive and useful to an organisation provided the demands made on them are appropriate to their abilities.

KEY POINTS

The INTELLIGENCE SPAN is a measure of people's ability to solve problems and take decisions.

The PRINCIPLE OF AUTONOMY applies to dispositions, dimensions, social roles and the intelligence span. There is no consistent, predictable relationship connecting dispositions, dimensions, social roles and the intelligence span to each other. In other words, the dispositions, dimensions, social roles and the intelligence span are all independent of each other.

YOUR NOTES (OPTIONAL AT YOUR OWN RISK)

How would you describe your intelligence span? For example, are you below average, above average or average?

What evidence are you using?

Do you know anyone personally or by reputation who is below average in the intelligence span?

What evidence are you using?

Do you know anyone personally or by reputation who is above average in the intelligence span?

What evidence are you using?

How would you describe your manager's or other appropriate individual's intelligence span?

What evidence are you using?

FURTHER NOTES

CHAPTER 15

Personality assessment headings

So far, we have discovered that our personality is described by five dispositions, five dimensions, seven social roles and the intelligence span. In other words, there are eighteen principal features to our personality. We call these eighteen constituent parts of our personality the 'personality characteristics', although we also refer to 'characteristics'. Each personality characteristic is a scale, which measures, for example, the intensity, influence or ability of that characteristic.

> **The PERSONALITY CHARACTERISTICS are the eighteen principal features of our personality and consist of the five dispositions, five dimensions, seven social roles and intelligence span. Each personality characteristic is a scale, which measures, for example, intensity, influence or ability.**

Our eighteen personality characteristics give our personalities eighteen degrees of freedom. In other words, there are eighteen principal ways in which an individual's personality characteristics can differ from, or be similar to, those of another person. People differ significantly in ways other than their personality characteristics. There are the visible physical variations in size and appearance. Moreover, people also differ, for example, in their energy, health, strength and interest in food. Some of these variations can also reveal the influence of personality characteristics.

The 'personality checklist' lists the eighteen personality characteristics.

The PERSONALITY CHECKLIST is a list of the eighteen personality characteristics.

The order of the personality characteristics on the personality checklist is the same as their order of appearance in Chapters 1 to 14. The personality checklist should be studied carefully, because, in later chapters, we often use this list as the basis for further discussions (see Table 15.1). The fascination, talents and vitality of a person cannot be expressed in a list. The personality checklist cannot capture people's uniqueness. It lists only their personality characteristics. In this way, it gives a framework to our understanding of their personalities.

In the first fourteen chapters, we have only considered aspects of a person. We have examined in turn the eighteen personality characteristics. We have also considered the personalities arising from two characteristics, for example the lifestyle consequences of the sociability disposition and the ways of thinking dimension discussed in Chapter 12. However, in our daily lives, we do not meet one or two personality characteristics but people with complex personalities. In order to understand people's personalities, it is necessary to establish the contribution each of the eighteen personality characteristics makes to their personality.

We need a means of describing where every person is located on each personality characteristic scale. So far, we have described some people as very high or very low in their

Table 15.1 Personality checklist detailing the eighteen personality
characteristics

PERSONALITY CHARACTERISTICS
A) DISPOSITIONS
1) Sociability
2) Emotion
3) Ambition
4) Curiosity
5) Uncertainty
B) DIMENSIONS
1) Ways of thinking – Facts / possibilities
2) Ways of interacting – Group / independent
3) Ways of relating – Own-feelings / others'-feelings
4) Social interests – Wide-interests / narrow-interests
5) Attitudes to the future – Optimistic / pessimistic
C) SOCIAL ROLES
1) Communicator
2) Cost-benefit calculator
3) Educator
4) Innovator
5) Lifelong learner
6) Organiser
7) Accumulator
D) INTELLIGENCE SPAN

Note: in order to save space, the names of the dimensions are omitted from
later lists.

dispositions. We have talked about people's very pronounced
traits. However, the requirement is for a system which

describes with sufficient accuracy every individual's location on each of the eighteen personality characteristics. For example, we need to be able to describe the location of a particular person on the sociability, emotion, ambition, curiosity and uncertainty dispositions compared to everyone else. Equally, we must be able to make the same assessment for the dimensions, social roles and intelligence span.

At work, managers and supervisors are required to judge employees' performance. At school or college, teachers have to assess students' assignments or examinations. Typical classification systems use seven headings, for example excellent, very good, good, satisfactory, unsatisfactory, poor and fail. Assessments based on these seven headings are matters of business or academic judgement. We also use seven 'personality assessment headings' for each of the eighteen personality characteristics, although we generally refer to 'assessment headings'. This number of assessment headings allows for a reasonably accurate description of an individual's location on each of the eighteen personality characteristics. More than seven assessment headings would be difficult to use, and fewer than seven would not make the distinctions required. The choice of seven headings is entirely practical.

PERSONALITY ASSESSMENT HEADINGS are used to describe an individual's location on each of the eighteen personality characteristics.

Unfortunately, the nature of the personality characteristics is too different to use the same personality assessment headings for all of them. Nevertheless, we can use the same assessment headings for the dispositions and intelligence span. The social role assessment headings only differ in one heading from those used for the dispositions and intelligence span. Dimensions need their own assessment headings. The

Table 15.2 The personality assessment headings

DISPOSITION AND INTELLIGENCE ASSESSMENT HEADINGS	SOCIAL ROLE ASSESSMENT HEADINGS	DIMENSION ASSESSMENT HEADINGS (*SEE NOTE BELOW EXPLAINING 'A' AND 'B')
Very high	Very high	Very pronounced trait 'A'
High	High	Pronounced trait 'A'
Above average	Above average	More trait 'A' than trait 'B'
Average	Average	Broadly equal
Below average	Below average	More trait 'B' than trait 'A'
Low	Low	Pronounced trait 'B'
Very low	Absent	Very pronounced trait 'B'

*Note: the illustration is of two traits ('A' and 'B') within a single dimension, for example the facts trait and the possibilities trait within the ways of thinking dimension.

assessment headings for the dispositions and intelligence span, social roles and dimensions are given in Table 15.2.

There are objective reasons or criteria which justify each assessment of employees' performance or students' work. In this way, different managers and teachers will grade the same performance consistently. Likewise, we need objective reasons or criteria for our personality assessment headings so that different people will arrive at largely the same personality assessment. However, in all assessments of this kind, whether of employees' performance, students' work or personality, the reliability of the judgement improves with practice and experience. We start with dispositions.

IMPORTANT

In employee or student assessment, business executives or teachers judge the merits of employees' or students' work. This is not true of personality assessment, which is not concerned with the merits of an individual's personality. One kind of personality is neither better nor worse than another. Our personalities are just different. This is a point of fundamental importance.

DISPOSITIONS

In Chapters 1 to 5, we have described the features of the five dispositions in the very high and very low assessment headings. The intervening five assessment headings for dispositions share aspects of the very high or very low headings to a greater or lesser extent. In this chapter, we use ambition as the example for our seven disposition assessment headings and associated assessment criteria.

If ambition dominates an individual's personality, the assessment heading is very high. In cases where the ambition plays a large part in an individual's personality, the assessment heading is high. Where a person's ambition is a significant feature of their personality, the assessment heading is above average. If a person displays an ordinary level of ambition, the assessment heading is average. If ambition plays a fairly small part in an individual's personality, its heading is below average. In cases where the ambition plays a small part in an individual's personality, the assessment heading is low. Where ambition only just features in an individual's personality, the assessment heading is very low. The disposition assessment headings and their associated criteria are summarised in Fig. 15.1 and Table 15.3.

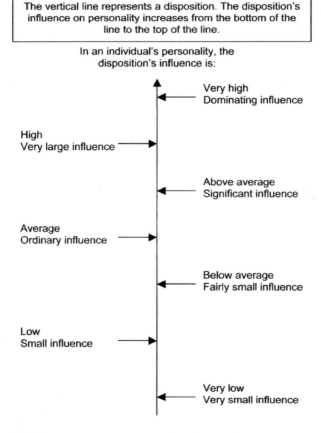

Fig. 15.1 Disposition assessment headings and assessment criteria

Table 15.3 Disposition assessment headings and assessment criteria

DISPOSITION ASSESSMENT HEADINGS	ASSESSMENT CRITERIA FOR DECIDING WHICH ASSESSMENT HEADING APPLIES TO AN INDIVIDUAL
	In an individual's personality, the disposition's influence is:
Very high	Dominating
High	Very large
Above average	Significant
Average	Ordinary
Below average	Fairly small
Low	Small
Very low	Very small

DIMENSIONS

Since the assessment headings in a dimension are symmetrical about the midpoint, we need consider only four trait assessment headings. We use the facts trait as our assessment example. If the primary facts trait plays a very dominant part in an individual's ways of thinking, with very little flexibility to use the secondary possibilities trait, the assessment heading is very pronounced facts. In cases where the primary facts trait plays a major part in an individual's ways of thinking, with some flexibility to use the secondary possibilities trait, the assessment heading is pronounced facts. Where the primary facts trait plays a significant part in an individual's ways of thinking, but with some real flexibility to use the secondary possibilities trait, the assessment heading is more facts than possibilities. The approximate midpoint of the dimension is described as broadly equal. At this point, both the facts trait and possibilities trait play a more or less equivalent part in the ways of thinking. We can illustrate the seven assessment headings for dimensions using the ways of thinking dimension:

- Very pronounced facts
- Pronounced facts
- More facts than possibilities
- Broadly equal
- More possibilities than facts
- Pronounced possibilities
- Very pronounced possibilities

The assessment headings and their associated assessment criteria for dimensions are summarised in Fig. 15.2 and Table 15.4.

SOCIAL ROLES

We use the cost-benefit calculator social role as the example for our seven social role assessment headings and assessment criteria. If people have the resources to complete correctly very difficult cost-benefit tasks, the assessment heading is very high. In cases where people have the resources to complete correctly difficult cost-benefit tasks, the assessment heading is high. Where cost-benefit tasks of some difficulty are completed appropriately, the assessment

The vertical rectangle represents one half of a dimension.

In a dimension, the assessment headings are:

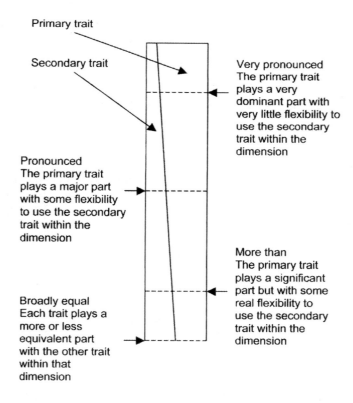

Primary trait

Secondary trait

Very pronounced
The primary trait
plays a very
dominant part with
very little flexibility to
use the secondary
trait within the
dimension

Pronounced
The primary trait
plays a major part
with some flexibility
to use the secondary
trait within the
dimension

More than
The primary trait
plays a significant
part but with some
real flexibility to
use the secondary
trait within the
dimension

Broadly equal
Each trait plays a
more or less
equivalent part
with the other trait
within that
dimension

Fig. 15.2 Dimension assessment headings and assessment criteria

heading is above average. If everyday cost-benefit tasks are
completed acceptably, the assessment heading is average. If
some everyday tasks are completed in a suitable manner, the
assessment heading is below average. If some simple tasks

Table 15.4 Dimension assessment headings and
assessment criteria

DIMENSION ASSESSMENT HEADINGS	ASSESSMENT CRITERIA FOR DECIDING WHICH ASSESSMENT HEADING APPLIES TO AN INDIVIDUAL
	In an individual's personality, the trait plays:
Very pronounced	A very dominant part with very little flexibility to use the secondary trait within the dimension
Pronounced	A major part with some flexibility to use the secondary trait within the dimension
More than	A significant part but with some real flexibility to use the secondary trait within the dimension
Broadly equal	A more or less equivalent part with the other trait within that dimension

can be completed adequately, the assessment heading is low.
If a person has no cost-benefit ability, the assessment
heading is absent. The social role assessment headings and
their associated criteria are summarised in Fig. 15.3 and
Table 15.5.

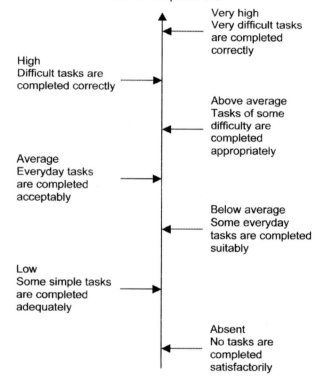

The vertical line represents a social role. The resources in the social role increase from the bottom of the line to the top of the line.

An individual's resources in a social role and the tasks that can be completed are:

Very high
Very difficult tasks are completed correctly

High
Difficult tasks are completed correctly

Above average
Tasks of some difficulty are completed appropriately

Average
Everyday tasks are completed acceptably

Below average
Some everyday tasks are completed suitably

Low
Some simple tasks are completed adequately

Absent
No tasks are completed satisfactorily

Fig. 15.3 Social role assessment headings and assessment criteria

THE INTELLIGENCE SPAN

If very difficult problems are solved correctly, the assessment heading for the intelligence span is very high. In cases where

Table 15.5 Social role assessment headings and assessment criteria

SOCIAL ROLE ASSESSMENT HEADINGS	ASSESSMENT CRITERIA FOR DECIDING WHICH ASSESSMENT HEADING APPLIES TO AN INDIVIDUAL
	An individual can use the social role resources to complete successfully:
Very high	Very difficult tasks
High	Difficult tasks
Above average	Tasks of some difficulty
Average	Everyday tasks
Below average	Some everyday tasks
Low	Some simple tasks
Absent	No tasks

difficult problems are solved correctly, the assessment heading is high. Where an individual's problems are of some difficulty and are solved appropriately, the assessment heading is above average. If everyday problems are solved acceptably, the assessment heading is average. If some everyday problems are solved adequately, the assessment heading is below average. In cases where only simple problems are solved adequately, the assessment heading is low. Where a person can only solve satisfactorily some very simple problems, the assessment heading is very low. The intelligence span assessment headings and their associated criteria are summarised in Fig. 15.4 and Table 15.6.

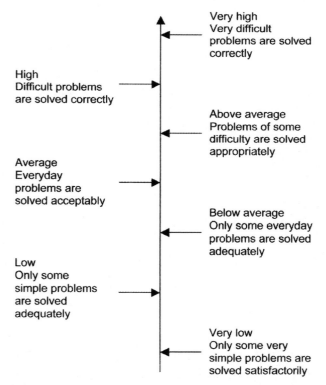

The vertical line represents the intelligence span, which increases from the bottom of the line to the top of the line.

An individual's intelligence and the problems that can be solved are:

Very high
Very difficult
problems are solved
correctly

High
Difficult problems
are solved correctly

Above average
Problems of some
difficulty are solved
appropriately

Average
Everyday
problems are
solved acceptably

Below average
Only some everyday
problems are solved
adequately

Low
Only some
simple problems
are solved
adequately

Very low
Only some very
simple problems are
solved satisfactorily

Fig. 15.4 The intelligence span assessment headings and assessment criteria

ASSESSMENT HEADINGS AS DESCRIPTIONS OF PEOPLE'S PERSONALITY CHARACTERISTICS

In applying assessment headings to the personality characteristics, we are evaluating evidence. For example, the

Table 15.6 Intelligence span assessment headings and
assessment criteria

INTELLIGENCE SPAN ASSESSMENT HEADINGS	ASSESSMENT CRITERIA FOR DECIDING WHICH ASSESSMENT HEADING APPLIES TO AN INDIVIDUAL
	Individuals can use their intelligence to solve successfully:
Very high	Very difficult problems
High	Difficult problems
Above average	Problems of some difficulty
Average	Everyday problems
Below average	Some everyday problems
Low	Simple problems
Very low	Very simple problems

ways of thinking assessment headings describe how
individuals solve problems and make decisions. The best we
can do with our description of the ways of thinking is to say,
for example, that one person has a very pronounced facts
trait, while another person has a very pronounced
possibilities trait. It is impossible to reach an exact
conclusion. Personality assessments are not measurements
using numbers like the measurements of temperature or
time. They are assessments based on understanding and
experience. Sound assessment only comes with knowledge

and practice.

Numbers are misleading if they are used as assessment headings for personality characteristics. The use of numbers for assessment headings suggests an accuracy that cannot be achieved. We can illustrate the mistake by attempting to use numbers as ways of thinking assessment headings. We could describe an individual whose personality assessment heading is more facts than possibilities as having, for example, a 'number one facts trait'. We could then describe an individual whose personality assessment heading is very pronounced facts as having a 'number three facts trait'. The danger is that we make a really serious error. We come to believe that a person assessed as having a number three facts trait has exactly three times as much of the facts trait as a person assessed as having a number one facts trait. Such conclusions are nonsense, because we are not describing quantities that can be measured in numbers. This example clearly reveals that numbers should not be used in personality assessment.

WELL-DEFINED PERSONALITY CHARACTERISTICS

In later chapters, we shall examine a number of individuals whose personality characteristics are assessed as follows:

- High, very high, low or very low assessment headings for most of their dispositions
- Pronounced or very pronounced assessment headings for most of their traits

These individuals often have clearly recognisable personality characteristics, which we describe as 'well-defined'.

WELL-DEFINED PERSONALITY CHARACTERISTICS describe

individuals who have high, very high, low or very low assessment headings for most of their dispositions and pronounced or very pronounced assessment headings for most of their traits.

FLEXIBLE PERSONALITY CHARACTERISTICS

People with flexible personality characteristics have the following assessment headings:

- Average, above average or below average assessment headings for most of their dispositions
- Broadly equal or more than assessment headings for most of their traits

FLEXIBLE PERSONALITY CHARACTERISTICS describe individuals who have average, above average or below average assessment headings for most of their dispositions and broadly equal or more than assessment headings for most of their traits.

CONCLUSION

When we correctly apply assessment headings to personality characteristics, we arrive at a clearer understanding of our and other people's personalities. We are now in the position to start exploring the complexity of the individual. In the next chapter, we examine the personality characteristics and assessment headings of some very interesting individuals. As has been stressed several times before, in establishing individuals' assessment headings, we are making no judgement about their worth as people.

KEY POINTS

> WARNING ABOUT PERSONALITY ASSESSMENT
> In employee or student assessment, business executives or teachers judge the merits of employees' or students' work. This is not true of personality assessment, which is not concerned with the merits of an individual's personality. One kind of personality is neither better nor worse than another. Our personalities are just different. This is a point of fundamental importance.

The PERSONALITY CHARACTERISTICS are the eighteen principal features of our personality and consist of the five dispositions, five dimensions, seven social roles and intelligence span. Each personality characteristic is a scale, which measures, for example, intensity, influence or ability.

The PERSONALITY CHECKLIST is a list of the eighteen personality characteristics.

PERSONALITY ASSESSMENT HEADINGS are used to describe an individual's location on each of the eighteen personality characteristics.

WELL-DEFINED PERSONALITY CHARACTERISTICS describe individuals who have high, very high, low or very low assessment headings for most of their dispositions and pronounced or very pronounced assessment headings for most of their traits.

FLEXIBLE PERSONALITY CHARACTERISTICS describe individuals who have average, above average or below average assessment headings for most of their dispositions and broadly equal or more than assessment headings for most of their traits.

FURTHER NOTES

CHAPTER 16

The personality profile

From Chapters 1 to 14, we have learned about the eighteen personality characteristics. We also have the means, explained in Chapter 15, to describe each of the eighteen personality characteristics by using an assessment heading. Our task is now to describe an individual's personality using personality characteristics and assessment headings. We do this by attaching an assessment heading to each of the eighteen personality characteristics. We call this description using personality characteristics and assessment headings the 'personality profile', although we sometimes refer to the 'profile'. A completed example of the personality profile for an imaginary person is given in Table 16.1.

The PERSONALITY PROFILE is a list of the eighteen personality characteristics with an assessment heading attached to each personality characteristic.

Eventually, we will need to be able to prepare an individual's personality profile from our knowledge of the individual. However, before we can do this, it is necessary to become more familiar with using the ideas and concepts involved in personality profiling. One good way of achieving

Table 16.1 The personality profile for an imaginary person

PERSONALITY CHARACTERISTICS	ASSESSMENT HEADINGS
A) DISPOSITIONS	
1) Sociability	Average
2) Emotion	High
3) Ambition	Very high
4) Curiosity	High
5) Uncertainty	Low
B) DIMENSIONS	
1) Facts / possibilities	Pronounced facts
2) Group / independent	Pronounced group
3) Own-feelings / others'-feelings	More others'-feelings than own-feelings
4) Wide-interests / narrow-interests	Pronounced narrow-interests
5) Optimistic / pessimistic	Broadly equal
C) SOCIAL ROLES	
1) Communicator	High
2) Cost-benefit calculator	Average
3) Educator	High
4) Innovator	Very high
5) Lifelong learner	Very high
6) Organiser	Average
7) Accumulator	Absent
D) INTELLIGENCE SPAN	High

this objective is to learn how to interpret a personality profile. In other words, we become familiar with the personality characteristics and personality assessment headings through understanding and explaining the personality profiles of individuals. Accordingly, our task in the remainder of this chapter is to describe the principal aspects of individuals' personalities from their personality profiles. In other words, we learn to describe the main features of individuals' personalities from their personality characteristics and assessment headings.

We interpret eight personality profiles. They are very distinctive and, for this reason, easier to describe. In each case, we assume that we are going to meet the person represented by the personality profile. We want to anticipate as fully as possible the character of the person we are going to meet. For simplicity, we assume that the personality profiles describe men. Each personality profile has some similarities to the personality of a historical individual. This person is identified after each interpretation.

The skill of describing an individual from a personality profile can be mastered only with practice. When examining a personality profile for the first time, it is as well to begin by reviewing the whole profile. Consequently, you should read and think about the whole profile before reading the suggested interpretation. We interpret the first five profiles together. Then, you have the opportunity to practice your skill at interpreting personality profiles. You can interpret the last three profiles yourself and then read the suggested answers.

PERSONALITY PROFILE NUMBER ONE

The profile in Table 16.2 should be read and studied before proceeding any further. We should note that this personality profile has well-defined personality characteristics, which is also the case for the remaining personality profiles in this chapter. Another aspect of the profile that stands out is that this individual has many very powerful resources in the social roles and intelligence span. We now review his dispositions, dimensions, social roles and intelligence span in turn.

Dispositions
(Above average sociability, high emotion, very high ambition, very high curiosity and low uncertainty)

This person is happy to work in the company of others but works effectively on his own. There is real passion behind his actions. He wants to achieve great things and is very inquisitive. However, he sees little point in seeking out unpredictable situations and, for example, experiencing danger.

Dimensions
(Very pronounced facts, pronounced group, pronounced own-feelings, pronounced wide-interests and broadly equal attitudes to the future)

He has factual reasons for everything he does. He considers the available information very carefully before making any decisions. His lifestyle is routine and planned, but his sociability leads to some flexibility. He is loyal to his communities. The wellbeing of his communities matters greatly to him. He is self-willed and very much guided by his own feelings. He takes little interest in other people's feelings and, from time to time, seriously misjudges their moods and

Table 16.2 Personality profile number one

PERSONALITY CHARACTERISTICS	ASSESSMENT HEADINGS
A) DISPOSITIONS	
1) Sociability	Above average
2) Emotion	High
3) Ambition	Very high
4) Curiosity	Very high
5) Uncertainty	Low
B) DIMENSIONS	
1) Facts / possibilities	Very pronounced facts
2) Group / independent	Pronounced group
3) Own-feelings / others'-feelings	Pronounced own-feelings
4) Wide-interests / narrow-interests	Pronounced wide-interests
5) Optimistic / pessimistic	Broadly equal
C) SOCIAL ROLES	
1) Communicator	Very high
2) Cost-benefit calculator	High
3) Educator	High
4) Innovator	Very high
5) Lifelong learner	Very high
6) Organiser	High
7) Accumulator	Absent
D) INTELLIGENCE SPAN	Very high

feelings. He is rude and impolite. In view of his passionate nature and own-feelings trait, he is somewhat quarrelsome with people who disagree with him. Society, social issues and politics are really important to him. He is realistic about the future.

Social roles
(Very high communicator, high cost-benefit calculator, high educator, very high innovator, very high lifelong learner, high organiser and absent accumulator)

His writing or speaking is excellent and is often intended to educate. He has good personal, commercial and business judgement. Original ideas flow in abundance. He often masters new skills and can manage other people with little difficulty.

Intelligence span
(Very high)

After careful consideration of the facts, he takes the right decisions and makes few mistakes even with the most difficult problems.

Conclusion
We must be careful when meeting this person. We are unlikely to be a match for this gentleman. We are expecting to meet a very impressive and rather complicated individual. He is approachable and loyal to his communities. However, he is self-centred, blunt and frank. On account of his great talents, he seems likely to be important in society. He could be very successful in business, writing, journalism, diplomacy, politics, inventing or scientific research. One individual who shared some similarities to this personality profile was, in fact, very successful in all these careers. He was a famous American, Benjamin Franklin (1706–90).

A very short biography of Benjamin Franklin

Benjamin Franklin was very successful in business as a printer, publisher, writer, newspaperman and postmaster. He retired a rich man from business in early middle age. He then became a leading scientist, for example in his investigations into electricity, and inventor, for example the lightning rod and bifocal glasses. He was much involved in community affairs and projects from early middle age. He did much to benefit society. As a young man, he was rude and arrogant. On retiring from business, he took a keen interest in politics, but, from time to time, seriously misjudged the public mood. Late in life, he played a prominent part in the achievement of American Independence, especially as a highly successful diplomat to France. He was one of America's Founding Fathers, who helped draft the American Constitution in 1787.

PERSONALITY PROFILE NUMBER TWO

The profile in Table 16.3 should be read and studied before proceeding any further. At first inspection, this individual also has some important resources in social roles and intelligence. We would again expect him to be a person of importance. His traits promise to make him a most distinctive individual.

Dispositions

(High sociability, very high emotion, very high ambition, average curiosity and very high uncertainty)

This person spends lots of time with other people. He is deeply moved by what he experiences. He wants to do great things. He is very attracted by the tension of unpredictable outcomes, especially risky activities and danger. He has a passion for perilous pastimes.

Dimensions
(Very pronounced possibilities, pronounced independent,
very pronounced own-feelings, very pronounced wide-
interests and pronounced optimistic)

His decisions are almost entirely based on assessing alternative outcomes. He is imaginative and capable of supplying an inspiring vision. His lifestyle is full of variety, and he rarely makes long-term plans. He has little loyalty to his communities. His own aims and objectives guide his actions and, in order to follow them, he is prepared to change sides or companies. He does not think or worry very much about other people's feelings. He is rude and bad-mannered. His interest is in society as a whole. His optimism leads him to expect success and helps him to recover quickly from disappointments and setbacks. He is cheerful and buoyant.

Social roles
(Very high communicator, low cost-benefit calculator, absent
educator, low innovator, high lifelong learner, high
organiser and absent accumulator)

He is a fine speaker or writer or both. However, he makes some bad decisions. His financial skills are poor. Even in later life, with a great deal of experience, he makes serious misjudgements, which significantly damage his career. On the positive side, he often learns new skills and is a good manager.

Intelligence span
(Very high)

His very high intelligence makes him very perceptive and insightful.

Table 16.3 Personality profile number two

PERSONALITY CHARACTERISTICS	ASSESSMENT HEADINGS
A) DISPOSITIONS	
1) Sociability	High
2) Emotion	Very high
3) Ambition	Very high
4) Curiosity	Average
5) Uncertainty	Very high
B) DIMENSIONS	
1) Facts / possibilities	Very pronounced possibilities
2) Group / independent	Pronounced independent
3) Own-feelings / others'-feelings	Very pronounced own-feelings
4) Wide-interests / narrow-interests	Very pronounced wide-interests
5) Optimistic / pessimistic	Pronounced optimistic
C) SOCIAL ROLES	
1) Communicator	Very high
2) Cost-benefit calculator	Low
3) Educator	Absent
4) Innovator	Low
5) Lifelong learner	High
6) Organiser	High
7) Accumulator	Absent
D) INTELLIGENCE SPAN	Very high

Conclusion

We should also be rather wary of this person. He follows his own agenda, is self-centred and is blunt in his comments. His very pronounced possibilities trait and very high intelligence mean he is exceptionally quick-witted and at his best in a sudden crisis. He is very interested in society as a whole. His fine communication skills are used to great advantage in his career. However, his lack of loyalty, poor judgement and preoccupation with self could significantly hold back his career at the very highest level. He does not attract personal loyalty. One person who shared some similarities to this personality profile was Winston Churchill (1874–1965), considered by many to be the greatest of all Englishmen.

A very short biography of Winston Churchill

Winston Churchill's first career was as a cavalry officer. He was a fine horseman and polo player. He enjoyed danger and, as a young military officer, travelled the world in order to take part in military conflict. He soon entered politics but was dedicated to his own objectives. He successfully changed political parties twice, an event almost unknown in British politics. He was rapidly promoted to senior political office. Fairly or otherwise, his impulsive actions and judgement were questioned during the First World War (1914–18), and, to his great shock, he was demoted. With his irrepressible optimism and great vigour, he soon returned to high office. He held senior political appointments in the 1920s. In the 1930s, his 'wilderness' years, his political judgement was generally poor and led to politically damaging outcomes. The very important exception was his fierce opposition to Adolf Hitler, the Nazi dictator. Churchill became British wartime Prime Minister during the great crisis of 1940.

PERSONALITY PROFILE NUMBER THREE

The profile in Table 16.4 should be read and studied before proceeding any further. Here, the social roles suggest general competence, although a less complicated person than our first two examples.

Dispositions

(Low sociability, high emotion, very high ambition, very high curiosity and very low uncertainty)

This person largely works alone but is driven by passion. His determination to achieve something important and his inquisitiveness shape his life.

Dimensions

(Very pronounced facts, pronounced group, pronounced others'-feelings, pronounced narrow-interests and broadly equal attitudes to the future)

This person relies almost completely on the reason and logic of facts. Decisions are justified by facts. His lifestyle is routine, and he plans far ahead. On account of his great curiosity and pronounced narrow-interests trait, he is interested in some kind of specialist subject. Although he mostly thinks alone, he is loyal to his communities. His sensitivity to the needs and views of others defines his personal relationships. He thinks much about the wellbeing of his few close companions and is devastated by personal loss. He is easily hurt and distressed by any kind of criticism. He has very little interest in politics.

Social roles

(Average communicator, average cost-benefit calculator, above average educator, very high innovator, above average lifelong learner, above average organiser and absent accumulator)

Only the very high innovator role, which combines

Table 16.4 Personality profile number three

PERSONALITY CHARACTERISTICS	ASSESSMENT HEADINGS
A) DISPOSITIONS	
1) Sociability	Low
2) Emotion	High
3) Ambition	Very high
4) Curiosity	Very high
5) Uncertainty	Very low
B) DIMENSIONS	
1) Facts / possibilities	Very pronounced facts
2) Group / independent	Pronounced group
3) Own-feelings / others'-feelings	Pronounced others'-feelings
4) Wide-interests / narrow-interests	Pronounced narrow-interests
5) Optimistic / pessimistic	Broadly equal
C) SOCIAL ROLES	
1) Communicator	Average
2) Cost-benefit calculator	Average
3) Educator	Above average
4) Innovator	Very high
5) Lifelong learner	Above average
6) Organiser	Above average
7) Accumulator	Absent
D) INTELLIGENCE SPAN	Very high

powerfully with his very high curiosity, stands out. We are dealing here with an original thinker. This person finds new explanations to questions posed by his curiosity. There are some useful other social roles which result in an all-round general competence.

Intelligence span
(Very high)

His very high intelligence, when combined with his low sociability, very high curiosity and very high innovator social role, results in a specialist career in a profession or advanced research.

Conclusion

The low sociability, pronounced others'-feelings trait and pronounced narrow-interests trait lead us to anticipate a quiet, sensitive, even withdrawn person. This individual is polite but, at best, distant. He gives away very little at a first meeting. His abiding interest is his own thoughts and problems. One person who shared some similarities to this personality profile was not a man but a woman. She was Marie Curie (1867–1934), the only scientist to have been awarded Nobel Prizes in two distinct sciences (jointly for physics (1903) and individually for chemistry (1911)).

A very short biography of Marie Curie

Marie Curie was a hard-working and brilliant student. Although she was born and brought up in Poland, her great ambition led her to study physics in France, where she excelled. There, she met her husband and had an all too short period of great family happiness. She was an outstanding scientific researcher and the most painstaking of individual experimenters. She worked for years on the same problem. The facts of science dominated her professional thinking. The early death of her husband was a devastating personal blow from which she never recovered. She retreated into her work.

PERSONALITY PROFILE NUMBER FOUR

The profile in Table 16.5 should be read and studied before proceeding any further. This person has four exceptional resources in social roles and intelligence. One intriguing question is the use to which he has put his very high communicator and innovator social roles when combined with his very high intelligence.

Dispositions
(Very high sociability, very high emotion, very high ambition, low curiosity and low uncertainty)

This person enjoys the company of others. He talks constantly to his friends and enjoys parties. If at all possible, he never spends his leisure time alone. His temper is powerful, and his feelings are passionate. At times, he becomes very angry. He is determined to be successful.

Dimensions
(Very pronounced possibilities, pronounced independent, pronounced others'-feelings, pronounced narrow-interests and broadly equal attitudes to the future)

His imagination guides nearly all of his actions. He takes immediate decisions based on exploring alternatives. He decides what to do at that instant in time. His lifestyle is impulsive and full of variety. He is restless, frequently on the move. There is little loyalty or identification with any community. His actions are generally kind and considerate. He is deeply concerned about people's reaction to his work.

Table 16.5 Personality profile number four

PERSONALITY CHARACTERISTICS	ASSESSMENT HEADINGS
A) DISPOSITIONS	
1) Sociability	Very high
2) Emotion	Very high
3) Ambition	Very high
4) Curiosity	Low
5) Uncertainty	Low
B) DIMENSIONS	
1) Facts / possibilities	Very pronounced possibilities
2) Group / independent	Pronounced independent
3) Own-feelings / others'-feelings	Pronounced others'-feelings
4) Wide-interests / narrow-interests	Pronounced narrow-interests
5) Optimistic / pessimistic	Broadly equal
C) SOCIAL ROLES	
1) Communicator	Very high
2) Cost-benefit calculator	High
3) Educator	Low
4) Innovator	Very high
5) Lifelong learner	Low
6) Organiser	Low
7) Accumulator	Low
D) INTELLIGENCE SPAN	Very high

His friendships are intense, but he has little interest in wider society.

Social roles
(Very high communicator, high cost-benefit calculator, low educator, very high innovator, low lifelong learner, low organiser and low accumulator)
He is excellent at expressing his very pronounced possibilities visions, which contain much originality. His cost-benefit skills ensure financial success.

Intelligence span
(Very high)
In his work, he takes extraordinarily good decisions and implements them to a very high standard.

Conclusion
We are expecting to meet a man driven by his very intense, very highly original and personal visions which are of the highest quality. They are implemented with great skill. He is very outgoing but has only a few very close friends. If we enter this circle of friends, we are always welcome in his company. His career depends on the nature of his very high communication talent and the expression of his very pronounced possibilities trait. However, he is financially well rewarded for his efforts. One historical person who had some similarities to this personality profile inevitably had to work alone at his art. He was Pablo Picasso (1881–1973), one of the best-known artists of the twentieth century, and, with Georges Braque, the inventor of Cubism.

A very short biography of Pablo Picasso
Pablo Picasso was Spanish but lived and stayed at many different addresses in France, very largely in Paris. He was a

prodigiously gifted artist from early childhood. With the sole exception of his work, which was of necessity a solitary occupation, Picasso was always socialising with other people. He was only interested in his own work and, during a long life, generally took very little interest in politics. He was extraordinarily financially successful. He was generous to his friends, though he was very domineering in old age. He was a prolific artist in many media (perhaps the most prolific).

PERSONALITY PROFILE NUMBER FIVE

The profile in Table 16.6 should be read and studied before proceeding any further. The combination of very high curiosity, a very high innovator social role and very high intelligence suggests someone of great talent.

Dispositions
(High sociability, very high emotion, high ambition, very high curiosity and very low uncertainty)
This person enjoys the company of others. He likes being and working with other people. He is very passionate. He hopes to achieve something important with his life. Curiosity shapes his life and actions. He has no interest in the tension of unpredictable outcomes and is completely bored by competitions.

Dimensions
(Pronounced possibilities, pronounced independent, pronounced own-feelings, broadly equal in social interests and broadly equal attitudes to the future)
Problems are largely solved by imagining and assessing alternative outcomes. His highly imaginative insights are

driven by his very high curiosity. His lifestyle is one of variety. Loyalty to communities plays little part in his decisions or life. He gives a high priority to his own interests and is self-centred. He is rude and blunt in his remarks.

Social roles
(Above average communicator, below average cost-benefit calculator, above average educator, very high innovator, average lifelong learner, low organiser and absent accumulator)

His abiding passion is solving by original thought the problems raised by his very high curiosity. His one very high social role (innovator) means that his originality combined with his curiosity are the principal influences on his life.

Intelligence span
(Very high)

His very high intelligence means that his mature judgements are generally of a very high standard.

Conclusion
Since he has high ambition, very high curiosity, a very high innovator social role and very high intelligence, we anticipate an important thinker. His high sociability means he likes to work with other people. It says nothing about the importance of his individual contributions. One historical person who shared some similarities to this personality profile was Albert Einstein (1879–1955), the famous physicist and considered by many to be one of the greatest scientists.

A very short biography of Albert Einstein
Albert Einstein's lifelong, dominating passion was his intense curiosity about nature. He liked to work with others. He made fundamental contributions of lasting

Table 16.6 Personality profile number five

PERSONALITY CHARACTERISTICS	ASSESSMENT HEADINGS
A) DISPOSITIONS	
1) Sociability	High
2) Emotion	Very high
3) Ambition	High
4) Curiosity	Very high
5) Uncertainty	Very low
B) DIMENSIONS	
1) Facts / possibilities	Pronounced possibilities
2) Group / independent	Pronounced independent
3) Own-feelings / others'-feelings	Pronounced own-feelings
4) Wide-interests / narrow-interests	Broadly equal
5) Optimistic / pessimistic	Broadly equal
C) SOCIAL ROLES	
1) Communicator	Above average
2) Cost-benefit calculator	Below average
3) Educator	Above average
4) Innovator	Very high
5) Lifelong learner	Average
6) Organiser	Low
7) Accumulator	Absent
D) INTELLIGENCE SPAN	Very high

importance in understanding mass, energy, space and time. His way of thinking was to imagine what it would be like, for example, to ride a beam of light or to fall freely in a gravitational field. In this way, he was able to question our basic assumptions about nature. He showed little loyalty to any institution. He put himself first. He was blunt, and his sharp wit could be unkind. As a young father, he had nothing to do with his daughter who was born outside of marriage. His first marriage ended in divorce. In science, he went his own way and achieved little in the second half of his life.

ADVICE FOR COMPLETING THE NEXT THREE PERSONALITY INTERPRETATIONS

You now have the opportunity to prepare your own interpretations of the next three personality profiles (six, seven and eight). Each interpretation should be completed before reading the suggested answer. However, if you wish to read the suggested answer immediately, there is still much to be learned about interpreting personality profiles. You can also learn a little about a historical person who shared some similarities to each personality profile.

PERSONALITY PROFILE NUMBER SIX

The profile in Table 16.7 should be read and studied carefully. Your interpretation of this individual's personality should be based on his personality profile.

Table 16.7 Personality profile number six

PERSONALITY CHARACTERISTICS	ASSESSMENT HEADINGS
A) DISPOSITIONS	
1) Sociability	Below average
2) Emotion	Very high
3) Ambition	Very high
4) Curiosity	Low
5) Uncertainty	Low
B) DIMENSIONS	
1) Facts / possibilities	Very pronounced possibilities
2) Group / independent	Very pronounced group
3) Own-feelings / others'-feelings	Pronounced others'-feelings
4) Wide-interests / narrow-interests	Very pronounced wide-interests
5) Optimistic / pessimistic	Very pronounced optimistic
C) SOCIAL ROLES	
1) Communicator	Very high
2) Cost-benefit calculator	Low
3) Educator	Low
4) Innovator	Low
5) Lifelong learner	Low
6) Organiser	Low
7) Accumulator	Absent
D) INTELLIGENCE SPAN	Above average

SUGGESTED ANSWER TO PERSONALITY PROFILE NUMBER SIX

This person is rather different from the earlier examples. He lacks the high or very high intelligence to help him achieve his very high ambition. One puzzle is how he may use his very high communicator social role.

Dispositions

(Below average sociability, very high emotion, very high ambition, low curiosity and low uncertainty)

He spends most of his time alone, but he has companions even if he lacks friends. An intense passion drives his great sense of destiny.

Dimensions

(Very pronounced possibilities, very pronounced group, pronounced others'-feelings, very pronounced wide-interests and very pronounced optimistic)

He takes spontaneous decisions based on exploring alternatives. He decides what to do at the time. His lifestyle is impulsive and full of variety. His very pronounced possibilities trait and below average sociability result in a life which is wholly guided by his own imagination. He is entirely inspired by his own passionate visions. The whole meaning of his life comes from his loyalty to, and identification with, his communities. He is very good at sensing the moods and feelings of others. He is very interested in society as a whole. He is totally convinced that he will succeed whatever setbacks he experiences.

Social roles

(Very high communicator, every other role is low except accumulator which is absent)

His one outstanding skill is to communicate information or emotion to others. In view of his very high emotion and very pronounced possibilities trait, he communicates the highly emotional contents of his imagination. The content comes from his intense loyalty to his communities and interest in society at large. His communication is especially effective because of his pronounced others'-feelings trait. He is sensitive to, and responds to, the moods of his audiences. His lack of resources in other social roles means that he is unsuccessful in many situations.

Intelligence span

(Above average)

He makes mistakes in situations which are difficult. He is unable to foresee the outcome of complex events. He appears to lack the intelligence for significant career success.

Conclusion

We must expect to meet an individual who is driven by his very high emotion, very high ambition and his very pronounced possibilities trait. His very pronounced optimistic trait leads to his belief that he will be successful. For that reason, he automatically assumes that he will achieve his ambitions. In view of his very high emotion, any failure to achieve his very high ambition would result in a severely disappointed and angry man. His very pronounced group trait means he is very loyal to his communities. His very pronounced wide-interests trait is seen in his great concern for society as a whole. The result is very strongly-held political beliefs which put his communities first. His one resource is his very high communicator social role, which his pronounced others'-feelings trait makes very effective. Adolf Hitler (1889–1945) shared some similarities to this personality profile.

A very short biography of Adolf Hitler

Adolf Hitler was the all-powerful Nazi dictator of Germany (1933–45). He was a racist, imperialist warlord, who seized power in highly disturbed times. His hypnotic speeches (his very high communicator social role) fed off the mass hysteria of his times (his pronounced others'-feelings trait) and resulted in his rise to power. He created a mass political party, which his speeches inspired, to achieve his fanatical visions. His driving nationalist inspiration (his very pronounced group trait) was of a Germany reborn in military greatness. His spontaneity, blind optimism, disregard of the facts and absurd visions for a German slave empire in Eastern Europe resulted in many successes through surprising his opponents. He started the Second World War (1939–45) to establish his slave empire. The resulting conflict caused tens of millions of deaths and devastated Europe. His other fanatical political goal was the racial purity of Germany. He blamed previous German failures on defenceless minorities both in Germany and abroad. In revenge, he ordered the Holocaust in which six million Jews, Gypsies and others were murdered. He committed suicide in 1945, a completely broken man with his world in ruins. He is generally regarded as the most evil person of all time.

PERSONALITY PROFILE NUMBER SEVEN

The profile in Table 16.8 should be read and studied carefully. Your own interpretation of this individual's personality should be based on his personality profile.

Table 16.8 Personality profile number seven

PERSONALITY CHARACTERISTICS	ASSESSMENT HEADINGS
A) DISPOSITIONS	
1) Sociability	Above average
2) Emotion	Very high
3) Ambition	Very high
4) Curiosity	Low
5) Uncertainty	Low
B) DIMENSIONS	
1) Facts / possibilities	Very pronounced facts
2) Group / independent	Very pronounced independent
3) Own-feelings / others'-feelings	Very pronounced own-feelings
4) Wide-interests / narrow-interests	Very pronounced wide-interests
5) Optimistic / pessimistic	Broadly equal
C) SOCIAL ROLES	
1) Communicator	Low
2) Cost-benefit calculator	Low
3) Educator	Low
4) Innovator	Low
5) Lifelong learner	Low
6) Organiser	High
7) Accumulator	Absent
D) INTELLIGENCE SPAN	High

SUGGESTED ANSWER TO PERSONALITY PROFILE
NUMBER SEVEN

We would do well to be rather cautious about our dealings
with this person. He is dedicated to pursuing his own aims
and objectives (very pronounced independent trait) and is
almost completely concerned with his own feelings (very
pronounced own-feelings trait).

Dispositions
(Above average sociability, very high emotion, very high
ambition, low curiosity and low uncertainty)
This person likes working with others, which points to a
career which involves social contacts. His profound sense of
destiny is fuelled by the strongest passion.

Dimensions
(Very pronounced facts, very pronounced independent,
very pronounced own-feelings, very pronounced wide-
interests and broadly equal attitudes to the future)
Decisions are justified by facts, which totally guide his
thinking. He is greatly impressed by the application of logic
to practical problems. His lifestyle has much routine, and he
plans years ahead. He nearly always puts his own aims and
objectives first. He has very little loyalty to any community.
He is much involved with his own feelings, and other
people's minds are largely closed to him. He does not think or
worry very much about other people's feelings. He is often
extremely blunt and very rude to other people. He is very
concerned about events in society.

Social roles
(High organiser, all others low except accumulator which is
absent)

He can impose his will on others by his personal presence. His lack of other social roles means that, in many situations, he is likely to make serious mistakes.

Intelligence span
(High)

His high intelligence means he can solve difficult problems, but he struggles when dealing with issues of great complexity.

Conclusion

We are again expecting to meet a person whose great desire to succeed is driven by intense emotion. His one high social role is that of organiser, which forms the basis of any success. His above average sociability, very pronounced facts trait and high intelligence suggest an administrative career. He plays an influential part in organisations, but his actions derive from his own aims and objectives. He ignores the feelings of other people. He is an effective manager, who rejects inappropriate traditions and is prepared to take unpleasant and difficult decisions concerning staff. Joseph Stalin (1879–1953) shared some similarities to this personality profile.

A very short biography of Joseph Stalin

Joseph Stalin was the Marxist-Leninist dictator of the Soviet Union (1924–53). He seized power shortly after the Communist revolution, using his control of the party bureaucracy, which was in charge of the country. His fanatical attempt to impose Communism in the Soviet Union resulted in utter disaster. Millions died of starvation. He then retained power through a reign of terror. Millions more innocent people were executed or imprisoned under terrible conditions. He personally arranged for the murder of his close family, long-standing colleagues, acquaintances and friends. He became increasingly obsessed with his historical reputation as the Great Man who implemented Communism. He attempted to destroy any evidence of his mistakes. Facts were hidden, and witnesses killed. Stalin died an isolated and lonely individual, who, in his last years, lived in perpetual fear of assassination. He is widely regarded as one of the most evil people of all time.

PERSONALITY PROFILE NUMBER EIGHT

The profile in Table 16.9 should be read and studied carefully. Your own interpretation of this individual's personality should be based on his personality profile.

SUGGESTED ANSWER TO PERSONALITY PROFILE NUMBER EIGHT

This person is interesting, because, unlike the previous examples, very high ambition is combined with low emotion. On first meeting, there is a real danger of underestimating this person. He may appear rather relaxed and lacking the drive of most successful people.

Dispositions
(High sociability, low emotion, very high ambition, low curiosity and above average uncertainty)
He very much enjoys working and socialising with other people. He wishes to achieve a great deal, but his low emotion results in an easy-going lifestyle. He lacks passionate beliefs and is content to let other people do the work. However, he does enjoy the tension caused by uncertainty and seeks out situations which involve unpredictability.

Table 16.9 Personality profile number eight

PERSONALITY CHARACTERISTICS	ASSESSMENT HEADINGS
A) DISPOSITIONS	
1) Sociability	High
2) Emotion	Low
3) Ambition	Very high
4) Curiosity	Low
5) Uncertainty	Above average
B) DIMENSIONS	
1) Facts / possibilities	Pronounced facts
2) Group / independent	Pronounced group
3) Own-feelings / others'-feelings	Very pronounced others'-feelings
4) Wide-interests / narrow-interests	Very pronounced wide-interests
5) Optimistic / pessimistic	More optimistic than pessimistic
C) SOCIAL ROLES	
1) Communicator	High
2) Cost-benefit calculator	Low
3) Educator	Low
4) Innovator	Low
5) Lifelong learner	Low
6) Organiser	High
7) Accumulator	Absent
D) INTELLIGENCE SPAN	High

Dimensions
(Pronounced facts, pronounced group, very pronounced others'-feelings, very pronounced wide-interests and more optimistic than pessimistic)

His decisions are generally based on facts. He is loyal to his various communities and, for this reason, inspires trust. His obvious sympathy and compassion make him very well-liked and popular. He is very interested in society at large. His optimism means that he responds positively to setbacks and is not disheartened by failure.

Social roles
(High communicator, high organiser, every other role is low except accumulator which is absent)

His communicator and organiser social roles are important resources for a career in a senior executive position. However, his lack of resources in other social roles means that he is capable of making mistakes and depends a great deal on advice from others. He is a poor investor and also lacks originality.

Intelligence span
(High)

He is unable to dominate intellectually people with a very high intelligence span.

Conclusion
We should be very cautious when dealing with this person. We expect to be completely charmed by his kindness and personal attention. Moreover, his humanity and tact make him highly likeable and give rise to significant personal loyalty. On account of his high sociability and very high ambition, he works effectively with others. His low emotion means that he is excellent at delegating. His ability to delegate may make up for his lack of good judgement. His composed

manner is useful in pacifying the anger of friends and opponents. Moreover, he does not panic in crises. He takes notice of the facts. He is also very interested in society at large. His cheerful outlook means that he is not disheartened by failure. He is a good communicator and has natural dignity and authority. Franklin D Roosevelt (1882–1945), considered by many to be one of America's greatest Presidents, shared some similarities to this personality profile.

A very short biography of Franklin D Roosevelt

Franklin D Roosevelt was the 32nd and the longest-serving President of America (1932–45). Voters found him very attractive. He could charm anyone, including the press. He responded to crises calmly and was undeterred by setbacks. He successfully dealt with the massive economic disruption of the 1930s, 'The Great Depression'. He also led America to victory in the Second World War (1941–5). All this was achieved despite the fact that he was largely paralysed from the waist down as a result of an illness in the early 1920s. He was distinguished by his willingness to listen and his ability to handle other politicians. Perhaps his greatest skill was his effective use of staff and his powers of delegation. He surrounded himself with the most able aides, who were deeply loyal to him personally. He relied very heavily on the judgement and advice of two very close associates. He was not a hard-working President and was dependent on others for his policy ideas. He was open to suggestions. He was prepared to abandon any of his policies which failed to produce results.

CONCLUSION

In this chapter, we have found a remarkable variety of personality profiles among only eight people. Nevertheless, the same personality characteristics are common to all our examples. The dispositions, dimensions, social roles and intelligence span successfully supply all the required concepts for a full account of eight very different individuals.

KEY POINTS

The PERSONALITY PROFILE is a list of the eighteen personality characteristics with an assessment heading attached to each personality characteristic.

FURTHER NOTES

CHAPTER 17

Personality assessment using the personality profile

In Chapter 16, we produced short descriptions of individuals from their personality profiles. In this chapter, we now reverse the process and produce personality profiles from short descriptions. The assessment of personality using the personality profile is a very important skill to acquire. We have seen in Chapter 16 that people can have very different personality profiles. Unless we can prepare accurate personality profiles, there will be significant gaps in our knowledge of people. If we want a good understanding of others, we have to be able to produce for ourselves, when required, a correct personality profile.

In order to improve our skills at personality profiling, some practice is essential. In this chapter, we prepare nine personality profiles from short descriptions of nine particularly interesting individuals. All the nine examples are men. Their personality profiles have some likenesses to the personality profiles of historical individuals who gained a widespread reputation in their lifetimes. At the end of each of the nine personality profiles, there is a short biography of the historical individual whose personality has some similarities to the profile. We prepare the first four profiles together, using the descriptions which are supplied. You are then invited to prepare your own personality profile for each of the remaining five individuals from the information supplied. The guidance notes to these five exercises are given immediately before the first exercise. These exercises require a working knowledge of Chapters 1 to 16.

We now describe the process of personality profiling used in this chapter by referring to the first paragraph of example number one, which reads as follows:

> 'This person was a highly successful military commander [above average uncertainty]. He always put the interests of the military before his own personal ambitions [very pronounced group]. He travelled a great deal [ambiguous – there are many reasons why people travel]. He worked very well in committees but also wrote and studied reports by himself [above average sociability]. He wanted to command the most important military operations [high ambition], although he did not expect to rise to the very high rank that he achieved [broadly equal attitudes to the future].'

You can see that there are some conclusions about this individual's personality characteristics and assessment headings which are identified within square brackets. For example, the first sentence is 'This person was a highly successful military commander [above average uncertainty]'. This square bracket means that, based on the evidence from the first sentence, the individual has an above average assessment heading in the uncertainty disposition.

We now summarise the assessment process used in the first sentence of example number one. In this sentence, we are told that the individual is a military commander. We can reasonably assume that military commanders enjoy the tension and thrill of uncertainty, which is a necessary feature of military action. Consequently, we draw the conclusion '[above average uncertainty]' at the end of the first sentence of his description. As it happens, there is no later evidence to make us change our minds, for example to revise our conclusion to high uncertainty. When we complete example number one's personality profile, we write 'above average' against the uncertainty disposition. This assessment process is repeated for the remainder of the description. Each sentence of the description is reviewed for evidence of personality characteristics and assessment headings which are then noted within square brackets. Finally, for each personality characteristic, we review all the evidence in order to arrive at an assessment heading for the personality profile.

Some of the information given about each individual is noted as irrelevant to personality or ambiguous. Other information may relate to more than one personality characteristic. You should treat the conclusions with regard to the personality profiles in this chapter cautiously. Reasonable people could make slightly different assessments from the same short description. It is sometimes especially difficult to make assessments near either end of a personality characteristic scale. For example, the decision whether a trait is pronounced or very pronounced is difficult from a short written description. It is really necessary to meet people and observe their personality characteristics closely. Inevitably, our assessments in this chapter are based on a small amount of written evidence. Where there is no evidence concerning a disposition or social role, it is probable that the assessment heading is low, very low or absent. Where there is no evidence concerning a dimension, it is probable that the assessment heading is broadly equal.

EXAMPLE NUMBER ONE

A short description of the individual in example number one

This person was a highly successful military commander [above average uncertainty]. He always put the interests of the military before his own personal ambitions [very pronounced group]. He travelled a great deal [ambiguous – there are many reasons why people travel]. He worked very well in committees but also wrote and studied reports by himself [above average sociability]. He wanted to command the most important military operations [high ambition], although he did not expect to rise to the very high rank that he achieved [broadly equal attitudes to the future].

He had a major responsibility for military planning at which he was very good [pronounced facts]. He insisted that there had to be long-term plans for operations and these had to be supported by detailed facts [pronounced facts]. All his decisions were carefully thought out and based on the best possible understanding of the situation [pronounced facts]. He tried to have as much information as was available when making a decision [pronounced facts]. He strongly criticised those who wanted to take spontaneous decisions based on their own sudden insights [pronounced facts]. At meetings, he had angry public arguments with those with whom he disagreed [high emotion]. He regularly lost his temper at these meetings [high emotion]. He assessed the likely success of each military operation [broadly equal attitudes to the future].

He had a natural dignity and immediately inspired great respect and confidence [very high organiser]. In his career, he played an important role in successfully managing extremely complex operations [very high organiser]. Much of his time was taken up with deciding the use of military resources, which he did very well [high cost-benefit calculator].

His decisions, which were very difficult to make, were far more often right than wrong [very high intelligence]. He was good at explaining his own point of view [above average communicator]. In order to win arguments, he took a close interest in the views of those who could influence decisions [very high intelligence]. His judgement of the personalities of his fellow officers and politicians was exceptionally good [very high organiser and very high intelligence].

He felt a genuine sympathy for others and understood how they felt [pronounced others'-feelings]. At the same time, he could take difficult military decisions which resulted in the deaths of many military personnel [very pronounced group]. He took a general interest in the news, politics and social controversies [broadly equal wide-interests and narrow-interests].

Our description of this man is very short, but it is sufficient to establish from our notes many of the assessment headings in his personality profile. Since we have only summary evidence, reasonable people could sensibly reach slightly different conclusions. We can now use the preceding analysis to prepare a personality profile (see Table 17.1).

A similar historical individual to example number one

Alan Brooke (1883–1963), Chief of the (British) Imperial General Staff (1941–6), had some similarities to the personality profile described in example number one. He was a loyal British career officer, who was devoted to his country, and was the most senior British military officer during the Second World War. He was highly intelligent, took very good cost-benefit decisions and was one of the leading strategists behind the Allied victory in Europe. He had an impressive personal presence and was highly effective when dealing with his senior officers. He was an exceptionally talented field commander, military planner and organiser.

Table 17.1 Example number one personality profile

PERSONALITY CHARACTERISTICS	ASSESSMENT HEADINGS
A) DISPOSITIONS	
1) Sociability	Above average
2) Emotion	High
3) Ambition	High
4) Curiosity	No evidence
5) Uncertainty	Above average
B) DIMENSIONS	
1) Facts / possibilities	Pronounced facts
2) Group / independent	Very pronounced group
3) Own-feelings / others'-feelings	Pronounced others'-feelings
4) Wide-interests / narrow-interests	Broadly equal
5) Optimistic / pessimistic	Broadly equal
C) SOCIAL ROLES	
1) Communicator	Above average
2) Cost-benefit calculator	High
3) Educator	No evidence
4) Innovator	No evidence
5) Lifelong learner	No evidence
6) Organiser	Very high
7) Accumulator	No evidence
D) INTELLIGENCE SPAN	Very high

Note: where there is no evidence concerning a disposition or social role, it is probable that the assessment heading is low, very low or absent. Where there is no evidence concerning a dimension, it is probable that the assessment heading is broadly equal.

EXAMPLE NUMBER TWO

A short description of the individual in example number two

This person achieved distinction in his profession, but his later fame came as a surprise to him [broadly equal attitudes to the future]. His own assessment was that he had achieved everything that was possible for him [irrelevant – feelings of self-satisfaction are not a personality characteristic]. He made important contributions to his profession and was highly regarded as an original thinker [very high innovator and very high intelligence].

His great desire was to understand what it meant to be human [very high ambition and very high curiosity]. He saw each individual as unique [ambiguous – either a facts or possibilities thinker could agree with this rather vague sentence]. In his view, when it came to understanding the individual, there were no general principles [ambiguous – for the same reason as before]. With regard to the inner life of the mind, he argued that there was nothing to be gained by scientific reasoning based on theory [ambiguous – for the same reason as before]. As a matter of principle, he believed at all times in his sudden insights [very pronounced possibilities].

By far the most important source of his insights was his own imagination [very pronounced possibilities]. He looked to the contents of his own mind, especially his many visions, for guidance, while very largely ignoring the world of experience and fact [very pronounced possibilities and pronounced independent]. He was certain that there was a spiritual world beyond the everyday world [irrelevant – the existence of spiritual beliefs (or lack of them) are unaffected by the facts or possibilities traits, although the nature of the beliefs can be expected to differ depending on the primary trait]. For part of his life, he became very interested in the secrets, which, in his opinion, were to be found hidden in some very old books [very high curiosity].

A sudden insight led him to decide on his future career [very pronounced possibilities]. He was spontaneous in his actions and decisions [very pronounced possibilities lifestyle]. In his profession and his writings, he generally worked alone [below average sociability]. He was confident in the correctness of his decisions, because they were based on the content of his dreams [very pronounced possibilities and pronounced independent]. He was greatly upset by his own intense feelings, which, at times, he thought would destroy him [very high emotion].

He wanted, above all, to be free to follow his own intellectual interests [pronounced independent]. His quarrels with close colleagues were intense [very high emotion]. He was only interested in his own ideas [pronounced independent]. As an adult, he refused to join any professional group except his own [pronounced independent]. He published many books, which were regarded as important contributions to spiritual awareness [high communicator, high educator, very high innovator and very high intelligence]. He was a teacher who gave many lessons to his patients [high educator]. Although he was largely uninterested in society at large [pronounced narrow-interests], he had a natural dignity and authority, which enabled him to exercise authority over larger groups [high organiser]. In his view, his intellectual interests separated him from other people [below average sociability]. Nevertheless, he was married with children [irrelevant – all kinds of people marry and have children]. He thoroughly enjoyed foreign travel [ambiguous – it could be high uncertainty, possibilities lifestyle or high accumulator social role or some combination of these personality characteristics].

He was indiscreet and unaware when he had upset other people [pronounced own-feelings]. He lacked sympathy for others [pronounced own-feelings]. He was rude, frank and unfeeling in his actions, comments and observations [pronounced own-feelings]. He displayed little interest in politics [pronounced narrow-interests]. He made great efforts to promote his own ideas [very high ambition]. We can now use this analysis to prepare a personality profile (see Table 17.2).

A similar historical individual to example number two

Carl Jung (1875–1961), a psychiatrist, was one of the leading religious thinkers of the twentieth century. He had some similarities to the personality profile described in example number two. He was both inspired and driven by his dreams, daydreams and fantasies. As a psychiatrist, he made important contributions to his profession. He was an early supporter of Sigmund Freud (1856–1939), but the two men later had major disagreements. He developed an important and influential theory of personality which was based on eight personality types. This aspect of Jung's work is discussed in Chapter 24.

EXAMPLE NUMBER THREE

A short description of the individual in example number three

For a while, this person was financially and commercially very successful in business [high cost-benefit calculator and very high intelligence], but later did much to harm his own company [ambiguous – harmful actions can have many different causes]. He was known for his unusual opinions [ambiguous – unusual opinions have many origins]. He was

Table 17.2 Example number two personality profile

PERSONALITY CHARACTERISTICS	ASSESSMENT HEADINGS
A) DISPOSITIONS	
1) Sociability	Below average
2) Emotion	Very high
3) Ambition	Very high
4) Curiosity	Very high
5) Uncertainty	No evidence
B) DIMENSIONS	
1) Facts / possibilities	Very pronounced possibilities
2) Group / independent	Pronounced independent
3) Own-feelings / others'-feelings	Pronounced own-feelings
4) Wide-interests / narrow-interests	Pronounced narrow-interests
5) Optimistic / pessimistic	Broadly equal
C) SOCIAL ROLES	
1) Communicator	High
2) Cost-benefit calculator	No evidence
3) Educator	High
4) Innovator	Very high
5) Lifelong learner	No evidence
6) Organiser	High
7) Accumulator	No evidence
D) INTELLIGENCE SPAN	Very high

convinced that unknowable forces ruled his life [very pronounced possibilities – the belief cannot depend on any facts]. He was certain he had lived a number of previous lives but admitted he lacked any factual evidence [very pronounced possibilities]. He used his 'experiences' from his previous lives to explain his beliefs [very pronounced possibilities].

He held passionate views about social and political issues [very high emotion and very pronounced wide-interests]. He started his own newspaper to publicise his opinions on society [very pronounced wide-interests]. He blamed all the evil in the world on a small number of individuals [very high emotion and very pronounced wide-interests]. He wanted to lead his nation [very high ambition and very pronounced wide-interests].

People judged him as ignorant because he was uninterested in facts [very pronounced possibilities]. He acted spontaneously [very pronounced possibilities]. He impulsively criticised employees' actions [very pronounced possibilities lifestyle]. In doing so, he revealed little interest in the feelings of his colleagues and employees [pronounced own-feelings]. He made important decisions spontaneously, which, on occasion, led to a great deal of criticism [very pronounced possibilities].

His commercial success arose from his improvements in production methods, great practical skills and highly original marketing vision [high cost-benefit calculator, very high innovator and very high intelligence]. His ideas changed an industry forever [very high innovator and very high intelligence]. His working hours were very irregular [very pronounced possibilities lifestyle]. He worked enormously hard to achieve his vision [very high ambition]. He could work well with a team or by himself [average sociability]. He was very interested in how industrialisation could be made to work better and more efficiently [very high innovator].

He insisted on managing his business alone and mostly ignored other people's advice [very pronounced independent]. He took little notice of the many people who warned him of his serious errors [very pronounced independent]. He was committed to his own objectives [very pronounced independent]. In time, he ruled his business as a tyrant [ambiguous – tyranny has many origins]. He was unable to accept responsibility for his own poor judgement [ambiguous – the inability to accept responsibility has many causes].

Audiences which contained more than a few people frightened him [low organiser]. He was scared of strong, talented managers, whom he sacked from his company [low organiser]. He imposed his authority on weak managers by deliberately illogical behaviour [pronounced own-feelings and low organiser]. He did not worry how his actions affected other people [pronounced own-feelings]. His lack of a personal presence meant that the image he presented to the world at large had to be created for him by an employee [low organiser]. His failure to improve his products led to his commercial failure [ambiguous – inaction can have many different causes]. In later life, he built a museum [high accumulator]. We can now use the preceding analysis to prepare a personality profile (see Table 17.3).

A similar historical individual to example number three
Henry Ford (1863–1947), the founder of the Ford Motor Company, had some similarities to the personality profile described in example number three. He was a brilliant engineer who was the first to understand the mass market for cars. He innovated in marketing, design and production

Table 17.3 Example number three personality profile

PERSONALITY CHARACTERISTICS	ASSESSMENT HEADINGS
A) DISPOSITIONS	
1) Sociability	Average
2) Emotion	Very high
3) Ambition	Very high
4) Curiosity	No evidence
5) Uncertainty	No evidence
B) DIMENSIONS	
1) Facts / possibilities	Very pronounced possibilities
2) Group / independent	Very pronounced independent
3) Own-feelings / others'-feelings	Pronounced own-feelings
4) Wide-interests / narrow-interests	Very pronounced wide-interests
5) Optimistic / pessimistic	No evidence
C) SOCIAL ROLES	
1) Communicator	No evidence
2) Cost-benefit calculator	High
3) Educator	No evidence
4) Innovator	Very high
5) Lifelong learner	No evidence
6) Organiser	Low
7) Accumulator	High
D) INTELLIGENCE SPAN	Very high

engineering. He designed the Model T, the first mass-produced car. He became very rich and an extremely popular folk hero with the ordinary Americans of his time. He used his wealth to publicise his passionate social and political convictions. However, he did not rise above the ignorance of his rural, uneducated background. His tyrannical management of the Ford Motor Company did lasting damage to the company. In business, he ignored obvious facts and refused to listen to advice. In spite of dominating the early mass car market in America, the Ford Motor Company was soon overtaken and outperformed by its rival, General Motors.

EXAMPLE NUMBER FOUR

A short description of the individual in example number four

This person was a successful writer and teacher [very high communicator and high educator]. He was punctual and reliable with regard to his employer [pronounced facts lifestyle]. He took a gloomy view of life and of personal relationships [pronounced pessimistic]. He took great care not to give offence [very pronounced others'-feelings]. For him, everything was in decline [pronounced pessimistic]. He looked on the past as some kind of golden age [pronounced pessimistic]. He was convinced that the world was directed by a divine purpose, which was personal in nature [irrelevant].

He was kindly and considerate [very pronounced others'-feelings]. As an adolescent, he obeyed his community's instructions, even if it caused him great sadness and pain [very pronounced group]. His interest in other people was deep and genuine [very pronounced others'-feelings]. He did not expect any personal happiness [pronounced pessimistic].

He did his duty [very pronounced group]. He was very loyal to his employer, country and religion [very pronounced group]. He identified very strongly with his place of birth and its people [very pronounced group]. He had little interest in politics, which he angrily condemned as a waste of time [high emotion and pronounced narrow-interests]. To him, the greatest virtue was sympathy for the suffering of others [very pronounced others'-feelings].

His great passion was for brilliantly reworking the ideas of earlier authors [high emotion and very high communicator]. Whenever he could find time, he worked very hard at his stories [very high ambition and very high communicator]. His efforts as a writer took more of his time than he could either spare or justify to himself [very high ambition]. In consequence, he failed to do some of his duties. For this reason, he was convinced that he lacked moral strength, which upset him greatly [high emotion and very pronounced group]. He was determined to produce work of the highest standard and, accordingly, took very many years to complete a story [very high ambition]. In his desire to reach the highest possible standards, he was often unable to finish a story [very high ambition]. His stories were full of detail [pronounced facts]. He took great care to make certain that the detail made sense [pronounced facts]. To his mind, his stories were a true history of a previous world [pronounced facts].

He worked by himself [below average sociability] but was married with children [irrelevant]. He was devoted to his family [irrelevant]. He liked to relax occasionally in the company of a small group of like-minded friends [pronounced narrow-interests and below average sociability]. He was strongly against 'progress' [high emotion]. His anger over the disappearance of much that he enjoyed from his childhood was intense [high emotion].

He was a brilliant student who was obsessed throughout his life with rediscovering ancient truths [very high intelligence and pronounced facts]. His small amount of professional research was of a very high quality [very high intelligence]. He made his career choices and personal decisions logically, based on the facts of his situation and the needs of others [pronounced facts and very pronounced others'-feelings]. His lifestyle was largely unchanging and contained much that was routine [pronounced facts lifestyle]. We can now use the preceding analysis to prepare a personality profile (see Table 17.4).

A similar historical individual to example number four

J R R Tolkien (1892–1973) had some similarities to the personality profile described in example number four. He was one of the most popular novelists of the twentieth century and the outstanding writer of fantasy. It is surprising that a writer of fantasy should have a pronounced facts trait. However, Tolkien believed that his stories were, in a vitally important sense, a true history which described a real past. For this reason, he took great care to ensure his stories made sense. His writings were never more than a time-consuming hobby. He was burdened by the fact that this hobby caused him to neglect his teaching and research duties. Although having little interest in politics, he was very conservative in outlook. He was a conventional Christian, devoted to the Roman Catholic Church, and believed in the monarchy and social order. The content of books often reveals a surprising amount about their authors' personalities, besides their high or very high communicator social role. In Tolkien's case, much of his personality (high emotion, pronounced facts, very pronounced group, very pronounced others'-feelings,

Table 17.4 Example number four personality profile

PERSONALITY CHARACTERISTICS	ASSESSMENT HEADINGS
A) DISPOSITIONS	
1) Sociability	Below average
2) Emotion	High
3) Ambition	Very high
4) Curiosity	No evidence
5) Uncertainty	No evidence
B) DIMENSIONS	
1) Facts / possibilities	Pronounced facts
2) Group / independent	Very pronounced group
3) Own-feelings / others'-feelings	Very pronounced others'-feelings
4) Wide-interests / narrow-interests	Pronounced narrow-interests
5) Optimistic / pessimistic	Pronounced pessimistic
C) SOCIAL ROLES	
1) Communicator	Very high
2) Cost-benefit calculator	No evidence
3) Educator	High
4) Innovator	No evidence
5) Lifelong learner	No evidence
6) Organiser	No evidence
7) Accumulator	No evidence
D) INTELLIGENCE SPAN	Very high

pronounced narrow-interests, pronounced pessimistic, very high communicator and very high intelligence) can be seen in his masterpiece *The Lord of the Rings*.

DETAILED ADVICE FOR COMPLETING THE EXERCISES

You are advised to complete for yourself the next five personality profiles from the information provided. However, if you wish to read the suggested answer immediately, there is still much to be learned about assessing personality. As mentioned earlier, these personality profiles have similarities to those of five historical individuals. There is a short biography at the end of each suggested answer.

Each of the short descriptions in the five exercises should be read several times before any assessments are made. The short description for each exercise contains a series of numbers. Each number represents an opportunity to identify a personality characteristic(s) and assessment heading(s). If supported by the evidence in the sentence, you may also be able to identify a lifestyle. Some of the assessment information may be irrelevant or ambiguous and should be noted as such in your answers. The numbers in each exercise provide you with the opportunity to check your conclusions with the suggested answer. For this reason, you need to record your answers using these numbers.

We now use the first paragraph of exercise number one as an example of how to complete these exercises. The paragraph reads as follows:

> 'He was wealthy [1]. He had an impressive personal presence, a natural authority [2] and was always cheerful and buoyant [3]. He was respected by

everyone for his management ability [4]. He was convinced he would succeed and was determined to achieve success [5]. In his view, he was carrying out his special destiny given to him by Providence [6].'

The first sentence of the first exercise states the individual was 'wealthy [1]'. This tells you nothing about his personality characteristics. For example, the money may have been inherited. Consequently, your answer will begin '1) irrelevant'. The second sentence states he had 'an impressive personal presence, a natural authority [2] and was always cheerful and buoyant [3]'. This tells you he was a very high organiser [2] and very pronounced optimistic [3]. You enter these answers for the exercise as follows:

1) Irrelevant
2) Very high organiser
3) Very pronounced optimistic

You then complete the remaining numbers. In some cases, you may have to change an earlier assessment heading because of later evidence. From your finished list, you can then complete the personality profile for exercise number one. You should then check your numbered answers and personality profile against the suggested answer. The exercises are hard work but excellent practice.

EXERCISE NUMBER ONE

A short description of the individual in exercise number one

He was wealthy [1]. He had an impressive personal presence, a natural authority [2] and was always cheerful and buoyant

[3]. He was respected by everyone for his management ability [4]. He was convinced he would succeed and was determined to achieve success [5]. In his view, he was carrying out his special destiny given to him by Providence [6].

He had a lifelong interest in his local community but was not concerned about society at large [7]. His personal financial dealings were honest [8]. He never questioned his community's beliefs or the guidance he received from his parents [9]. One consequence of following his community's guidance was his lifelong generosity to good causes [10]. The reasons that he offered for his actions were facts [11].

His overriding, passionate desire was to make money [12]. He was prepared to do almost anything to increase his company's size and profitability [13]. His company paid bribes in order to destroy competitors [14]. He soon learned to hide his very strong temper [15]. He was widely respected in the industry for his politeness [16]. However, if sufficiently upset, he became very angry, especially if his loyalty to his company was criticised [17]. He had a small number of close friends [18]. He was capable of working by himself, but he worked very closely with another senior executive during his best years [19].

He enjoyed his largely unchanging daily routine and was exceptionally methodical in all his decisions and actions [20]. He managed his business by detailed plans [21]. He was obsessive in his pastimes [22]. He had to be the best in all his hobbies [23]. He was punctual for meetings [24]. He believed passionately that business decisions had to be based on a detailed assessment of all the facts [25]. He insisted that facts and figures had to be accurate and presented fairly [26]. His view was that if you understood the facts correctly, you would make the right decisions [27]. He was very careful in his decision making [28]. However, once a decision was made, he had no doubts, unless the factual situation changed [29].

Other employees supplied all the technological developments [30]. His great skill was to assess the business consequences of other people's ideas [31]. He could easily develop accurate financial plans [32]. His success was largely due to his ability with financial information [33]. He was nearly always right in his business decisions [34]. He was not discouraged even by repeated disappointments [35]. He started in business at the age of twenty, using borrowed money [36].

He was a very effective sales person [37]. He liked talking to customers and fully understood their feelings [38]. His skills at handling people were exceptional [39]. He revealed a genuine personal interest in the lives of many of his employees [40]. He was an exceptionally hard worker, who wanted to win [41]. His greatest talent was his ability to create and manage the best management teams [42]. He could solve the most difficult business problems but was prepared to let the other senior managers question all of his decisions [43]. Although he was almost always correct in his business judgement, he insisted on a broad agreement before moving forward [44]. He refused to accept poor performance from himself or anyone else [45].

He showed little interest in politics [46]. He largely ignored the intense public criticism of his company for its abuse of its control of the market [47]. For many years, he managed the business from head office and was reluctant to travel because of the change to his daily routine [48]. His loyalty to his company was complete [49]. In his private life, he believed in discipline, but his children loved him [50]. His personality profile should be summarised in Table 17.5.

A suggested answer to exercise number one

The suggested answer for the personality profile is in Table 17.6.

Table 17.5 Exercise number one personality profile
(to be completed by readers)

PERSONALITY CHARACTERISTICS	ASSESSMENT HEADINGS
A) DISPOSITIONS	
1) Sociability	
2) Emotion	
3) Ambition	
4) Curiosity	
5) Uncertainty	
B) DIMENSIONS	
1) Facts / possibilities	
2) Group / independent	
3) Own-feelings / others'-feelings	
4) Wide-interests / narrow-interests	
5) Optimistic / pessimistic	
C) SOCIAL ROLES	
1) Communicator	
2) Cost-benefit calculator	
3) Educator	
4) Innovator	
5) Lifelong learner	
6) Organiser	
7) Accumulator	
D) INTELLIGENCE SPAN	

Table 17.6 Exercise number one suggested personality profile

PERSONALITY CHARACTERISTICS	ASSESSMENT HEADINGS
A) DISPOSITIONS	
1) Sociability	Above average
2) Emotion	Very high
3) Ambition	Very high
4) Curiosity	Low
5) Uncertainty	No evidence
B) DIMENSIONS	
1) Facts / possibilities	Very pronounced facts
2) Group / independent	Very pronounced group
3) Own-feelings / others'-feelings	Pronounced others'-feelings
4) Wide-interests / narrow-interests	Pronounced narrow-interests
5) Optimistic / pessimistic	Very pronounced optimistic
C) SOCIAL ROLES	
1) Communicator	Above average
2) Cost-benefit calculator	Very high
3) Educator	No evidence
4) Innovator	No evidence
5) Lifelong learner	No evidence
6) Organiser	Very high
7) Accumulator	No evidence
D) INTELLIGENCE SPAN	Very high

Suggested answers for each numbered item in exercise number one

1) irrelevant, 2) very high organiser, 3) very pronounced optimistic, 4) very high organiser, 5) very high ambition and very pronounced optimistic, 6) very high ambition, 7) very pronounced group and pronounced narrow-interests, 8) irrelevant – whether people behave well or badly does not depend on their personality profile, 9) low curiosity, 10) very pronounced group, 11) very pronounced facts, 12) very high emotion and very high ambition, 13) very high ambition, 14) ambiguous – very different personality profiles can resort to unlawful activity and for very different reasons, 15) very high emotion, 16) pronounced others'-feelings, 17) very high emotion and very pronounced group, 18) above average sociability and pronounced narrow-interests, 19) above average sociability, 20) very pronounced facts and very pronounced facts lifestyle, 21) very pronounced facts lifestyle, 22) ambiguous – obsessions have very different origins, 23) very high ambition, 24) very pronounced facts lifestyle, 25) very high emotion and very pronounced facts, 26) very pronounced facts, 27) very pronounced facts, 28) very pronounced facts lifestyle, 29) very pronounced facts, 30) irrelevant – the evidence is about other employees, 31) very high cost-benefit calculator, 32) very high cost-benefit calculator, 33) very pronounced facts and very high cost-benefit calculator, 34) very high cost-benefit calculator and very high intelligence, 35) very pronounced optimistic, 36) ambiguous, but is perhaps some evidence of ambition – very different personality profiles are found in young businesspeople, 37) above average sociability and above average communicator, 38) above average sociability and pronounced others'-feelings, 39) very high organiser, 40) pronounced others'-feelings, 41) very high ambition, 42) very high organiser, 43) very pronounced group, very high

organiser and very high intelligence, 44) very pronounced group and very high intelligence, 45) very high ambition, 46) pronounced narrow-interests, 47) pronounced narrow-interests, 48) very pronounced facts lifestyle, 49) very pronounced group, 50) irrelevant – whether people are good parents is unconnected with their personality profile.

A similar historical individual to that described in exercise number one

John D Rockefeller (1839–1937), the founder of Standard Oil, had some similarities to the personality profile described in exercise number one. Rockefeller was, in all probability, the richest businessperson of all time in terms of his share of the world's business wealth. Standard Oil established an effective American monopoly in kerosene for lamps. Rockefeller was very optimistic. He was, perhaps, fortunate that the opportunities for the oil business were so great that they exceeded his most optimistic expectations. Eventually, Standard Oil's monopoly was broken up by the American courts as being against the public interest. Rockefeller's very pronounced group and pronounced narrow-interests traits meant he seriously underestimated the importance of public criticism of his ruthless business practices. As far as Rockefeller was concerned, Standard Oil was entitled to do anything which advanced the business interests of Standard Oil. Rockefeller was noted for his generosity to charity.

EXERCISE NUMBER TWO

A short description of the individual in exercise number two

He was a successful entertainer, who did nearly all of the creative and commercial work for his very profitable business

[1]. He made a great deal of money [2]. He was convinced that individual lives were ruled by the mysterious hand of fate [3]. He worked exceptionally hard and often acquired new skills [4].

He was unpredictable and his employees could not anticipate his next action [5]. His decisions, which were often without reasons, were spontaneous [6]. He was very irregular in his working life [7]. He believed that the ordinary person strongly disliked everyone who was in a position of power [8]. He spent some of his leisure time on his own and took long walks by himself [9]. However, when necessary for commercial reasons, he convincingly appeared friendly to everyone [10]. For large parts of his life, he had few close friends [11]. He did not assume his artistic creations would be either successful or unsuccessful [12].

He was a good investor, buying and selling shares at the right time [13]. His leisure time mattered much more to him than social issues or politics [14]. He was very considerate to other people [15]. He cried easily and was very nervous before a performance [16]. His artistic skills and talents, especially his bodily movement and timing, were extraordinarily good [17]. The serious illness or death of someone known to him greatly upset him [18].

At work, he insisted everything had to be done his way [19]. His artistic judgement was rarely wrong [20]. He publicly admitted that he was only prepared to fight in a war for his own beliefs and would never fight merely out of a sense of loyalty to a nation [21]. He retired to a foreign country [22]. He was determined to reach the top [23]. Everything about his work had to be of the highest quality [24]. If this could not be achieved, he gave up a project [25]. Initially, as a young man, he was shy [26].

He was responsible for many technical advances in the industry [27]. He started each new project with no idea of what to do [28]. If he met an artistic difficulty, he sat for hours looking at a wall, waiting for some ideas to come [29]. He never planned ahead but knew immediately when he had the right idea, even if he could offer no reasons [30]. He married several times on impulse and was soon bored by people and situations [31]. In his view, artistic vision was far more important than any fact [32].

His employees could not openly disagree with him at work, but he had the personal presence to inspire everyone [33]. He was brilliant at teaching those working for him how to produce the performance he needed [34]. Everyone, including himself, had to practice until reaching the highest standards [35]. His talent in entertaining an audience was legendary [36]. He was easily hurt and distressed by criticism [37]. He was unable to dismiss or criticise his staff and was prepared to apologise for his bad behaviour [38]. For him, pity was the highest moral feeling [39]. He was known for his strong likes and dislikes [40]. People who knew him well described him as, above all, a visionary [41]. His personality profile should be summarised in Table 17.7.

A suggested answer to exercise number two
The suggested answer for the personality profile is in Table 17.8.

Suggested answers for each numbered item in exercise number two
1) very high communicator, high cost-benefit calculator and very high intelligence, 2) high cost-benefit calculator (he made the money himself), 3) irrelevant – beliefs of this kind are independent of the personality profile, 4) very high ambition and high lifelong learner, 5) very pronounced possibilities lifestyle, 6) very pronounced possibilities, 7) very pronounced

Table 17.7 Exercise number two personality profile
(to be completed by readers)

PERSONALITY CHARACTERISTICS	ASSESSMENT HEADINGS
A) DISPOSITIONS	
1) Sociability	
2) Emotion	
3) Ambition	
4) Curiosity	
5) Uncertainty	
B) DIMENSIONS	
1) Facts / possibilities	
2) Group / independent	
3) Own-feelings / others'-feelings	
4) Wide-interests / narrow-interests	
5) Optimistic / pessimistic	
C) SOCIAL ROLES	
1) Communicator	
2) Cost-benefit calculator	
3) Educator	
4) Innovator	
5) Lifelong learner	
6) Organiser	
7) Accumulator	
D) INTELLIGENCE SPAN	

Table 17.8 Exercise number two suggested personality profile

PERSONALITY CHARACTERISTICS	ASSESSMENT HEADINGS
A) DISPOSITIONS	
1) Sociability	Below average
2) Emotion	Very high
3) Ambition	Very high
4) Curiosity	No evidence
5) Uncertainty	No evidence
B) DIMENSIONS	
1) Facts / possibilities	Very pronounced possibilities
2) Group / independent	Very pronounced independent
3) Own-feelings / others'-feelings	Pronounced others'-feelings
4) Wide-interests / narrow-interests	Pronounced narrow-interests
5) Optimistic / pessimistic	Broadly equal
C) SOCIAL ROLES	
1) Communicator	Very high
2) Cost-benefit calculator	High
3) Educator	High
4) Innovator	High
5) Lifelong learner	High
6) Organiser	High
7) Accumulator	No evidence
D) INTELLIGENCE SPAN	Very high

possibilities lifestyle, 8) very pronounced independent, 9) below average sociability, 10) very high communicator and very high intelligence, 11) below average sociability, 12) broadly equal attitudes to the future, 13) high cost-benefit calculator, 14) pronounced narrow-interests, 15) pronounced others'-feelings, 16) very high emotion, 17) very high communicator and very high intelligence, 18) very high emotion and pronounced narrow-interests, 19) very pronounced independent, 20) very high intelligence, 21) very pronounced independent, 22) very pronounced independent, 23) very high ambition, 24) very high ambition, 25) very high ambition, 26) below average sociability and pronounced others'-feelings, 27) high innovator, 28) very pronounced possibilities lifestyle, 29) very pronounced possibilities, 30) very pronounced possibilities lifestyle and very pronounced possibilities, 31) very pronounced possibilities lifestyle, 32) very pronounced possibilities, 33) high organiser, 34) high educator, 35) very high ambition, 36) very high communicator, 37) pronounced others'-feelings, 38) pronounced others'-feelings, 39) pronounced others'-feelings, 40) very high emotion, 41) very pronounced possibilities.

A similar historical individual to that described in exercise number two

Charles Chaplin (1889–1977), the comic actor, film director, writer and producer, had some similarities to the personality profile described in exercise number two. There have been few more talented individuals than Chaplin, who, in his lifetime, achieved an extraordinary worldwide fame. He acted in, wrote, produced and directed his own exceptionally popular films. He was also a successful manager, businessperson and financial investor. He even composed music for his films, while the first eleven chapters of his autobiography (written completely by himself) were a masterpiece. Nevertheless, he made some serious misjudgements and mistakes.

EXERCISE NUMBER THREE

A short description of the individual in exercise number three

This person spent much of his time looking for the truth [1]. He wanted to become a famous scientist, who made important contributions to his science [2]. He was confident his researches would lead to success [3]. However, his career was damaged by bad mistakes and errors of judgement [4]. Nevertheless, his books sold well [5]. He was successful as a self-employed consultant, who met his clients individually [6].

He was interested in facts [7]. He was sometimes very indiscreet, blunt and rude in his words and actions [8]. He could not stop asking questions and suggesting answers [9]. He produced many generally poor new ideas [10]. He completely ignored the work of other researchers [11]. He wanted to exercise a natural authority over others but was unable to do so [12]. However, he could be guided by others on a personal level and had great respect for several close colleagues [13]. In time, he became very angry about his dependence on these people, and his liking for them was replaced by an equally intense dislike [14]. He soon regained his self-confidence after failures [15].

For him, the truth was to be found in facts [16]. He felt the answers would be obvious if he studied the facts for long enough [17]. However, his scientific judgement was sometimes poor, and he placed far too much importance on a few facts [18]. Some of his theories were very strange [19]. He attempted to explain some human illnesses by arithmetic [20].

He actively and unwisely advised the widespread use of a highly dangerous drug [21].

His life was very regular, very punctual and routine [22]. He was happily married and much liked by his children [23]. He worked by himself and took walks alone [24]. He ignored invited guests at his home, if he had nothing to say to them [25]. Some of his guests found the silence very embarrassing, but he paid no attention to their unhappiness [26].

He easily became angry, which he tried to hide as best he could [27]. He was easily deceived, and repeated deceptions made him very distrustful of other people [28]. He was self-centred and self-satisfied [29]. His inability to understand other people led to many jealousies and personal conflicts [30]. He was a very poor judge of character [31]. He was insensitive and unable to keep a secret [32].

He saw no reason for social rules [33]. To his mind, his own judgement was far better than any agreed set of rules [34]. He hated being dependent on other people [35]. He was a good lecturer [36]. He took little interest in politics [37]. During his lifetime, he built up a large collection of ideas and ancient books [38]. His personality profile should be summarised in Table 17.9.

A suggested answer to exercise number three
The suggested answer for the personality profile is in Table 17.10.

Suggested answers for each numbered item in exercise number three
1) very high curiosity, 2) very high ambition, 3) pronounced optimistic, 4) only high intelligence (not the very high intelligence which was essential to achieve his goals), 5) high communicator, 6) low sociability and at least average cost-benefit calculator, 7) very pronounced facts, 8) very

Table 17.9 Exercise number three personality profile
(to be completed by readers)

PERSONALITY CHARACTERISTICS	ASSESSMENT HEADINGS
A) DISPOSITIONS	
1) Sociability	
2) Emotion	
3) Ambition	
4) Curiosity	
5) Uncertainty	
B) DIMENSIONS	
1) Facts / possibilities	
2) Group / independent	
3) Own-feelings / others'-feelings	
4) Wide-interests / narrow-interests	
5) Optimistic / pessimistic	
C) SOCIAL ROLES	
1) Communicator	
2) Cost-benefit calculator	
3) Educator	
4) Innovator	
5) Lifelong learner	
6) Organiser	
7) Accumulator	
D) INTELLIGENCE SPAN	

pronounced own-feelings, 9) very high curiosity, 10) very high innovator (a very high innovator is not necessarily a very good innovator!), 11) very pronounced independent, 12) absent organiser, 13) absent organiser, 14) very high emotion and very pronounced independent, 15) pronounced optimistic, 16) very pronounced facts, 17) very pronounced facts, 18) very pronounced facts and only high intelligence, 19) only high intelligence, 20) only high intelligence, 21) only high intelligence, 22) very pronounced facts lifestyle, 23) irrelevant – the state of a person's family life is independent of their personality profile, 24) low sociability, 25) low sociability and very pronounced own-feelings, 26) very pronounced own-feelings, 27) very high emotion, 28) very pronounced own-feelings, 29) very pronounced own-feelings, 30) very high emotion and very pronounced own-feelings, 31) very pronounced own-feelings, 32) very pronounced own-feelings, 33) very pronounced independent, 34) very pronounced independent, 35) very pronounced independent, 36) high communicator and high educator, 37) pronounced narrow-interests, 38) high accumulator.

A similar historical individual to that described in exercise number three

Sigmund Freud (1856–1939), a psychiatrist, had some similarities to the personality profile described in exercise number three. As a result of his personality profile, his professional relationships with colleagues were often difficult. This was largely because he did not listen to constructive criticism. In particular, the very high emotion, very pronounced independent and very pronounced own-feelings traits and the absence of an organiser role were responsible for some very angry disagreements with professional colleagues. These four personality characteristics also led to unfortunate outcomes when combined with his low

Table 17.10 Exercise number three suggested personality profile

PERSONALITY CHARACTERISTICS	ASSESSMENT HEADINGS
A) DISPOSITIONS	
1) Sociability	Low
2) Emotion	Very high
3) Ambition	Very high
4) Curiosity	Very high
5) Uncertainty	No evidence
B) DIMENSIONS	
1) Facts / possibilities	Very pronounced facts
2) Group / independent	Very pronounced independent
3) Own-feelings / others'-feelings	Very pronounced own-feelings
4) Wide-interests / narrow-interests	Pronounced narrow-interests
5) Optimistic / pessimistic	Pronounced optimistic
C) SOCIAL ROLES	
1) Communicator	High
2) Cost-benefit calculator	Average
3) Educator	High
4) Innovator	Very high
5) Lifelong learner	No evidence
6) Organiser	Absent
7) Accumulator	High
D) INTELLIGENCE SPAN	High

sociability, very high ambition, very high curiosity, very pronounced facts trait, pronounced optimistic trait and his, in this context, only high intelligence. He was responsible for a great many poor ideas and a few good ones. His difficulty was that he could not tell the difference. None of this stopped Freud becoming one of the most controversial and best-known thinkers of the twentieth century, largely because of his arguments in favour of sexual freedom. Freud's own assessment of his contributions was well-founded and far better than that of his followers. He saw himself as no more than an intellectual adventurer, who might open the way for others.

EXERCISE NUMBER FOUR

A short description of the individual in exercise number four

He was a well-known and successful inventor [1]. He worked on many projects at the same time in order to prevent boredom [2]. He believed in an ever-present spirit world and the power of unseen forces [3]. He sometimes tried to understand the nature of reality but without using any facts [4]. His inventions arose from sudden insights [5]. His marriages were the result of spontaneous decisions, and he made no attempt to find suitable brides [6]. He was unconcerned about the needs and wants of other people [7].

His thinking was disorganised [8]. From early in his career, he managed his own research laboratory [9]. He soon lost interest in a project [10]. He personally carried out the important tests and experiments [11]. He was restless and did not stay for long in one place, unless he had no alternative [12]. He never asked for outside advice or help [13]. He wanted to follow his own objectives and to be without obligations to other people [14]. He successfully carried out many difficult experiments using his great talents and insights [15].

Failure hardly ever discouraged him [16]. He was convinced he could find a solution [17]. Repeated disappointments only strengthened his determination and his belief in his final success [18]. He wanted to revolutionise technology [19] and, even as a young man, was convinced he had the necessary ability [20]. He was a very hard worker, who was determined to succeed [21]. He tried to find original designs by which machines could be made to perform more and more tasks [22]. He made many important inventions [23]. Some of his greatest achievements were in making highly significant improvements to existing machines, but some of his inventions were entirely original [24]. He was completely unsystematic in his research [25]. He only became angry for a good reason [26].

He had sufficient friends and associates for his business purposes [27]. He was able to manage his work assistants reasonably well [28]. He was blunt, rude and insensitive and he played practical jokes [29]. He was a good businessman who was financially very successful [30]. After early mistakes, he soon learned to invent products which had profitable markets [31]. He revealed little interest in politics [32]. His personality profile should be summarised in Table 17.11.

A suggested answer to exercise number four
The suggested answer for the personality profile is in Table 17.12.

Suggested answers for each numbered item in exercise number four
1) very high innovator and very high intelligence, 2) very pronounced possibilities lifestyle, 3) irrelevant – spiritual beliefs

Table 17.11 Exercise number four personality profile
(to be completed by readers)

PERSONALITY CHARACTERISTICS	ASSESSMENT HEADINGS
A) DISPOSITIONS	
1) Sociability	
2) Emotion	
3) Ambition	
4) Curiosity	
5) Uncertainty	
B) DIMENSIONS	
1) Facts / possibilities	
2) Group / independent	
3) Own-feelings / others'-feelings	
4) Wide-interests / narrow-interests	
5) Optimistic / pessimistic	
C) SOCIAL ROLES	
1) Communicator	
2) Cost-benefit calculator	
3) Educator	
4) Innovator	
5) Lifelong learner	
6) Organiser	
7) Accumulator	
D) INTELLIGENCE SPAN	

Table 17.12 Exercise number four suggested personality profile

PERSONALITY CHARACTERISTICS	ASSESSMENT HEADINGS
A) DISPOSITIONS	
1) Sociability	Average
2) Emotion	Average
3) Ambition	Very high
4) Curiosity	Very high
5) Uncertainty	No evidence
B) DIMENSIONS	
1) Facts / possibilities	Very pronounced possibilities
2) Group / independent	Very pronounced independent
3) Own-feelings / others'-feelings	Pronounced own-feelings
4) Wide-interests / narrow-interests	Pronounced narrow-interests
5) Optimistic / pessimistic	Pronounced optimistic
C) SOCIAL ROLES	
1) Communicator	No evidence
2) Cost-benefit calculator	High
3) Educator	No evidence
4) Innovator	Very high
5) Lifelong learner	No evidence
6) Organiser	Above average
7) Accumulator	No evidence
D) INTELLIGENCE SPAN	Very high

(or lack of them) are unaffected by the facts or possibilities traits, 4) very high curiosity and very pronounced possibilities, 5) very pronounced possibilities, 6) very pronounced possibilities lifestyle and very pronounced possibilities, 7) pronounced own-feelings, 8) very pronounced possibilities, 9) above average organiser, 10) very pronounced possibilities lifestyle, 11) very pronounced independent, 12) very pronounced possibilities lifestyle, 13) very pronounced independent, 14) very pronounced independent, 15) very high intelligence, 16) pronounced optimistic, 17) pronounced optimistic, 18) pronounced optimistic, 19) very high ambition, 20) pronounced optimistic, 21) very high ambition, 22) very high innovator, 23) very high innovator and very high intelligence, 24) very high innovator and very high intelligence, 25) very pronounced possibilities lifestyle, 26) average emotion, 27) average sociability, 28) above average organiser, 29) pronounced own-feelings, 30) high cost-benefit calculator, 31) high cost-benefit calculator, 32) pronounced narrow-interests.

A similar historical individual to that described in exercise number four

Thomas Edison (1847–1931), generally considered to be the most prolific and successful inventor of all time, had some similarities to the personality profile described in exercise number four. He started one of the world's first industrial research laboratories. He was a legend in his own lifetime. The media of his time called him the 'Wizard of Menlo Park', after the name of one of his research laboratories. His more important inventions included the first commercially-viable incandescent electric light, the gramophone and the mass generation and distribution of electricity. He played a crucial role in many of the inventions which supplied the technology for the remarkable and sustained economic growth of the twentieth century.

EXERCISE NUMBER FIVE

A short description of the individual in exercise number five

He was a most distinguished scientist. He spent his whole life asking questions and seeking answers [1]. He made many highly original contributions to his science [2]. He was only concerned with facts and their meanings [3]. As a young man, his objective was to discover a few important scientific facts, but, by the end of his career, he had discovered the theoretical basis for his science [4]. He was a very accurate observer of facts [5].

He lived a life of great regularity [6]. You could tell the time by some of his daily activities [7]. For much of his life, one day was almost the same as the next [8]. He thought very carefully about his future actions [9]. When it was time to marry, he deliberately looked for (and found) a loving, gentle, pretty, unsociable wife, who would let him continue his work undisturbed [10].

He was very methodical in his studies [11]. He worked on one problem for twenty years [12]. He was completely determined to learn the scientific truth about nature [13]. He always tried to keep an open mind [14]. He gave up any of his theories if they were contradicted by facts [15]. Although he was not an abstract thinker and it took him time to understand a topic, he discovered important new and true explanations for many aspects of nature [16]. His greatest intellectual joy was to discover general laws of nature in the facts [17].

His books sold very well, and he was financially successful [18]. He was a good investor [19]. He saved much of his large income but feared financial ruin and poverty [20]. He worried that his children would be too unhealthy to earn a living [21]. He expected to be strongly condemned by society for his scientific work [22]. He worked by himself [23]. He was happily married and adored by his children [24]. He was kind and considerate to his servants, who thought highly of him [25]. He and his wife neither entertained nor went to parties [26].

He took decisions by listing the factual arguments for and against [27]. Routine was essential to his wellbeing [28]. He kept detailed financial records of his household expenditure [29]. He showed some interest in politics but took no active part [30]. He played no significant part in any organisation [31]. As a young man, he was excellent at hunting, shooting and riding [32]. His father criticised his excessive interest in these pastimes [33]. As a scientist, he was a skilful and very clever experimenter [34].

He had a temper and could become very angry [35]. However, losing his temper upset him greatly, because it seriously disturbed his routine [36]. He could not watch others suffer and, in consequence, gave up medical training [37]. It upset him that his scientific discoveries made other people unhappy [38]. He was widely known for his kindly, tender, sympathetic and considerate nature [39]. He sometimes discussed his work with scientists who supported his views [40]. Above all, he wanted their admiration and respect [41]. He worked very hard [42]. He followed his own research interests and refused to agree with other scientists unless convinced by the factual evidence [43].

All his life, he had the most magnificent collections which included minerals and insects [44]. He was very proud of his collections [45]. His collection and retention of experiences, facts and things proved to be very useful in his scientific work [46]. Above all, he wanted to explain and understand the world of nature [47]. His personality profile should be summarised in Table 17.13.

A suggested answer to exercise number five
The suggested answer for the personality profile is in Table 17.14.

Table 17.13 Exercise number five personality profile
(to be completed by readers)

PERSONALITY CHARACTERISTICS	ASSESSMENT HEADINGS
A) DISPOSITIONS	
1) Sociability	
2) Emotion	
3) Ambition	
4) Curiosity	
5) Uncertainty	
B) DIMENSIONS	
1) Facts / possibilities	
2) Group / independent	
3) Own-feelings / others'-feelings	
4) Wide-interests / narrow-interests	
5) Optimistic / pessimistic	
C) SOCIAL ROLES	
1) Communicator	
2) Cost-benefit calculator	
3) Educator	
4) Innovator	
5) Lifelong learner	
6) Organiser	
7) Accumulator	
D) INTELLIGENCE SPAN	

Suggested answers for each numbered item in exercise number five

1) very high curiosity, 2) very high innovator and very high intelligence, 3) very pronounced facts, 4) very high ambition, very pronounced facts, very high innovator and very high intelligence, 5) very pronounced facts, 6) very pronounced facts lifestyle, 7) very pronounced facts lifestyle, 8) very pronounced facts lifestyle, 9) very pronounced facts lifestyle, 10) low sociability, very high ambition and very pronounced facts, 11) very pronounced facts lifestyle, 12) very pronounced facts lifestyle, 13) very high ambition and very high curiosity, 14) very high intelligence, 15) very pronounced facts and very high intelligence, 16) very high innovator and very high intelligence, 17) very pronounced facts, 18) high communicator and high cost-benefit calculator, 19) high cost-benefit calculator, 20) pronounced pessimistic, 21) pronounced pessimistic, 22) pronounced pessimistic, 23) low sociability, 24) irrelevant – whether or not you are happily married does not depend on your personality profile, 25) very pronounced others'-feelings, 26) low sociability, 27) very pronounced facts, 28) very pronounced facts lifestyle, 29) very pronounced facts lifestyle, 30) broadly equal wide-interests and narrow-interests, 31) pronounced independent, 32) very high intelligence, 33) irrelevant – criticism from your parents does not depend on your personality profile, 34) very high intelligence, 35) high emotion, 36) high emotion, very pronounced others'-feelings and very pronounced facts lifestyle, 37) very pronounced others'-feelings, 38) very pronounced others'-feelings, 39) very pronounced others'-feelings, 40) low sociability, 41) very pronounced others'-feelings, 42) very high ambition, 43) very pronounced facts and pronounced independent, 44) very high accumulator, 45) very high accumulator, 46) very high accumulator, 47) very high ambition and very high curiosity.

Table 17.14 Exercise number five suggested personality profile

PERSONALITY CHARACTERISTICS	ASSESSMENT HEADINGS
A) DISPOSITIONS	
1) Sociability	Low
2) Emotion	High
3) Ambition	Very high
4) Curiosity	Very high
5) Uncertainty	No evidence
B) DIMENSIONS	
1) Facts / possibilities	Very pronounced facts
2) Group / independent	Pronounced independent
3) Own-feelings / others'-feelings	Very pronounced others'-feelings
4) Wide-interests / narrow-interests	Broadly equal
5) Optimistic / pessimistic	Pronounced pessimistic
C) SOCIAL ROLES	
1) Communicator	High
2) Cost-benefit calculator	High
3) Educator	No evidence
4) Innovator	Very high
5) Lifelong learner	No evidence
6) Organiser	No evidence
7) Accumulator	Very high
D) INTELLIGENCE SPAN	Very high

A similar historical individual to that described in exercise number five

Charles Darwin (1809–82), the famous biologist, considered by many to be one of the greatest scientists, had some similarities to the personality profile described in exercise number five. He and his wife rarely socialised. He worked very hard for twenty years by himself on his great problem (the origin of species) and was determined to succeed. He had a very routine lifestyle and lived in the same house for very many years. Nevertheless, as a very high accumulator, he went on a long voyage (HMS *Beagle*, 1831–6), where he collected many scientific facts and specimens. He followed his own scientific interests. However, he was anxious not to upset people's religious feelings. He expected the worst and feared a deeply hostile public reaction to his publication of the theory of evolution by natural selection. In the event, although condemned by a small minority, his ideas met with general approval. His scientific reputation has grown ever larger with the passing of the years.

PERSONALITY PROFILE CHART

We can represent an individual's personality profile by seven diagrams (see Figs. 17.1 to 17.7). The first six diagrams are taken from earlier chapters. We call the seven diagrams a 'personality profile chart'.

A PERSONALITY PROFILE CHART **represents an individual's personality profile by seven diagrams.**

As before, in each diagram, the font size of the personality characteristic and the thickness of the arrow describe each personality characteristic. The larger the font size and thicker the arrow, the higher or more pronounced is the personality characteristic. We use the personality profile of example number four in this chapter as the basis for a personality profile chart. However, the dispositions and social roles for which we had no evidence are now described as low or very low. As noted earlier, J R R Tolkien had some similarities to the personality profile of example number four.

PERSONALITY PROFILE CHART OF EXAMPLE NUMBER FOUR

A) Dispositions

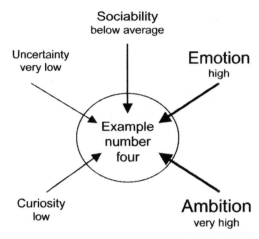

Fig. 17.1 The dispositions of example number four

B) Dimensions

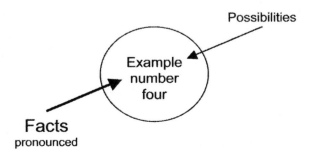

Fig. 17.2 The ways of thinking of example number four

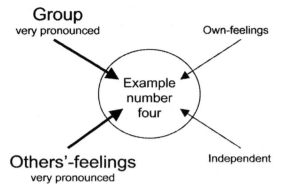

Fig. 17.3 The ways of interacting and ways of relating bundle of example number four

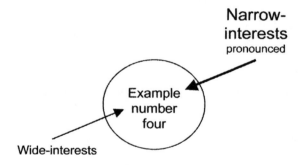

Fig. 17.4 The social interests of example number four

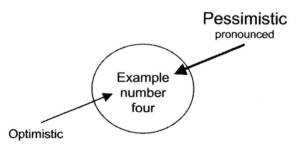

Fig. 17.5 The attitudes to the future of example number four

C) Social roles

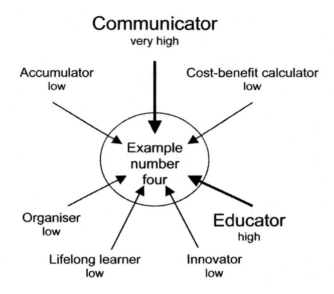

Fig. 17.6 The social roles of example number four

D) Intelligence span

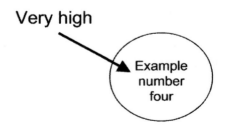

Fig. 17.7 The intelligence span of example number four

CONCLUSION

Successful personality profiling requires a sound knowledge of the personality profile, an adequate experience of people and sufficient previous practice. The first step in preparing an individual's personality profile is to collect the evidence, which, in real life, can take a great deal of time. In order to be of any value, a personality profile has to be based on sufficient knowledge of the person concerned. In this chapter, this demanding task has been done already for you, even if only in outline. The second step is to interpret the evidence. We have to decide what we can say about an individual's personality characteristics and assessment headings from the evidence. The final step in preparing a personality profile is to enter the assessment headings on the profile.

One serious practical difficulty is that similar behaviour can have its origins in very different personality profiles. A thoughtful person avoids coming to an early conclusion. For example, from time to time, a person is called 'a loner'. This generally means the individual has no close personal relationships. As we shall see in Chapter 20, people with very different personality profiles can lack close personal relationships. Only detailed investigation will reveal a loner's true personality profile.

KEY POINTS

A PERSONALITY PROFILE CHART represents an individual's personality profile by seven diagrams.

A NOTE ON PERSONALITY SELF-ASSESSMENT

Some of the following tasks involve personality self-assessment. There are real difficulties in accurate self-assessment. We may easily make mistakes in assessing our own personality. We may give ourselves the assessment headings which we think are desirable. For example, if we believe that people with very high emotion are more successful, we may assess ourselves higher in emotion than we really are. We may self-assess ourselves as pronounced or very pronounced others'-feelings, because we believe that people with this trait and these assessment headings are widely admired. We may over-estimate our social roles and intelligence span assessment headings, because we like to see ourselves as having many resources. We may give ourselves assessment headings that are possessed by our role models, people we admire or who are highly regarded in our work, communities or culture.

YOUR NOTES (OPTIONAL AT YOUR OWN RISK)

What are your assessment headings for the five dispositions? (For this question and the next three questions, you can also enter your answers into Table 17.15 (your own personality profile) by putting a tick in the relevant box.)

What evidence are you using?

What are your assessment headings for the five dimensions?

What evidence are you using?

What are your assessment headings for the seven social roles?

What evidence are you using?

What is your assessment heading for the intelligence span?

What evidence are you using?

Are your personality characteristics more accurately described as well-defined or flexible?

What evidence are you using?

If your personality characteristics are more accurately described as well-defined, which of your personality characteristics make you well-defined?

What evidence are you using?

If your personality characteristics are more accurately described as flexible, which of your personality characteristics make you flexible?

What evidence are you using?

Do you know personally or by reputation any people with well-defined or flexible personality characteristics?

What evidence are you using?

If their personality characteristics are well-defined, which of their personality characteristics make them well-defined?

What evidence are you using?

If their personality characteristics are flexible, which of their personality characteristics make them flexible?

What evidence are you using?

Table 17.15 Your own personality profile

PERSONALITY CHARACTERISTICS	ASSESSMENT HEADINGS						
A) DISPOSITIONS	V. high	High	Above av.	Aver-age	Below av.	Low	V. low
1) Sociability							
2) Emotion							
3) Ambition							
4) Curiosity							
5) Uncertainty							
B) DIMENSIONS	TRAIT 'A'				TRAIT 'B'		
TRAIT 'A' / TRAIT 'B'	V. pron.	Pron.	More than	Br. equal	More than	Pron.	V. pron.
1) Facts / possibilities							
2) Group / independent							
3) Own-feelings / others'-feelings							
4) Wide-interests / narrow-interests							
5) Optimistic / pessimistic							
C) SOCIAL ROLES	V. high	High	Above av.	Aver-age	Below av.	Low	Ab-sent
1) Communicator							
2) Cost-benefit calculator							
3) Educator							
4) Innovator							
5) Lifelong learner							
6) Organiser							
7) Accumulator							
	V. high	High	Above av.	Aver-age	Below av.	Low	V. low
D) INTELLIGENCE SPAN							

Note: av. = average; V. = Very; Pron. = Pronounced; Br. = Broadly

FURTHER NOTES

CHAPTER 18

The explanation of personality

We have learned how to describe and assess personality using the personality profile. In order to make best use of personality assessment, we need to understand the nature and origins of personality. In particular, we need to know why our personality profiles have eighteen principal characteristics which consist of the dispositions, dimensions, social roles and intelligence span. We also need to explain why individuals vary so much in their assessment headings. This understanding will eventually help us to take much better decisions at work concerning individuals and their organisation.

OUR HUNTER-GATHERER PAST

Scientists have discovered that the earth's climate is, and has been, highly unstable, subject to large-scale, short-term and long-term changes. In the past, dramatic climate change has occurred over a few decades. Moreover, the earth's climate has, over the longer term, become increasingly unstable. The outcome is that, for hundreds of thousands of years, our ancestors had to cope with highly variable and increasingly unstable environments. We also know that, until the last few thousand years, we lived as nomadic hunter-gatherers with only simple technology, for example spears, baskets and fire.

The social organisation of known hunter-gatherers followed an almost universal pattern, which was determined by the constraints of the hunter-gatherer way of life. Hunter-gatherers spent their time in an extended family containing, on average, some thirty or so individuals. The membership of a hunter-gatherer extended family varied over time. Relations and friends came and went. The extended families also belonged to a larger association, usually containing between 500 and 2,000 individuals. Intermarriage, language and beliefs held this larger association together. From the preceding facts and assumptions, we can propose a hypothesis that explains our personality profiles.

We begin by considering the effect that a highly variable environment, driven by intense, sudden climate change, would have on hunter-gatherers. Abrupt transformations could occur without warning. The natural vegetation and animals, the sole sources of food, could alter greatly over a few decades. An extended family's home territory could change from being well-watered to a semi-desert in a few generations and then change back again. The challenges of a highly variable environment would be very serious for an extended family of hunter-gatherers. These rapid, large alterations to their territory would provide the most difficult intellectual challenge. They certainly needed their intelligence and practical skills.

For our hunter-gatherer ancestors, the amount of food within their territory would be a matter of great importance. Rich territories with plentiful food could support larger populations. People would be freer to move between extended families. In poor territories with little food, populations would be smaller and spread over wider areas.

Members of an extended family would be much more dependent on each other in poor territories. Neighbours could easily have disputes over food and water resources. Rules governing the membership of, and competition between, extended families would be much more important and stricter. Consequently, the social demands of rich and poor territories would be very different.

Large variations in the amount of available food would force significant social and economic change on hunter-gatherers. They would have to make many alterations to their social organisation, traditions and values. In other practical matters, for example in the search for food, existing knowledge and traditions might become largely useless. New problems would require original solutions. The question we must ask ourselves is this: what kind of personality profiles would be essential for reasoning hunter-gatherers to succeed in these most challenging circumstances, when territories altered rapidly in the amount of available food?

Rapid environmental change would demand a wide range of individual abilities in thought and action. In particular, members of an extended family would have to supply a rich variety of individual talents, which, other than their basic technology, would be their only resource. This is the clue that solves the mystery of our personalities. Only complex and very different personality profiles would ensure that the extended family and its neighbours had the necessary skills to overcome all their problems. A great variety in hunter-gatherer personality profiles would mean that they had a wide range of abilities and talents. There would be sufficient variety of human resources available within a hunter-gatherer extended family and its neighbours to overcome successfully any challenge that may arise from intense climate variability.

We survived because of the complexity of our personality profiles. In this straightforward way, we can explain the complexity and variety of our personality profiles. However, we still need to find reasons for each of our eighteen personality characteristics. We now look again at the personality characteristics in the light of this new understanding, still following the order of the personality profile.

> The HUNTER-GATHERER PERSONALITY HYPOTHESIS states that people have the highly varied, complex personality profiles of reasoning, social, nomadic, tool-using, omnivorous hunter-gatherers adapted to intense environmental variability.

DISPOSITIONS

Every hunter-gatherer would need the five dispositions. Sociability would be the basis of the hunter-gatherer extended family. Emotion would provide the drive to action. Ambition would supply the family's aims and objectives. Curiosity would bring about the increase in understanding, while the pleasure derived from uncertainty would make the unpredictability of the hunter-gatherer way of life attractive.

Sociability

Hunter-gatherers could not survive as individuals. They could only succeed in communities. Consequently, our sociability was essential to us all. Variations in our sociability would result in very adaptable behaviour. Whatever the task that needed to be done, someone in the extended family would have a broadly appropriate sociability disposition. If an individual was required to sit alone for hours at a time making baskets or fishing, somebody in the family with low sociability would enjoy this task. If teams had to be formed to collect berries or hunt animals, other family members, who had higher sociability, would enjoy this team task. The sociability disposition gave us a large number of personal and organisational resources to do many kinds of tasks.

Emotion

Everyone needs emotions in order to drive and direct the actions which are essential to our wellbeing. Members of a hunter-gatherer extended family with high or very high emotion would inspire other family members in their tasks. In difficult circumstances, those with strong emotions could bring about exceptional efforts from others. Equally important, people with low or very low emotion could take a calm approach. They could stop others being too strongly influenced by their emotions in their actions. Members with very different locations on the emotion disposition would ensure that in every context the extended family would have alternative responses to consider. This variation in emotion would be a vital resource for an extended family.

Ambition

Everyone requires some ambition, if only to stay alive. The variable nature of ambition between individuals would be essential if an extended family were to function effectively. From time to time, members with a strong determination to achieve some goal would supply new aims and objectives to guide their own and the family's decisions. The achievement of difficult personal or family objectives would require a determined effort. However, if all members of the family were highly ambitious, the extended family could be torn apart by competing ambitions. Indeed, family members who had low or very low ambition would fulfil a valuable restraining function. They would raise the necessary objections if the targets proposed were unreasonable. Sometimes, it would be better for a hunter-gatherer extended family to be satisfied with undemanding goals.

Curiosity

Our understanding of the environment and ourselves is essential to our success. The greater our knowledge and experience, the more likely we are to take correct decisions, especially when the environment is changing rapidly. Our curiosity drives the increase in our knowledge and understanding. Consequently, everyone in the extended family would be curious to an extent, inquisitive about their natural and social environment. Each person would add to individual and family understanding. Members of the extended family with high or very high curiosity would frequently ask questions and seek answers. In all cases, there could be the chance that something really useful and valuable might be learned. There would be many interesting questions a hunter-gatherer might ask. In what kinds of territories do we find certain fruits, berries or roots? What factors lead one to expect a bountiful yield? Where do certain kinds of animals eat, drink or sleep? Could a better basket be made? Would this stone make a tool? What are the characteristics of a really good camp site? What kind of social organisation would be best for the extended family? Why does a certain individual behave in a particular way?

Uncertainty

Our ancestors were nomadic hunter-gatherers. Consequently, their lives would be full of uncertainties. When existing territories were exhausted, they would have to move on to new ones. The outcome would be unpredictable. The enjoyment of the tension of uncertainty, to see what lay in the next valley or over the next hill, would push hunter-gatherers from old, exhausted territories to new and more rewarding ones. Most days, hunter-gatherers would make an unpredictable search for food. Tension would arise from whether today's hunting and gathering would be a success or failure. The pleasure derived from this uncertainty would be a powerful encouragement to their nomadic way of life and search for food. Furthermore, the additional tension which was the result of the competition and rivalry between families and family members would also be an important motivation to greater achievement.

Hunter-gatherers would also need to accept perils and dangers. Hazardous situations would be unavoidable for hunter-gatherers, who would have to take risks to survive. They would inevitably be exposed to danger from predators, for example lions. The additional pleasure derived from the tension found in these dangerous and risky outcomes would add real enjoyment to their daily routine. The ensuing excitement from the uncertainty would make the risks and dangers seem worthwhile. Enjoyment of the tension of unpredictable outcomes would be essential to hunter-gatherers.

Sometimes, in order to make large gains, it would be necessary to take big risks. The extended family would benefit from individual variability in the uncertainty disposition. In particular, it would be useful to have one or two individuals who thrived on the tension of taking significant, even highly dangerous risks, especially if the possible rewards were exceptional. In these situations, the risk would be of death or of injury, which, for hunter-gatherers, could mean death. Accordingly, careful consideration of the wisdom of any risky activity would be essential to avoid unnecessary injuries or deaths. Those members of the family who had low or very low uncertainty would oppose hazardous activities which lacked sufficient justification.

DIMENSIONS

As a result of intense environmental variability, hunter-gatherers would face many serious, social, technical and organisational challenges, which would test their problem-solving and decision-making skills to the limit. There are many different, but equally valid ways, to solve social, technical and organisational problems. Hunter-gatherers would need to have this variety of approaches in order to take better decisions. The variability in people's personality dimensions would give extended families this essential resource.

The ways of thinking dimension meant people would make very different uses of facts or of assessing alternatives in decision making. Equally, as a result of the ways of interacting dimension, they would differ in the priority they gave to community aims and objectives. As a consequence of the ways of relating dimension, they would disagree about the importance to be attached to other people's feelings. The social interests dimension would mean some people would be interested in the community at large, while others would be interested in their immediate companions. The optimists and pessimists would make their own conflicting contribution to decisions. All these alternative points of view would have their own value and merits in a family discussion.

Hunter-gatherer extended families would benefit from these many different approaches to problem solving and decision making. Moreover, it would help if each point of view could be expressed clearly and with conviction. With regard to traits, this would necessitate well-defined personality characteristics among some family members. Other family members would need to assess the merits of all these different approaches. They would need flexible personality characteristics with regard to their traits.

In summary, the variations in the personality traits of extended family members would be responsible for very different approaches to problem solving and decision making. Some of the most clear-cut views would be from family members with well-defined personality characteristics, whose arguments would reflect their pronounced or very pronounced traits. Their contribution would be assessed by others in the extended family with flexible personality characteristics, whose more adaptable approach would reflect their broadly equal and more than traits. We now explore these issues in more detail by looking at each dimension in turn.

Ways of thinking: facts and possibilities

Members with primary facts traits and those with primary possibilities traits would significantly increase the problem solving resources of the family. For any particular problem, they would use information or assess alternatives in seeking an answer. Other members of the extended family with broadly equal facts and possibilities traits would also work on the problem and would help to select a solution.

Lifestyles

The pronounced and very pronounced facts (planned) and the pronounced and very pronounced possibilities (spontaneous) lifestyles would supply another essential resource to the daily life of hunter-gatherers. Some foods could be hunted or gathered only as the result of careful planning. It would be necessary to be at the right place at the right time. For example, some fruits, berries or animals might only be found in certain places at specific times of the year. However, other foods could only be taken at the moment when the opportunity occurred. These unexpected occasions would need immediate action. For example, honey was much prized by hunter-gatherers. The honey from a bees' nest needed to be taken as and when the nest was found, whatever might be the planned activities for the day. The differing lifestyles made both these alternative responses (planned and spontaneous) available within an extended family.

Ways of interacting: group and independent

Members with a pronounced and very pronounced group trait would be loyal and dedicated to the aims and objectives of their extended family. These members would be trusted because of their devotion to the family as a whole. They would put the family before their personal needs. Moreover, they would strive to develop and maintain unity within the family. They would be prepared to undertake the most unpleasant tasks on behalf of the extended family. Members with a pronounced and very pronounced independent trait would put forward their own values and objectives. In this way, they would bring their individual viewpoints to the attention of their family. Consequently, the dangers of a herd mentality (unquestioningly doing what others do) could be avoided. For the preceding reasons, the group and independent traits would be essential to extended family problem solving and decision making.

Ways of relating: own-feelings and others'-feelings

The family members with a pronounced or very pronounced own-feelings trait would be frank. Their comments about others might be blunt, but at least the truth would be told. Also, they would argue in favour of distressing but necessary actions. They would face up to difficult situations. For example, among nomadic peoples, very ill or dying members could present the cruellest dilemma, especially for those with a pronounced or very pronounced others'-feelings trait. Sometimes, for hunter-gatherers, one dying close relative might have to be left behind so that the family could survive. Those with a pronounced or very pronounced own-feelings trait would accept the inevitability of this decision and, in the process, persuade the family of its necessity.

Family members with a pronounced or very pronounced others'-feelings trait would bring sympathy and compassion to the family. Their interest in the feelings of others would identify dissatisfaction and unhappiness among other members or even other extended families. These members with a pronounced or very pronounced others'-feelings trait would strive to find the means to minimise or eliminate the sadness or anger of others. Members with widely differing locations on the ways of relating dimension would produce from within the extended family a broad variety of sometimes conflicting attitudes to individuals. In this way, the ways of relating dimension would enrich the social and individual actions, problem solving and decision making within an extended family.

Social interests: wide-interests and narrow-interests

This dimension would produce valuable, but different contributions from within a hunter-gatherer extended family. Matters that affected the extended family and its neighbours as a whole would be the concern of those with a primary wide-interests trait. For example, if working arrangements within the family needed to be altered, those with a primary wide-interests trait would concern themselves with this problem. They would also want to deal with the relationships between the extended families within the larger association. Those family members with a primary narrow-interests trait would be interested in matters which affected their immediate companions. Thus, those with a primary narrow-interests trait would take or demand action on behalf of any close companion.

Attitudes to the future: optimistic and pessimistic

In a highly uncertain hunting and gathering environment, the extended family's attitudes to the future would be of great importance. Misjudgements about the future could have disastrous consequences. Optimism could result in underestimating the difficulties involved in any course of action and could lead to activities with poor chances of success. However, in a rich environment, an optimistic attitude may lead to great rewards. In any situation, pessimism could result in overestimating the difficulties and lead to inaction. Furthermore, it could bring about the unnecessary rejection of advantageous courses of action. However, a pessimist's advice could sometimes avoid disaster. In an approaching famine, the pessimist's view would be that the famine was inevitable. Consequently, pessimists would argue that the only sensible action would be to do nothing. In this way, the least amount of food would be needed. This argument, if correct and accepted, may rescue the family. The saving of food from this inaction may avoid death by starvation.

In any event, optimists and pessimists would give their very different views about the future to their extended family. The other members could then assess the value of each prediction. Of course, the attitudes to the future of family members would be well-known to their companions. However, their arguments for their conflicting points of view would raise all the issues and could greatly assist in taking better decisions.

SOCIAL ROLES

The seven social roles would satisfy the essential requirements of reasoning, social, nomadic, tool-using, omnivorous hunter-gatherers who were adapted to intense environmental variability and lived in extended families. Communicators would express, among other things, emotions, ambitions, experiences and information to other family members. Cost-benefit calculators would take the decisions which involved assessing the short-term and long-term advantages and disadvantages of actions. Educators would pass on the family's culture and knowledge. Innovators would find original solutions. Lifelong learners would continue to master new skills. Organisers would coordinate the family. Finally, accumulators would collect and retain experiences.

The extended family would need a few members with at least a high assessment heading in each one of the seven social roles. These individuals could then use their resources in the social role to guide or help the others. The possession of high or very high social roles by many family members would add nothing to the success of family actions and decision making. On the contrary, it might well lead to confusion and disputes.

Communicators

The effective sharing of information and feelings would be fundamental to the unity and efficient operation of a hunter-gatherer extended family. The few members of an extended family who were high or very high communicators would contribute significantly to social bonding and cooperation by exchanging information and passing on experiences. In this way, everyone would be united by shared understanding, attitudes and knowledge. Everyone would become acquainted with the needs of the family and the views of its individual members. Communication in its widest context includes the unifying myths and rituals represented by song, dance, art and stories as well as more everyday matters of experiences, facts and emotions.

Cost-benefit calculators

The hunting and gathering lifestyle would be one of choices, especially about the short-term and long-term advantages and disadvantages of proposed actions. These kinds of decisions would arise in all aspects of hunter-gatherer life. However, they would be particularly important with regard to the vital economic choices related to hunting and gathering. Hunter-gatherers would have to decide whether the benefit likely to be gained from a particular hunting or gathering trip would be worth the effort. For a family of hunter-gatherers to prosper, it would be essential that, over a period of time, the rewards in terms of food collected or hunted would exceed the efforts made in obtaining that food. This would be especially true in environments where food was scarce. In these territories, it might be necessary to travel long distances to find suitable plants and animals. The effort had to be worthwhile. An extended family would need to have one or two members who were especially good at making these cost-benefit judgements.

Educators

The teaching of hunter-gatherer culture, knowledge and skills would be essential to the extended family's continued existence. Long-term survival would depend on passing on the extended family's experience and technology to the next generation. In particular, the education of the young in the family's values, traditions and skills would be of the greatest importance. There would be two aspects to this education. First, it would be essential to ensure that, in matters which affected everyone, each family member reached the required basic standard. Second, it would be necessary to make certain that, where a very high standard of performance was essential in an activity, a few people achieved the required level. Consequently, several educators would be needed within an extended family to carry out these necessary tasks. A high or very high educator of all would maintain the general standard, while a high or very high educator of the talented would ensure the continuance of the specialist skills, especially by educating gifted children and young people.

Innovators

Innovation would be essential to discover the new ideas which improved the way the extended family and its wider community performed their tasks. This would be especially important in territories where the environmental variability was increasingly rapid and severe. The discovery of new food sources and technologies could be essential to survival. All long-term progress would depend on the skills and talents of members with a high or very high innovator social role. They could offer the extended family chances of significant and permanent increases in productivity through, for example, new hunting and gathering methods or improved tools. Nevertheless, a large majority of family members would need to concern themselves with meeting immediate requirements with tried and trusted methods.

Lifelong learners

Significant changes in a hunter-gatherer territory would necessitate some adults learning new skills to cope with novel challenges. For example, new kinds of food may require different ways of preparation, perhaps invented or suggested by others. Members with a high or very high lifelong learner social role would be admirably fitted for this task.

Organisers

The extended family and its tasks would need to be organised, for example when moving camp, meeting with neighbours or arranging hunting and gathering trips. One or two members of the extended family who had the natural dignity and authority to coordinate the actions of others would be invaluable. Furthermore, individual tasks would need to be shared out to the most appropriate people. This could be a difficult and demanding process, where the resources of members with a high or very high organiser social role would be exceptionally useful. However, too many with this resource within an extended family would lead to disputes and difficulties.

Accumulators

In a highly uncertain environment, there would be no way to establish in advance which additional hunter-gatherer experiences might be useful in the future. Accordingly, there would be a significant advantage in a few members of an extended family accumulating experiences, even if they had no obvious, useful purpose. Many different kinds of information or experiences could be collected and retained, for example concerning places, plants and animals. At some future time, these could be of great practical value.

INTELLIGENCE SPAN

Our intelligence is the origin of our adaptability, which is our ability to take decisions according to the situation that exists at the time. Indeed, since adaptability was essential for us to deal with intense, rapid climate variability and the consequent sudden, severe environmental change, we should rather say that our intelligence, our adaptability, was the result of intense climate variability.

In conditions of intense environmental variability, some members of the extended family would need to be of high or very high intelligence in order to solve the really difficult intellectual challenges faced by hunter-gatherers. While an average level of intelligence among most of the extended family would be necessary, only a few people would need to work at the most difficult problems. In particular, the most intelligent members could make suggestions to the others concerning social organisation, social values, improvements in technology, camp sites, setting priorities or reconciling disputes.

A family might not have had the required personality characteristics and assessment headings to meet the challenges of intense climate variability. The deliberate selection of some new members could well have been a most important feature in correcting this situation. We can assume that hunter-gatherers would have the intelligence and experience to alter, if necessary, their extended family membership. They could exchange, for example by marriage, individuals with other related families to ensure they had a sufficient range of personality profiles within their own extended family. Management of the family's membership would have demanded very high intelligence. Research into hunter-gatherer societies has shown that, at least during the last hundred or so years, the membership of extended families continually changed. Consequently, individuals could move around until they found an extended family in which their personality profiles were particularly productive and, therefore, welcome.

CONCLUSION

Our hunter-gatherer past makes sense of our personalities. In this context, we can explain our eighteen personality characteristics. The dispositions, dimensions, social roles and intelligence span are natural consequences of the hunter-gatherer way of life. Intense climate variability is a straightforward explanation of the great variety in our assessment headings. Our complex personalities are one of our most important resources. In Chapters 22 and 23, we learn how to apply this knowledge at work. The aim is to maximise the opportunities and productivity of individuals and organisations. However, we first need to understand the part played by childhood, life experiences and self-awareness in the development of our individual personalities.

KEY POINTS

The HUNTER-GATHERER PERSONALITY HYPOTHESIS states that people have the highly varied, complex personality profiles of reasoning, social, nomadic, tool-using, omnivorous hunter-gatherers adapted to intense environmental variability.

YOUR NOTES (OPTIONAL AT YOUR OWN RISK)

If you were a hunter-gatherer, and bearing in mind your personality profile:

- What hunter-gatherer tasks would you have chosen to do?
- What part would you have played in a hunter-gatherer extended family?

FURTHER NOTES

CHAPTER 19

Children's personalities

When we recruit students from school or college, we need to assess their personalities in order to decide on their suitability for particular careers. Children's personalities are also important to many organisations and individuals, especially those concerned with children's upbringing and education. For example, children's choices of school subjects and college courses often depend on their personalities. In this chapter, we use the personality profile to assess children's personalities. We examine the personalities of twelve children whose adult personality profiles appear in Chapters 16 and 17. There are short descriptions of each child. Together, we profile the first six children. Then, you can profile the next six children for yourself. After each profile, we indicate a well-known historical person, who, as a child, had some similarities to this personality profile.

In the following descriptions of children, the small amount of evidence from their childhoods means that our conclusions about their childhood assessment headings are often less certain than our conclusions about their adult assessment headings. For this reason, the personality assessment headings of these children are likely to be nearer the average than their adult assessment headings. For example, these children are generally assessed as high intelligence, even if their adult assessment heading is very high intelligence.

Furthermore, there may be little evidence from childhood on which to base an assessment of some personality characteristics. This is particularly true of the social interests dimension and the social roles, for example innovator and organiser. In any event, the lifelong learner social role cannot be revealed in childhood. Where there is little evidence about a child's personality characteristics, we leave the assessment heading blank. Childhood is considered to end around seventeen years of age. The descriptions are all assumed to be of boys.

EXAMPLE NUMBER ONE

This child enjoyed schoolwork and worked very hard to become first in his class [high ambition and high intelligence]. He was excellent at remembering facts and solving problems based on facts [pronounced facts]. He worked for long periods on his own [low sociability]. He even continued studying during mealtimes [high ambition]. His beliefs were based on reasoning with facts [pronounced facts]. His life consisted of a daily and weekly routine [pronounced facts lifestyle]. He was very sensitive to criticism and was deeply upset when people were angry with him [high emotion and pronounced others'-feelings]. He was careful not to give offence [pronounced others'-feelings]. He did what his family, school and community expected of him [pronounced group]. His personality profile is summarised in Table 19.1.

As a child, Marie Curie's personality profile had some similarities to the child in example number one.

Table 19.1 Example number one personality profile

PERSONALITY CHARACTERISTICS	ASSESSMENT HEADINGS
A) DISPOSITIONS	
1) Sociability	Low
2) Emotion	High
3) Ambition	High
4) Curiosity	
5) Uncertainty	
B) DIMENSIONS	
1) Facts / possibilities	Pronounced facts
2) Group / independent	Pronounced group
3) Own-feelings / others'-feelings	Pronounced others'-feelings
4) Wide-interests / narrow-interests	
5) Optimistic / pessimistic	
C) SOCIAL ROLES	
1) Communicator	
2) Cost-benefit calculator	
3) Educator	
4) Innovator	
5) Lifelong learner	
6) Organiser	
7) Accumulator	
D) INTELLIGENCE SPAN	High

Note: on children's personality profiles, where there is little evidence, we leave the assessment heading blank.

EXAMPLE NUMBER TWO

This child has some similarities to example number one. He learned facts easily, produced good arguments based on facts and liked the routine of school [pronounced facts and pronounced facts lifestyle]. However, he played no part in school life [pronounced independent]. He did not try to do well in subjects he disliked [pronounced independent]. His leisure time was spent by himself [low sociability]. At an early age, he began to ask questions and seek his own answers which were surprisingly good for a child of his age [high curiosity, pronounced independent and high intelligence]. In the same way as example number one, he was deeply concerned about other people's reactions to him [pronounced others'-feelings]. He was very sensitive to criticism and was very upset when people were angry with him [high emotion and pronounced others'-feelings]. His childhood collections of coins and shells were impressive [high ambition and high accumulator]. He was a kind boy [pronounced others'-feelings]. His personality profile is summarised in Table 19.2.

As a child, Charles Darwin's personality profile had some similarities to the child in example number two.

Table 19.2 Example number two personality profile

PERSONALITY CHARACTERISTICS	ASSESSMENT HEADINGS
A) DISPOSITIONS	
1) Sociability	Low
2) Emotion	High
3) Ambition	High
4) Curiosity	High
5) Uncertainty	
B) DIMENSIONS	
1) Facts / possibilities	Pronounced facts
2) Group / independent	Pronounced independent
3) Own-feelings / others'-feelings	Pronounced others'-feelings
4) Wide-interests / narrow-interests	
5) Optimistic / pessimistic	
C) SOCIAL ROLES	
1) Communicator	
2) Cost-benefit calculator	
3) Educator	
4) Innovator	
5) Lifelong learner	
6) Organiser	
7) Accumulator	High
D) INTELLIGENCE SPAN	High

EXAMPLE NUMBER THREE

He enjoyed playing with other boys, whom he often organised [above average sociability and high organiser]. As a boy, he was a successful inventor and was able to improve his sporting performance with his inventions [high innovator]. He liked the routine of school [pronounced facts lifestyle]. He was very good at school subjects, particularly those that used logic to reason about facts [pronounced facts]. He enjoyed reading [below average sociability] as well as debating with other boys [high sociability] (the below average sociability and high sociability combine to produce a flexible above average sociability assessment).

He was very angry when he paid too much for a toy [high emotion]. He much disliked being told what to do by his older brother, and they had frequent angry arguments [high emotion]. He often upset his parents by telling them that he would run away [pronounced own-feelings]. He wanted to be a writer and carefully set about improving his English style over several years [high ambition and high communicator]. He learned much from listening to his father's discussions with friends and neighbours [high intelligence]. His personality profile is summarised in Table 19.3.

As a child, Benjamin Franklin's personality profile had some similarities to the child in example number three.

Table 19.3 Example number three personality profile

PERSONALITY CHARACTERISTICS	ASSESSMENT HEADINGS
A) DISPOSITIONS	
1) Sociability	Above average
2) Emotion	High
3) Ambition	High
4) Curiosity	
5) Uncertainty	
B) DIMENSIONS	
1) Facts / possibilities	Pronounced facts
2) Group / independent	
3) Own-feelings / others'-feelings	Pronounced own-feelings
4) Wide-interests / narrow-interests	
5) Optimistic / pessimistic	
C) SOCIAL ROLES	
1) Communicator	High
2) Cost-benefit calculator	
3) Educator	
4) Innovator	High
5) Lifelong learner	
6) Organiser	High
7) Accumulator	
D) INTELLIGENCE SPAN	High

EXAMPLE NUMBER FOUR

He often spent time by himself and, as a child, had few friends [low sociability]. He liked to use his imagination and daydream [pronounced possibilities]. Around the age of fourteen, he became a successful entertainer [high ambition and high communicator]. Even as a child, he had a natural gift to entertain an audience [high communicator]. He made little sense of his school lessons, because facts meant nothing to him [pronounced possibilities]. Even in his early teens, he was bad at reading but was a born story teller [high communicator]. He was not upset by the many changes in his childhood circumstances [pronounced possibilities lifestyle]. As a boy, he was kind and considerate to other people [pronounced others'-feelings]. He had a talent for thinking up and carrying out his own successful money-making schemes, which did something to lessen the hardship of his boyhood [high cost-benefit calculator and high intelligence]. The suffering he saw as a child upset him greatly [high emotion and pronounced others'-feelings]. His personality profile is summarised in Table 19.4.

As a child, Charles Chaplin's personality profile had some similarities to the child in example number four.

Table 19.4 Example number four personality profile

PERSONALITY CHARACTERISTICS	ASSESSMENT HEADINGS
A) DISPOSITIONS	
1) Sociability	Low
2) Emotion	High
3) Ambition	High
4) Curiosity	
5) Uncertainty	
B) DIMENSIONS	
1) Facts / possibilities	Pronounced possibilities
2) Group / independent	
3) Own-feelings / others'-feelings	Pronounced others'-feelings
4) Wide-interests / narrow-interests	
5) Optimistic / pessimistic	
C) SOCIAL ROLES	
1) Communicator	High
2) Cost-benefit calculator	High
3) Educator	
4) Innovator	
5) Lifelong learner	
6) Organiser	
7) Accumulator	
D) INTELLIGENCE SPAN	High

EXAMPLE NUMBER FIVE

He was exceptionally quick and clever in his conversation [high intelligence]. He was often in trouble [ambiguous – children can be in trouble for all sorts of reasons]. He was disorganised, late and forever losing things [pronounced possibilities lifestyle]. His impulsive actions [pronounced possibilities lifestyle] and frank remarks [pronounced own-feelings] often resulted in punishment. His school performance was only average, because he did very badly in any subject that mostly consisted of learning and applying facts or rules, for example Latin [pronounced possibilities]. However, he did very well in creative writing which required the use of his imagination [pronounced possibilities, high communicator and high intelligence]. He was often very unhappy during his school years [high emotion].

He liked the company of other boys [high sociability] and played practical jokes [pronounced own-feelings]. He copied the work of other boys in order to gain the necessary grades [ambiguous – cheating can have a variety of explanations]. He consistently ignored the school rules and traditions [pronounced independent]. Nevertheless, he enjoyed sporting competitions, wanted to win and achieved sporting success [high ambition, high uncertainty and high intelligence]. His personality profile is summarised in Table 19.5.

As a child, Winston Churchill's personality profile had some similarities to the child in example number five.

Table 19.5 Example number five personality profile

PERSONALITY CHARACTERISTICS	ASSESSMENT HEADINGS
A) DISPOSITIONS	
1) Sociability	High
2) Emotion	High
3) Ambition	High
4) Curiosity	
5) Uncertainty	High
B) DIMENSIONS	
1) Facts / possibilities	Pronounced possibilities
2) Group / independent	Pronounced independent
3) Own-feelings / others'-feelings	Pronounced own-feelings
4) Wide-interests / narrow-interests	
5) Optimistic / pessimistic	
C) SOCIAL ROLES	
1) Communicator	High
2) Cost-benefit calculator	
3) Educator	
4) Innovator	
5) Lifelong learner	
6) Organiser	
7) Accumulator	
D) INTELLIGENCE SPAN	High

EXAMPLE NUMBER SIX

From the age of six or seven, he was very interested in the nature of the world [high curiosity]. Later, a favourite hobby was solving difficult mathematical problems, which often took some time [high ambition, high curiosity and high intelligence]. By his early teens, he was excited by the way geometry could answer so many questions [high curiosity]. He only made an effort at subjects which interested him [pronounced independent]. He worked best in the company of friends and family [high sociability]. He was overjoyed when he solved a particularly difficult problem [high emotion and high intelligence]. The answers to problems came to him suddenly [pronounced possibilities]. He very much disliked the routine of school [pronounced possibilities lifestyle]. He was uninterested in facts [pronounced possibilities]. This meant that he was slow and uncertain in lessons involving facts [pronounced possibilities]. He hated examinations [high emotion].

As a young child, he could be angry and violent, especially towards his teachers [high emotion and pronounced own-feelings]. His bad temper often upset his companions [high emotion and pronounced own-feelings]. Other boys disliked him, because he said competitions were stupid [pronounced own-feelings and low uncertainty]. In his early teens, he liked playing music, especially with others [high sociability]. His personality profile is summarised in Table 19.6.

As a child, Albert Einstein's personality profile had some similarities to the child in example number six.

Table 19.6 Example number six personality profile

PERSONALITY CHARACTERISTICS	ASSESSMENT HEADINGS
A) DISPOSITIONS	
1) Sociability	High
2) Emotion	High
3) Ambition	High
4) Curiosity	High
5) Uncertainty	Low
B) DIMENSIONS	
1) Facts / possibilities	Pronounced possibilities
2) Group / independent	Pronounced independent
3) Own-feelings / others'-feelings	Pronounced own-feelings
4) Wide-interests / narrow-interests	
5) Optimistic / pessimistic	
C) SOCIAL ROLES	
1) Communicator	
2) Cost-benefit calculator	
3) Educator	
4) Innovator	
5) Lifelong learner	
6) Organiser	
7) Accumulator	
D) INTELLIGENCE SPAN	High

ADVICE FOR COMPLETING THE EXERCISES

You are advised to complete the next six personality profiles of children from the information provided. It is hard work but well worthwhile. The same working procedures should be adopted as were used to complete the exercises for adults in Chapter 17. As before, some of the information supplied may be irrelevant or ambiguous with regard to personality profiles and should be noted as such in your comments. After each answer, we indicate a well-known historical person, who, as a child, had some similarities to this personality profile.

EXERCISE NUMBER ONE

A short description of the child in exercise number one

He was a sociable boy who had his share of friends but could study effectively by himself [1]. He was a very calculating child who based his decisions on facts [2]. He enjoyed school debates and relied on facts and logic to win the argument [3]. His responsibilities to his family and school were very important to him [4]. He did whatever his school told him [5]. He would not think of playing if he had any duties to do [6]. He worked hard at his studies and was determined to succeed [7].

He was a considerate boy who did not upset his close family and friends [8]. Even as a boy, he played an important part in managing the family business [9]. By his early teens, his greatest desire was to make a lot of money [10]. He was certain that he would succeed [11]. Even as a child, he made successful financial investments and was very good at arithmetic [12]. You should summarise his profile in Table 19.7.

A suggested answer to exercise number one

The suggested answer for the personality profile is in Table 19.8.

Table 19.7 Exercise number one personality profile (to be completed by readers)

PERSONALITY CHARACTERISTICS	ASSESSMENT HEADINGS
A) DISPOSITIONS	
1) Sociability	
2) Emotion	
3) Ambition	
4) Curiosity	
5) Uncertainty	
B) DIMENSIONS	
1) Facts / possibilities	
2) Group / independent	
3) Own-feelings / others'-feelings	
4) Wide-interests / narrow-interests	
5) Optimistic / pessimistic	
C) SOCIAL ROLES	
1) Communicator	
2) Cost-benefit calculator	
3) Educator	
4) Innovator	
5) Lifelong learner	
6) Organiser	
7) Accumulator	
D) INTELLIGENCE SPAN	

Table 19.8 Exercise number one suggested personality profile

PERSONALITY CHARACTERISTICS	ASSESSMENT HEADINGS
A) DISPOSITIONS	
1) Sociability	Above average
2) Emotion	
3) Ambition	High
4) Curiosity	
5) Uncertainty	
B) DIMENSIONS	
1) Facts / possibilities	Pronounced facts
2) Group / independent	Pronounced group
3) Own-feelings / others'-feelings	Pronounced others'-feelings
4) Wide-interests / narrow-interests	
5) Optimistic / pessimistic	Pronounced optimistic
C) SOCIAL ROLES	
1) Communicator	
2) Cost-benefit calculator	High
3) Educator	
4) Innovator	
5) Lifelong learner	
6) Organiser	High
7) Accumulator	
D) INTELLIGENCE SPAN	High

Suggested answers for each numbered item in exercise number one

1) above average sociability, 2) pronounced facts, 3) pronounced facts, 4) pronounced group, 5) pronounced group, 6) pronounced group, 7) high ambition, 8) pronounced others'-feelings, 9) high organiser and high intelligence, 10) high ambition, 11) pronounced optimistic, 12) high cost-benefit calculator and high intelligence.

A similar historical child to that described in exercise number one

As a child, John D Rockefeller's personality profile had some similarities to the child in exercise number one.

EXERCISE NUMBER TWO

A short description of the child in exercise number two

At school, he had no interest in school life and, in lessons, just looked at the classroom wall lost in his own dreams [1]. However, he was not disruptive, because he very much disliked upsetting other children or his teachers [2]. Although obviously intelligent, he could make no sense of factual subjects [3]. At playtime, he spent the time talking to the other children [4]. At home, his favourite hobby, which occupied most of his time, was to draw imaginative pictures to a surprisingly high standard [5]. He was nearly always late for school [6]. He ignored the school rules and would, without the teacher's permission, spontaneously leave the classroom for a chat with a friend [7]. You should summarise his profile in Table 19.9.

A suggested answer to exercise number two

The suggested answer for the personality profile is in Table 19.10.

Table 19.9 Exercise number two personality profile (to be completed by readers)

PERSONALITY CHARACTERISTICS	ASSESSMENT HEADINGS
A) DISPOSITIONS	
1) Sociability	
2) Emotion	
3) Ambition	
4) Curiosity	
5) Uncertainty	
B) DIMENSIONS	
1) Facts / possibilities	
2) Group / independent	
3) Own-feelings / others'-feelings	
4) Wide-interests / narrow-interests	
5) Optimistic / pessimistic	
C) SOCIAL ROLES	
1) Communicator	
2) Cost-benefit calculator	
3) Educator	
4) Innovator	
5) Lifelong learner	
6) Organiser	
7) Accumulator	
D) INTELLIGENCE SPAN	

Table 19.10 Exercise number two suggested personality profile

PERSONALITY CHARACTERISTICS	ASSESSMENT HEADINGS
A) DISPOSITIONS	
1) Sociability	High
2) Emotion	
3) Ambition	High
4) Curiosity	
5) Uncertainty	
B) DIMENSIONS	
1) Facts / possibilities	Pronounced possibilities
2) Group / independent	Pronounced independent
3) Own-feelings / others'-feelings	Pronounced others'-feelings
4) Wide-interests / narrow-interests	
5) Optimistic / pessimistic	
C) SOCIAL ROLES	
1) Communicator	High
2) Cost-benefit calculator	
3) Educator	
4) Innovator	
5) Lifelong learner	
6) Organiser	
7) Accumulator	
D) INTELLIGENCE SPAN	High

Suggested answers for each numbered item in exercise number two

1) pronounced possibilities and pronounced independent, 2) pronounced others'-feelings, 3) pronounced possibilities and high intelligence, 4) high sociability, 5) high ambition, pronounced possibilities, high communicator and high intelligence, 6) pronounced possibilities lifestyle, 7) pronounced possibilities lifestyle, high sociability and pronounced independent.

A similar historical child to that described in exercise number two

As a child, Pablo Picasso's personality profile had some similarities to the child in exercise number two.

EXERCISE NUMBER THREE

A short description of the child in exercise number three

As a boy, he confidently saw himself becoming a sporting hero or scientific genius [1]. His great desire was to be someone special [2]. He spent nearly all his leisure time doing school work by himself [3]. He had no close friends and for relaxation went walking alone [4]. His school grades were often the highest, and he was very good at learning facts and arguing from facts [5]. He was highly organised and was not late for school [6]. Nevertheless, he was not loyal to his school and played no part in school life [7]. He expected everything to be organised for his benefit and was totally unconcerned with how this affected his companions [8]. You should summarise his profile in Table 19.11.

A suggested answer to exercise number three

The suggested answer for the personality profile is in Table 19.12.

Table 19.11 Exercise number three personality profile
(to be completed by readers)

PERSONALITY CHARACTERISTICS	ASSESSMENT HEADINGS
A) DISPOSITIONS	
1) Sociability	
2) Emotion	
3) Ambition	
4) Curiosity	
5) Uncertainty	
B) DIMENSIONS	
1) Facts / possibilities	
2) Group / independent	
3) Own-feelings / others'-feelings	
4) Wide-interests / narrow-interests	
5) Optimistic / pessimistic	
C) SOCIAL ROLES	
1) Communicator	
2) Cost-benefit calculator	
3) Educator	
4) Innovator	
5) Lifelong learner	
6) Organiser	
7) Accumulator	
D) INTELLIGENCE SPAN	

Table 19.12 Exercise number three suggested personality profile

PERSONALITY CHARACTERISTICS	ASSESSMENT HEADINGS
A) DISPOSITIONS	
1) Sociability	Low
2) Emotion	
3) Ambition	High
4) Curiosity	
5) Uncertainty	
B) DIMENSIONS	
1) Facts / possibilities	Pronounced facts
2) Group / independent	Pronounced independent
3) Own-feelings / others'-feelings	Pronounced own-feelings
4) Wide-interests / narrow-interests	
5) Optimistic / pessimistic	Pronounced optimistic
C) SOCIAL ROLES	
1) Communicator	
2) Cost-benefit calculator	
3) Educator	
4) Innovator	
5) Lifelong learner	
6) Organiser	
7) Accumulator	
D) INTELLIGENCE SPAN	High

Suggested answers for each numbered item in exercise number three

1) high ambition and pronounced optimistic, 2) high ambition, 3) low sociability and high ambition, 4) low sociability, 5) pronounced facts and high intelligence, 6) pronounced facts lifestyle, 7) pronounced independent, 8) pronounced own-feelings.

A similar historical child to that described in exercise number three

As a child, Sigmund Freud's personality profile had some similarities to the child in exercise number three.

EXERCISE NUMBER FOUR

A short description of the child in exercise number four

He had no close friends and often played alone [1]. His mind was full of dreams and daydreams [2]. He found in nature a secret fantasy world [3]. The content of his imagination raised many questions for him and he often tried to find answers [4]. He hated the routine and order of school, which made him very unhappy [5]. He secretly made drawings of his imaginary worlds [6]. Nevertheless, his school results were good [7]. His spontaneous actions led to many accidents [8]. He attacked and hurt a boy who upset him [9]. He sometimes stayed away from school by successfully pretending to be ill [10]. He started to work hard at school, when he became worried that he would be unable to have a career [11]. He often upset his teachers and fellow students [12]. He had no loyalty to his school, whose rules he often broke [13]. You should summarise his profile in Table 19.13.

Table 19.13 Exercise number four personality profile
(to be completed by readers)

PERSONALITY CHARACTERISTICS	ASSESSMENT HEADINGS
A) DISPOSITIONS	
1) Sociability	
2) Emotion	
3) Ambition	
4) Curiosity	
5) Uncertainty	
B) DIMENSIONS	
1) Facts / possibilities	
2) Group / independent	
3) Own-feelings / others'-feelings	
4) Wide-interests / narrow-interests	
5) Optimistic / pessimistic	
C) SOCIAL ROLES	
1) Communicator	
2) Cost-benefit calculator	
3) Educator	
4) Innovator	
5) Lifelong learner	
6) Organiser	
7) Accumulator	
D) INTELLIGENCE SPAN	

A suggested answer to exercise number four

The suggested answer for the personality profile is in Table 19.14.

Table 19.14 Exercise number four suggested personality profile

PERSONALITY CHARACTERISTICS	ASSESSMENT HEADINGS
A) DISPOSITIONS	
1) Sociability	Low
2) Emotion	High
3) Ambition	High
4) Curiosity	High
5) Uncertainty	
B) DIMENSIONS	
1) Facts / possibilities	Pronounced possibilities
2) Group / independent	Pronounced independent
3) Own-feelings / others'-feelings	Pronounced own-feelings
4) Wide-interests / narrow-interests	
5) Optimistic / pessimistic	
C) SOCIAL ROLES	
1) Communicator	
2) Cost-benefit calculator	
3) Educator	
4) Innovator	
5) Lifelong learner	
6) Organiser	
7) Accumulator	
D) INTELLIGENCE SPAN	High

Suggested answers for each numbered item in exercise number four

1) low sociability, 2) pronounced possibilities, 3) pronounced possibilities, 4) high curiosity and pronounced possibilities, 5) high emotion and pronounced possibilities lifestyle, 6) pronounced possibilities, 7) high intelligence, 8) pronounced possibilities lifestyle, 9) high emotion and pronounced own-feelings, 10) high intelligence, 11) high ambition and pronounced independent, 12) pronounced own-feelings, 13) pronounced independent.

A similar historical child to that described in exercise number four

As a child, Carl Jung's personality profile had some similarities to the child in exercise number four.

EXERCISE NUMBER FIVE

A short description of the child in exercise number five

He enjoyed playing with other boys [1]. Nevertheless, he could spend some time by himself at school working effectively [2]. He liked telling other boys what to do [3]. He was good at learning facts and using logical arguments based on facts [4]. His school results were good, and he was punctual and reliable at school [5]. Eventually, he came to hate his teachers' authority over him and openly told his teachers that he greatly disliked them [6]. By his early teens, he began to see himself as a great hero, who would save his country [7]. He fought other boys in order to be more important than them, but he often lost the fights, which made him very angry [8]. His pride drove him to fight still stronger and bigger boys [9]. He always wanted revenge for his defeats [10]. In his youth, he was easily and often deceived by his companions, which made him very angry, deeply suspicious and highly mistrustful [11]. You should summarise his profile in Table 19.15.

Table 19.15 Exercise number five personality profile
(to be completed by readers)

PERSONALITY CHARACTERISTICS	ASSESSMENT HEADINGS
A) DISPOSITIONS	
1) Sociability	
2) Emotion	
3) Ambition	
4) Curiosity	
5) Uncertainty	
B) DIMENSIONS	
1) Facts / possibilities	
2) Group / independent	
3) Own-feelings / others'-feelings	
4) Wide-interests / narrow-interests	
5) Optimistic / pessimistic	
C) SOCIAL ROLES	
1) Communicator	
2) Cost-benefit calculator	
3) Educator	
4) Innovator	
5) Lifelong learner	
6) Organiser	
7) Accumulator	
D) INTELLIGENCE SPAN	

A suggested answer to exercise number five

The suggested answer for the personality profile is in Table 19.16.

Table 19.16 Exercise number five suggested personality profile

PERSONALITY CHARACTERISTICS	ASSESSMENT HEADINGS
A) DISPOSITIONS	
1) Sociability	Above average
2) Emotion	High
3) Ambition	High
4) Curiosity	
5) Uncertainty	
B) DIMENSIONS	
1) Facts / possibilities	Pronounced facts
2) Group / independent	Pronounced independent
3) Own-feelings / others'-feelings	Pronounced own-feelings
4) Wide-interests / narrow-interests	Pronounced wide-interests
5) Optimistic / pessimistic	
C) SOCIAL ROLES	
1) Communicator	
2) Cost-benefit calculator	
3) Educator	
4) Innovator	
5) Lifelong learner	
6) Organiser	High
7) Accumulator	
D) INTELLIGENCE SPAN	High

Suggested answers for each numbered item in exercise number five

1) above average sociability, 2) above average sociability, 3) high organiser, 4) pronounced facts, 5) pronounced facts lifestyle and high intelligence, 6) high emotion, pronounced independent and pronounced own-feelings, 7) high ambition and pronounced wide-interests, 8) high emotion, high ambition and pronounced own-feelings, 9) high ambition, 10) high emotion, 11) high emotion and pronounced own-feelings.

A similar historical child to that described in exercise number five

As a child, Joseph Stalin's personality profile had some similarities to the child in exercise number five.

EXERCISE NUMBER SIX

A short description of the child in exercise number six

During his childhood, he spent much time alone and lived by his daydreams [1]. He dreamed of fame and was certain that one day he would be famous because of his great talent [2]. He only enjoyed the few school lessons which described and praised his country's greatness [3]. He liked to listen to stories about his country's many successes and its great leaders [4]. He could make no sense of facts and did badly at school [5]. The resulting criticism of his poor grades by his teachers upset him greatly [6]. He was no better than average at practical subjects [7]. He cared a great deal about what people said about him and was easily hurt by their criticism [8]. He wanted to be part of the school community and was very upset and angry about his rejection by the school authorities [9]. His favourite teenage pastimes were solitary war games and reading adventure stories alone [10]. You should summarise his profile in Table 19.17.

Table 19.17 Exercise number six personality profile (to be completed by readers)

PERSONALITY CHARACTERISTICS	ASSESSMENT HEADINGS
A) DISPOSITIONS	
1) Sociability	
2) Emotion	
3) Ambition	
4) Curiosity	
5) Uncertainty	
B) DIMENSIONS	
1) Facts / possibilities	
2) Group / independent	
3) Own-feelings / others'-feelings	
4) Wide-interests / narrow-interests	
5) Optimistic / pessimistic	
C) SOCIAL ROLES	
1) Communicator	
2) Cost-benefit calculator	
3) Educator	
4) Innovator	
5) Lifelong learner	
6) Organiser	
7) Accumulator	
D) INTELLIGENCE SPAN	

A suggested answer to exercise number six

The suggested answer for the personality profile is in Table 19.18.

Table 19.18 Exercise number six suggested personality profile

PERSONALITY CHARACTERISTICS	ASSESSMENT HEADINGS
A) DISPOSITIONS	
1) Sociability	Low
2) Emotion	High
3) Ambition	High
4) Curiosity	
5) Uncertainty	
B) DIMENSIONS	
1) Facts / possibilities	Pronounced possibilities
2) Group / independent	Pronounced group
3) Own-feelings / others'-feelings	Pronounced others'-feelings
4) Wide-interests / narrow-interests	Pronounced wide-interests
5) Optimistic / pessimistic	Pronounced optimistic
C) SOCIAL ROLES	
1) Communicator	
2) Cost-benefit calculator	
3) Educator	
4) Innovator	
5) Lifelong learner	
6) Organiser	
7) Accumulator	
D) INTELLIGENCE SPAN	Average

Suggested answers for each numbered item in exercise number six

1) low sociability and pronounced possibilities, 2) high ambition and pronounced optimistic, 3) pronounced group and pronounced wide-interests, 4) pronounced group and pronounced wide-interests, 5) pronounced possibilities, 6) high emotion and pronounced others'-feelings, 7) average intelligence, 8) high emotion and pronounced others'-feelings, 9) high emotion and pronounced group, 10) low sociability.

A similar historical child to that described in exercise number six

As a child, Adolf Hitler's personality profile had some similarities to the child in exercise number six.

CONCLUSION

If our personality profiles only developed at the beginning of adulthood, we would have neither the time nor the opportunity to use our personality characteristics and assessment headings during childhood. In other words, we would be inefficient adults until we had learned how to take full advantage of our personality profiles. In order to avoid this unproductive adult period, we can anticipate that people would learn how to use their personality characteristics and assessment headings during childhood. Our small sample of children is consistent with this expectation. Moreover, these children's personality profiles last a lifetime. The continuation of childhood personality profiles into adulthood can be seen by comparing the same individual's childhood and adult profiles from Chapters 16, 17 and 19. This is hardly an original insight. We have evidence that, for hundreds of years, perceptive people have realised that childhood personality continues into adulthood. James Boswell (1740–95) in his *The Life of Samuel Johnson, LL.D.*, published in 1791, is one example. He noted the common observation of his time that the child is the adult 'in miniature; and that the distinguishing characteristics of each individual are the same, through the whole course of life.'

The evidence from the small sample in this chapter also supports the view that the personality profiles and lifestyles of some children are very different from each other. We identified six children with a pronounced facts trait and another six children with a pronounced possibilities trait. Children with a pronounced facts trait did well at school, liked the school routine and were praised for learning facts and for their reasoning skills. Sometimes, they may have been bored but could still easily learn the facts required for their school education. These children all gained self-esteem from their success at school. Children who had a pronounced possibilities trait did less well at school than their intelligence suggested. They were less able to learn facts and disliked the routine of school.

YOUR NOTES (OPTIONAL AT YOUR OWN RISK)

As a child, what was your personality profile? You may wish to do this personality profiling exercise by completing Table 19.19.

Table 19.19 Your childhood personality profile

PERSONALITY CHARACTERISTICS	ASSESSMENT HEADINGS						
A) DISPOSITIONS	V high	High	Above av.	Aver-age	Below av.	Low	V. low
1) Sociability							
2) Emotion							
3) Ambition							
4) Curiosity							
5) Uncertainty							
B) DIMENSIONS	TRAIT 'A'				TRAIT 'B'		
TRAIT 'A' / TRAIT 'B'	V. pron.	Pron.	More than	Br. equal	More than	Pron.	V. pron.
1) Facts / possibilities							
2) Group / independent							
3) Own-feelings / others'-feelings							
4) Wide-interests / narrow-interests							
5) Optimistic / pessimistic							
C) SOCIAL ROLES	V. high	High	Above av.	Aver-age	Below av.	Low	Ab-sent
1) Communicator							
2) Cost-benefit calculator							
3) Educator							
4) Innovator							
5) Lifelong learner							
6) Organiser							
7) Accumulator							
	V. high	High	Above av.	Aver-age	Below av.	Low	V. low
D) INTELLIGENCE SPAN							

Note: av. = average; V. = Very; Pron. = Pronounced; Br. = Broadly

FURTHER NOTES

CHAPTER 20

Life experiences

There are important aspects of personality which are not explained by the personality profile. For example, we may describe an individual as at ease, contented, helpful, open, secure, sincere, supportive or trusting. Alternatively, we may describe someone else as anxious, apprehensive, defiant, fearful, intimidated, stressed, suspicious, tense or worried. In these two cases, we are largely, but not entirely, identifying the effect on people of their life experiences, which are the significant events in an individual's personal history.

LIFE EXPERIENCES are the significant events in an individual's personal history.

Life experiences result in an important variable aspect of personality. People's life experiences can influence their personalities. For this reason, people's personalities can alter noticeably from one time to another. For example, an individual's personality could change from trusting to suspicious over a few weeks. Many kinds of life experiences can change people's personalities. However, important life experiences for many people are their family lives, friendships, health and careers. Successes or disappointments in any of these life experiences can have a significant short- or long-term effect on personality. A secure family life, strong friendships, good health and a successful career are positive life experiences, which increase a person's feelings of wellbeing.

> **POSITIVE LIFE EXPERIENCES increase a person's feelings of wellbeing.**

Loneliness, unemployment, poor health, an unhappy family life, poverty and discrimination are negative life experiences, which decrease a person's feelings of wellbeing.

> **NEGATIVE LIFE EXPERIENCES decrease a person's feelings of wellbeing.**

Children are socialised largely within the family and at school. In these situations, children begin to use their personality characteristics. However, if a child's family is unsatisfactory or if the child is alienated from school or the community, there are significant risks for that child. An inadequate upbringing or schooling may have a harmful influence on a child's personality and, therefore, on the community to which the child belongs. This is more likely to be the case if children have well-defined personality characteristics, because they have less flexible personalities. The effects of negative childhood experiences can be particularly long lasting.

The effects of life experiences vary greatly between people because of their differing personality profiles. An individual's personality profile sometimes determines which life experiences are either positive or negative. For example, the same life experiences can benefit a person with some personality characteristics and assessment headings but harm another with different personality characteristics and assessment headings. This is particularly true with regard to lifestyle, for example the amount of time spent with other people. An individual with very high sociability may find even a short separation from others worrying and experience immediate anxiety. The same short period of separation may seem secure and relaxing to an individual with very low sociability. Equally, an individual who has very low sociability may find even a short period with others worrying and experience immediate anxiety. Again, the same short period with others may seem secure and relaxing to a person with very high sociability. In these examples, we have only described short-term effects. However, if these experiences last longer, the effects on personality may also last longer and be more severe.

A routine or spontaneous lifestyle can also have very different effects on people with differing primary traits within the ways of thinking. A person with a pronounced or very pronounced facts trait feels secure with a routine lifestyle, while a person with a pronounced or very pronounced possibilities trait is distressed by the same routine lifestyle. A person with a pronounced or very pronounced possibilities trait enjoys frequent change, while a person with a pronounced or very pronounced facts trait is distressed by the same variety.

Similar comments can be made about many of the other personality characteristics. If people differ significantly in their personality profiles, then the same situation can be favourable for some but unfavourable to others. For example, individuals with very high ambition are unhappy with a lack of opportunities, while those with very low ambition do not even notice their absence. The same applies to the dimensions. People with a pronounced or very pronounced facts trait are distressed if they have to solve problems by thinking in terms of possible alternatives. Equally, those with a pronounced or very pronounced possibilities trait are distressed if they have to solve problems by the detailed study of facts. Again, individuals with a pronounced or a very pronounced group trait are troubled if forced to make decisions on the basis of their own interests. Equally, those with a pronounced or a very pronounced independent trait are troubled if they have to make decisions on the basis of community interests. We can make similar points about the remaining dimensions. People who have a particular social role with a high or very high assessment heading enjoy tasks for which their social role is appropriate. Those who lack the social role are distressed by their inability to complete the same tasks. People feel frustrated if required to carry out tasks for which they do not have the appropriate intelligence span.

There are some personality characteristics and assessment headings which significantly increase the effects of negative life experiences. One is high or very high emotion. An emotional person reacts strongly to, for example, failure. Another is a pronounced or very pronounced pessimistic trait. Negative life experiences can have a long-term, damaging effect on those with a pronounced or very pronounced pessimistic trait. This is particularly true if, for example, any failure is seen as evidence that their gloomy expectations are correct. Consequently, a series of disappointments and setbacks for emotional pessimists may lead to long-term feelings of anxiety and stress.

SELF-WORTH

People's assessment of their own achievements, their view as to their self-worth, can also significantly affect their personalities.

SELF-WORTH **is people's assessment of their own achievements.**

People who achieve their ambitions are likely to feel secure. They have high feelings of self-worth.

HIGH SELF-WORTH describes individuals' satisfaction with their achievements.

People who do not achieve their ambitions are likely to feel insecure. They have low feelings of self-worth.

LOW SELF-WORTH describes individuals' dissatisfaction with their achievements.

Two people may have nearly the same career successes but have very different feelings of self-worth, depending on whether their ambitions have, or have not, been achieved. Hardly surprisingly, Winston Churchill had high feelings of self-worth in his later years. He felt that he had achieved his destiny as British wartime Prime Minister. As we shall see in the following case study, Adolf Hitler, although he benefited from many years of political and military good fortune, always retained the low feelings of self-worth experienced in his early life. He felt humiliated and rejected as a result of his failure at school.

This book is largely an explanation of the personality profile. A full discussion of the effects of life experiences on people would take us too far away from this topic. These life experiences are too many to be discussed here in full. However, many important aspects are revealed in the following short case study.

A CASE STUDY ON LIFE EXPERIENCES

In exploring the effect of life experiences, it is interesting to compare two people whose lives both affected each other and had very evil consequences for their times. In the following case study, we explore the personalities of two heartless tyrants, Adolf Hitler and Joseph Stalin. The aim is to understand their adult personalities in terms of both their personality profiles and life experiences. We have already very broadly identified their personality profiles in exercises numbers six and seven of Chapter 16, which you may find useful to reread at this point. First, using these profiles, we enter both Hitler's and Stalin's adult personality assessment headings onto a personality profile (see Table 20.1).

We now compare Hitler's and Stalin's personality profiles using Table 20.1. We can see that Hitler and Stalin had many differences in their assessment headings. Nevertheless, their profiles with regard to their dispositions were very similar, differing only in their sociability. Hitler had below average sociability, while Stalin had above average sociability. However, their primary traits in four of the five dimensions were different. They only shared a very pronounced wide-interests trait. Their involvement in society at large reflects this shared, very pronounced wide-interests trait. Interestingly, they both had only one social role which was high or very high. Hitler was very high in his communicator social role, while Stalin had a high organiser social role. As a consequence of being low or absent in all their other social roles, they both lacked complexity and talents, which added to their insecurity.

Hitler's and Stalin's childhood experiences had very bad effects on the whole of their lives. We have already looked at childhoods with similarities to Hitler's and Stalin's in Chapter 19 (exercises number five and six), which you may find useful to reread at this point. Both descriptions identify very negative childhood life experiences. Although Hitler did reasonably well at school up to the age of eleven, he was

Table 20.1 Hitler's and Stalin's assessment headings

PERSONALITY CHARACTERISTICS	HITLER	STALIN
A) DISPOSITIONS		
1) Sociability	Below average	Above average
2) Emotion	Very high	Very high
3) Ambition	Very high	Very high
4) Curiosity	Low	Low
5) Uncertainty	Low	Low
B) DIMENSIONS		
1) Facts / possibilities	V. P. possibilities	V. P. facts
2) Group / independent	V. P. group	V. P. independent
3) Own-feelings / others'-feelings	P. others'-feelings	V. P. own-feelings
4) Wide-interests / narrow-interests	V. P. wide-interests	V. P. wide-interests
5) Optimistic / pessimistic	V. P. optimistic	Broadly equal
C) SOCIAL ROLES		
1) Communicator	Very high	Low
2) Cost-benefit calculator	Low	Low
3) Educator	Low	Low
4) Innovator	Low	Low
5) Lifelong learner	Low	Low
6) Organiser	Low	High
7) Accumulator	Absent	Absent
D) INTELLIGENCE SPAN	Above average	High

Note: V. = Very; P. = Pronounced

deeply embarrassed and humiliated by his almost complete failure at secondary school. With his very pronounced possibilities trait, he could make no sense of a facts-based education. His very high ambition and very pronounced optimistic trait led him to expect success and not his educational 'failure'. As a result of his very high emotion, very pronounced group trait and pronounced others'-feelings trait, Hitler's rejection by his school community was extremely painful for him. His alienation from authority and society was almost total. On the other hand, Hitler's family life as a child was largely secure.

Stalin's alienation started when he was a young child. His drunken father violently assaulted Stalin and his mother. Stalin's childhood failure to become a gang leader was a great personal disappointment. By his late teens, Stalin's very pronounced independent trait had led to a complete rejection of traditional beliefs, which he found wholly unconvincing. His very pronounced independent trait and very pronounced own-feelings trait also contributed to his deep hatred of school, religion and the state, whose authority he rejected. His very pronounced own-feelings trait meant that he was easily deceived, which resulted in a very suspicious nature. At his secondary school, spies and informers reported on the students, which also added to Stalin's suspiciousness. Stalin was also disaffected because a foreign power, Russia, repressed and occupied his country, Georgia. As with Hitler, Stalin's alienation from authority and society was almost total. One consequence of all these negative life experiences was that Stalin learned in his childhood how to maintain a ruthless tyranny and to control a society through fear and terror.

Hitler's ambitions as a teenager were unrealistic. His great optimism meant that he expected to be accepted as a student in an art college. His totally unexpected failure to become an art student came as a devastating shock. The death of his mother, whom he nursed through her final illness, also added to his confusion. He dropped out of society and, for a while, became a tramp. These extremely negative life experiences resulted in lifelong feelings of great hatred and anger towards authority and those with power and money.

Nevertheless, Hitler's very pronounced group trait found full expression when he joined the German army at the beginning of the First World War. It was the happiest period of his life. He was a dedicated, loyal corporal, who was decorated for his bravery. Germany's total defeat destroyed his short-lived happiness. For Hitler, it was a personal disaster and negative life experience of the worst kind. His wide-interests aim for the remainder of his life became to gain revenge for Germany's defeat and to restore Germany to its former military greatness.

Like others, Hitler needed somebody to blame for Germany's defeat. The popular choice was imagined Marxist-Jewish traitors. There was no truth in this explanation. Nevertheless, Hitler violently denounced the treachery of the Jews as the cause of Germany's defeat. Above all, Hitler wanted revenge on these imagined traitors. Hitler's explanations were the outcome of fantasies accepted as true because of his very pronounced possibilities trait. For him, his fantasies were completely convincing.

From then on, Hitler's very high ambition, very high emotion, very pronounced wide-interests and very high communicator social role were reflected in his actions to bring about the military rebirth of Germany and revenge on its 'traitors'. His ambition was to save the German people and punish its enemies. His solution revealed his lack of intelligence. He wanted a war of conquest to create a slave empire in Eastern Europe for the German people. His other equally senseless objective was the racial 'purity' of Germany by removing the Jews, Gypsies and others. In the event, his 'final solution' for these innocent people was their mass murder.

It may seem surprising that Hitler with a pronounced others'-feelings trait could be such a heartless tyrant and murderer. However, as a result of his very negative childhood life experiences, Hitler felt the strongest feelings of hatred and desires for revenge. Moreover, his pronounced others'-feelings trait was limited to the German 'race'. Hitler was convinced that people like the Jews, who were outside his German 'race', were 'subhuman' with no more rights than animals. It followed, according to Hitler's merciless reasoning, that the Jews and other minorities could be murdered. Perhaps equally surprisingly, Hitler's very pronounced possibilities and very pronounced group traits also meant that he was not worried about individual German military casualties. Only the German nation of his imagination mattered to the fantasising Hitler, not the lives of individual Germans.

During Stalin's childhood, he found his wide-interests objectives in the ideas of Karl Marx (1818–83). Marx predicted that the ordinary people would eventually rise up in an extremely violent and bloody revolution and destroy their rulers, the capitalists. The very high emotion and very high ambition found in Marx's wide-interests writings were the same as Stalin's personality profile. Marx's prediction of violence also agreed with the lessons of Stalin's life experiences. Stalin was convinced by his upbringing that ruthless violence was essential for success. Stalin's very pronounced independent trait eventually led him to see himself as the only person who could bring about Marx's prophecies.

Stalin, with his very pronounced facts trait, accepted the logical basis of Marx's predictions. Marx's ideas became the foundation of Stalin's reasoning. Stalin explained everything by Marxist logic (as later updated by the Russian revolutionary leader, Vladimir Lenin (1870–1924)). Accordingly, Stalin's Marxist-Leninist beliefs were held with a fanatical certainty. Consequently, when the Marxist-Leninist revolution resulted in disaster, Stalin could only blame traitors. As a result of his life experiences and personality profile, Stalin was full of suspicion about everyone. Accordingly, he destroyed all opposition by killing millions of loyal party members, colleagues and even his family in a series of purges. He accepted no personal responsibility for the millions of people who died of starvation as a result of his mistakes.

One unexpected outcome of Hitler's and Stalin's very different personalities was their description as loners. Neither Hitler nor Stalin could establish close personal relationships with another individual. Hitler took decisions in isolation, because, with his below average sociability and very pronounced possibilities thinking, he lived in his own world. He was unable to justify his visions to another person. Moreover, he did not have the intelligence to win an argument. Stalin was a loner because of his very pronounced independent trait and very pronounced own-feelings trait. His very pronounced own-feelings trait left him alone in a world which almost entirely consisted of his own feelings. He was unable to enter the minds of other people. In the case of both Hitler and Stalin, their very pronounced traits and negative life experiences completely alienated them from other individuals and the rest of society. When in power, they could not, and did not, share decision making with anyone else. All this contributed to their evil actions.

For very different reasons, Hitler and Stalin came to believe fanatical absurdities which satisfied their very high emotion and very high ambition. They were convinced their fanatical beliefs fully justified the violent revenge they took on many millions of innocent people. None of this explains why both men were able to carry out such ruinous and totally depraved policies. Admittedly, Hitler's pronounced others'-feelings trait and very high communicator social role enabled him to take advantage of the hatred and hysteria felt by many Germans. His visions of a Germany betrayed and reborn convinced many of them. His very pronounced group trait meant he was loyal to, and trusted, his followers, who repaid his trust with total personal loyalty. He only once decided to kill a few hundred of his own supporters for, as he saw it, reasons of political necessity. Stalin's above average sociability, very pronounced facts thinking and high organiser social role made him a successful administrator. His very pronounced independent and very pronounced own-feelings traits meant he could take the ruthless decisions necessary to destroy all his rivals. Nevertheless, as individuals, Hitler and Stalin could do relatively little harm. Their great evil came from the total control that both men achieved.

Their ability to take this control had nothing to do with their personalities. The first half of the twentieth century was an exceptionally troubled time. Industrialisation and new knowledge had confused people. Earlier traditions and certainties of belief had disappeared without being replaced. Meanwhile, war and empires were still acceptable to public opinion. Many people still believed that war was good for a country. Deep hatreds and fears between communities were common and were often deliberately made worse by weak rulers in order to strengthen their hold on power. The Communist revolution in the Soviet Union was both strongly welcomed by some and greatly feared by others. At the time, there was also a belief in the 'great man', who was also a 'man of destiny'. Georg Hegel (1770–1831), an influential German thinker, had praised these warlords. He even made the shameful suggestion that these warlords could behave as they pleased. Marx took much from Hegel. In addition to all this, there was an absence in Germany and the Soviet Union of any traditions of freedom, representative democracy, constitutional government and the rule of law.

In these confused times, two individuals with well-defined personality characteristics, who had become exceptionally angry and totally alienated as a result of very negative life experiences, were able to take control. Their very high emotion and very high ambition guided their decisions. Both believed fanatical nonsense, which, in their view, fully justified their hatred and violence. For different reasons, neither of them valued the life of an individual. They both took advantage of the intellectual and moral failure of the time. The situation was made for them. With the benefit of much good fortune, they lied and cheated their way to power. Their absurd beliefs led to merciless decisions. Once in control, their fanaticism was given full expression, and they were able to take whatever actions they wished. Tens of millions of ordinary people died or were killed for senseless reasons.

CONCLUSION

People can only live together according to the social and intellectual beliefs of their community. We cannot say how people would have behaved if their community, personality profile or life experiences had been different. For example, we cannot know how Hitler would have behaved later if he had been accepted into an art college. Equally, we cannot know how Stalin would have behaved as an adult if, as a child, he had not been cruelly beaten by his father, harshly repressed in his secondary school and, as seems almost certain, so easily deceived in his childhood gangland fights. The community, personality profile and life experiences are inseparable in their effect on the individual whose actions we wish to understand.

KEY POINTS

LIFE EXPERIENCES are the significant events in an individual's personal history.

POSITIVE LIFE EXPERIENCES increase a person's feelings of wellbeing.

NEGATIVE LIFE EXPERIENCES decrease a person's feelings of wellbeing.

SELF-WORTH is people's assessment of their own achievements.

HIGH SELF-WORTH describes individuals' satisfaction with their achievements.

LOW SELF-WORTH describes individuals' dissatisfaction with their achievements.

YOUR NOTES (OPTIONAL AT YOUR OWN RISK)

How would you describe your life experiences? For example, which of your life experiences were positive and which were negative?

What evidence are you using?

What events among your life experiences still affect you today?

What evidence are you using?

To what extent are you or anybody known to you affected by negative life experiences, high or very high emotion and pronounced or very pronounced pessimistic traits?

What evidence are you using?

Do you know anyone personally or by reputation whose personality has changed as a result of their life experiences?

What evidence are you using?

How secure are your feelings of self-worth?

What evidence are you using?

Do you know anyone personally or by reputation who has feelings of high self-worth?

What evidence are you using?

Do you know anyone personally or by reputation who has feelings of low self-worth?

What evidence are you using?

FURTHER NOTES

CHAPTER 21

Self-awareness

From the first twenty chapters, we have learned to understand our personalities. However, at work, increased knowledge only has value if it improves our performance. In this chapter, we start to explore how our new insights into our own personalities can benefit our careers. 'Self-awareness of personality' is people's insight into their own personality profiles and into the effect on their personalities of their life experiences.

> **SELF-AWARENESS OF PERSONALITY is people's understanding of their own personality profiles and life experiences.**

Charles Darwin was able to describe his personality with great accuracy in his short autobiography. He clearly identified his personality, and, in particular, those aspects of his personality which were a benefit to his scientific work. He also described how he had learned important lessons from experience.

> **People with HIGH SELF-AWARENESS have considerable insight into their personalities and life experiences.**

Other people have little insight into their personalities and life experiences. Henry Ford revealed no significant self-knowledge of his personality. After his initial success, he showed little awareness that his well-defined personality characteristics might lead to poor management and bad commercial decisions.

People with LOW SELF-AWARENESS have little insight into their personalities and life experiences.

We look at some benefits of high self-awareness and some risks from low self-awareness. In general, we consider people with assessment headings which are high, very high, low, very low, absent, pronounced and very pronounced, because these individuals illustrate the issues in their clearest form. We are particularly interested in those aspects of the personality profile and of life experiences where self-awareness leads to improved performance. As always, we follow the order of the personality profile and start with the dispositions.

NOTE
In this chapter, for reasons of simplicity and saving space, the assessment headings high, low and pronounced should be read as including very high, very low, absent and very pronounced.

DISPOSITIONS

Emotion

There are significant advantages and disadvantages for people with either high or low emotion. Experienced business leaders assert that only passionate executives (those with high emotion) produce results. Very often, the business team or individual with the most passion is the one that succeeds. We have already seen the benefits of high emotion with John D Rockefeller and Charles Chaplin. Both men were able to inspire those who worked for them. The disadvantage is that passionate individuals can be carried away by the strength of their own feelings. Henry Ford destroyed employees' work when intensely angry.

Self-awareness brings important advantages for managers with high emotion. Employees are often frightened of managers with high emotion who openly show their anger or irritation. In these situations, employees learn to hide their mistakes and refuse to tell their managers bad news. The performance of the organisation can decline significantly as a result. Consequently, many managers with high emotion become skilled at disguising their feelings. They learn from experience the wisdom of hiding anger or annoyance. In this case, the drive supplied by high emotion is kept but without the disadvantages and bad reputation which can follow from revealing an unpleasant temper. For this reason, John D Rockefeller hid his very high emotion. Staff, colleagues and associates respect these managers' effective self-control.

People with low emotion can do very well at work, but they need to choose careers where either personal hard work or unpleasant work is not essential to success. In some careers, effective management depends on delegation or on a few important decisions which can be taken at leisure. Alternatively, people with low emotion can choose a career which they enjoy, for example as a writer. In this case, the hard work is a pleasure. As well as literary careers, some sporting careers can be chosen largely for enjoyment. Low emotion can supply a major competitive advantage. Decisions and actions taken with little emotion can be more objective than those taken while experiencing considerable emotion. Additionally, managers with low emotion are not strongly attached to earlier decisions and can more easily change their minds.

Ambition

Strong determination is a defining aspect of high ambition. If one approach fails, individuals with high ambition try and try again. Sometimes, their determination is highly beneficial, while on other occasions, it achieves nothing at all. Isaac Newton (1642–1727), the famous physicist, considered by many to be one of the greatest scientists, illustrates the gains from determination. As a student, Newton found René Descartes' (1596–1650) book on geometry very difficult. He kept reaching parts of the book that he could not understand but he refused to be defeated. Instead, every time he could not understand Descartes' book, he started again from the beginning. This re-reading of the book continued until Newton had self-taught himself the whole work. However, in other areas of study, Newton's determination was much less successful. He wasted large amounts of time researching and experimenting in alchemy. His enormous efforts in this area produced no results.

Even if an ambitious person's goals are attainable, too much determination can still be damaging. People are rarely, if ever, capable of perfection. J R R Tolkien's ambition was to give his country, England, a truly worthy mythology (an example of his very pronounced group trait). In fact, he was so persistent in his search for perfection that much of his work was unfinished at his death.

People who are self-aware can successfully disguise their high ambition. Benjamin Franklin benefited by hiding his very high ambition. Many people feel threatened by individuals with high ambition, particularly, as in Franklin's case, those who have a pronounced own-feelings trait. In order to hide his very high ambition, Franklin stopped putting forward his suggestions for improvements as his own ideas. Rather, he pretended that these suggestions were the ideas of other people who wished to remain anonymous. He said that he was merely acting on their behalf. He found that this small deception resulted in a much better reception of his ideas.

Emotion and ambition

High emotion and high ambition result in a great determination to succeed, which helps talented people to achieve their goals. Individuals who are high in emotion and high in ambition commonly share the following:

- An intense need to succeed which often necessitates a single-mindedness of purpose
- A passionate desire to see the job done properly which enables them to demand from themselves and others the highest standards of performance
- A willingness to work very hard

High emotion and high ambition do not guarantee success. There are emotional, ambitious failures.

Some famous people have low emotion and high ambition, for example Franklin D Roosevelt. Ambitious individuals who have low emotion need the self-awareness to avoid direct personal competition from people with high emotion. Otherwise, they can be overcome by the greater efforts and appeal of people with high emotion in struggles for success and influence. Roosevelt achieved his ambitions by appealing to a majority of voters. Other people with low emotion and high ambition have succeeded over more emotional rivals by using the power that comes from owning the business or being a family member in a family company.

DIMENSIONS

Ways of thinking

People with a pronounced facts trait can be slow to act in a crisis because of their need to collect and review the evidence before taking a decision. They have to establish the facts with reasonable certainty. Since they need to have sufficient time to take decisions, they should avoid situations where quick decisions are essential. People with a pronounced facts trait are concerned with what is already known, but the past is not always a good guide to the future. From time to time, there are highly significant changes, for example in markets and products, which are difficult to predict from existing facts. Consequently, those with a pronounced facts trait should be cautious in situations which are subject to innovation or rapid change, because their decisions may be invalidated by unanticipated events or trends.

People with a pronounced possibilities trait are often at risk in situations outside their experience, which may also make them indecisive. For example, Pablo Picasso, who had a very pronounced possibilities trait, found it very difficult to take a decision which changed significantly his personal circumstances. Young people's lack of experience can also cause difficulties for people with a pronounced possibilities trait, even if they have high intelligence. Albert Einstein, who had a pronounced possibilities trait, went against the advice of family and friends in making an unfortunate first marriage. He lacked the necessary experience of personal relationships to realise that his dreams of future married happiness were mistaken. People with a pronounced possibilities trait should be cautious in situations where decisions either require a careful, detailed analysis of the facts or where they have insufficient experience on which to base their decisions.

People with pronounced ways of thinking traits are also at risk of error, because they are less likely to change their beliefs than those with broadly equal traits. People with a pronounced facts trait are convinced by their facts, theories and logic. They are little influenced by new possibilities. People with a pronounced possibilities trait are convinced by their assessment of alternative outcomes. They are little influenced by new facts. Thus, people with pronounced ways of thinking traits are less likely to change earlier conclusions than those with broadly equal traits, who can effectively use both their facts and possibilities traits. Albert Einstein is an example of a scientist with a pronounced possibilities trait whose beliefs were unaffected by new facts. Einstein never accepted the truth of quantum mechanics in spite of ever stronger factual evidence in its favour. He disregarded this evidence, because it was inconsistent with how he imagined the world to be.

People with different pronounced traits within the ways of thinking may be unable to predict each others' actions. Adolf Hitler, with his very pronounced possibilities trait, was hesitant and indecisive. He had little experience of his enemies. His decisions relied on his daydreams and fantasies. Joseph Stalin had a very pronounced facts trait. His conclusions were based on facts. In 1941, Stalin's assessment of the facts was that a Nazi invasion of the Soviet Union would be madness. Stalin was certain that Hitler would be unable to conquer the vast spaces of the Soviet Union and would be left with a disastrous war on two fronts. Consequently, to Stalin's factual mind, there was no risk of a

Nazi invasion in 1941. For this reason, Stalin made totally inadequate preparations against a Nazi invasion. This was, perhaps, the most important reason why the Soviet army and people suffered such enormous casualties during the early stages of the Nazi attack. We can now understand the reason for Joseph Stalin's most serious military blunder, which was his failure to foresee Hitler's invasion of the Soviet Union in 1941. Stalin's fundamental error was to assume that Hitler's decisions were made in the same way as his own. He wrongly believed that Hitler would consider the facts. Hitler's invasion shocked Stalin. For a week, he was unable take decisions.

Even without Hitler and Stalin, there are many examples of poor decisions by individuals as a result of their pronounced facts or possibilities traits. These people do not apply the correct kind of reasoning to the problems before them. Those who have pronounced ways of thinking traits need to be self-aware about when they can use their primary traits. As individuals, they should only try to solve the kinds of problems which are appropriate to their ways of thinking, knowledge and experience.

Ways of interacting

Loyalty is often an admired quality in business. However, people with a pronounced group trait can be too loyal to their organisations. John D Rockefeller's devotion to Standard Oil resulted in long-term harm to the business. His ruthless pursuit of Standard Oil's commercial interests and his harsh enforcement of its monopoly eventually led to the break up of the business. People with a pronounced independent trait tend not to seek or accept advice because they are interested in their own objectives and values. We have already seen this unwillingness to listen to others in Henry Ford and the young Albert Einstein.

Ways of relating

Individuals with a pronounced own-feelings trait may upset or misjudge colleagues. As a young man, Benjamin Franklin, with his pronounced own-feelings trait was unaware that his arrogance upset others. He only realised the extent to which he antagonised people when this was pointed out to him. Franklin, with his very high intelligence, decided to disguise his pronounced own-feelings trait. He stopped behaving as a blunt, quarrelsome, rude and proud young man and acted in an outwardly polite and respectful manner. He soon discovered that his assumed good manners were far more effective in achieving his aims than displays of bad temper and pride. Franklin's appearance of politeness took, at first, a considerable effort. He later admitted that his inner feelings were unchanged by the disguise.

Nevertheless, frankness has its virtues. Winston Churchill's own-feelings trait enabled him to warn bluntly in the middle to late 1930s about the dangers from the Nazis. He often pointed out the desperate need for British re-armament. In doing so, he was prepared to upset many people. Churchill fiercely denounced the 1938 Munich agreement which gave in to Hitler's demands over Czechoslovakia. Churchill attacked this agreement even though his criticisms caused great offence.

In business, there is often a deep reluctance by those executives with a pronounced others'-feelings trait, for example Charles Chaplin, to criticise or dismiss inadequate employees or make employees redundant. At best, these tasks have to be done by another manager, which gives the unfortunate impression of a lack of moral courage. Young adults who have a pronounced others'-feelings trait can sometimes be held back in their careers, because they have a great reluctance to hurt others' feelings. Wolfgang Amadeus Mozart (1756–91), the great music composer, had a very pronounced others'-feelings trait. He was twenty-five before he was able to break free of his family in order to pursue his own professional career.

Social interests dimension

People with a pronounced narrow-interests trait need to be very careful about their dealings with governments and in politics. There is a risk that any involvement may be based on ignorance. Carl Jung, with his pronounced narrow-interests trait, had little interest in politics. However, in the 1930s, he became unwisely involved with his profession in Nazi Germany in order to promote his own ideas. Equally, Charles Chaplin had a pronounced narrow-interests trait and also suffered from an ill-considered participation in American politics.

Attitudes to the future

People with a pronounced optimistic or pessimistic trait need to accept that they will expect more good or bad outcomes than the general population. In any particular circumstances, they may be right. After all, the future is unknown.

SOCIAL ROLES

People should avoid tasks at work which require a higher social role assessment heading than they possess. Otherwise, they may attempt tasks which are beyond their abilities. The cost-benefit calculator social role and organiser social role are the only two social roles that are generally required in management.

Cost-benefit calculators

Decisions about future benefits and costs are of great importance in our working lives. A low assessment heading in the cost-benefit calculator social role is often a serious disadvantage at work. People who have a low assessment heading in this social role need to be self-aware that they have difficulty in making correct decisions about the future in terms of advantages (benefits) and disadvantages (costs). The reason is that while they take account of short-term benefits and costs, they ignore long-term benefits and costs. This is not a question of intelligence span. Some people with very high intelligence are unable to take account of the long term in their cost-benefit decisions. People who have a low assessment heading in the cost-benefit calculator social role will need to take and follow advice from those who have a high assessment heading when considering issues which involve long-term benefits and costs.

People who are high cost-benefit calculators take much better decisions about using resources than those in whom this social role is low. For example, Charles Chaplin was a high cost-benefit calculator, while Winston Churchill was low in the social role. Chaplin was a highly successful investor and businessperson, while Churchill almost always lost money with his investments. Moreover, Churchill's lack of a cost-benefit calculator social role meant that, despite his very high intelligence, he continued to satisfy his very pronounced uncertainty disposition by heavy gambling. He also had pronounced own-feelings and pronounced independent traits, which often add to the difficulties of those with a low cost-benefit calculator social role. These traits tend to separate people from their communities and reduce the amount of advice they receive and accept from others. A low sociability disposition, which may also separate people from their communities, can have the same effect.

Organisers

We have already seen in Chapter 17, example number three (Henry Ford), the harm which can arise from a manager who is low in the organiser social role. These mangers find great difficulty in coordinating teams which consist of more than two or three members. They cannot manage a discussion between more than three people and cannot limit the length of each person's contribution. They may give their own opinions without looking for contributions from others. At the end of a meeting, they are unable to state the meeting's conclusions, explain the meeting's views or bring the meeting to an agreed action plan. It is unwise for people who are low in the organiser social role to put themselves forward as managers of teams with more than two or three members.

INTELLIGENCE SPAN

People should avoid tasks at work which require a higher assessment heading in the intelligence span than they possess. Otherwise, they may attempt tasks which are beyond their abilities. Intelligence has an important influence on self-awareness. Charles Darwin's very high intelligence and its constructive effect on his self-awareness were demonstrated in his scientific work. Darwin was highly critical of his own ideas. He learned from experience that his very high curiosity and very pronounced facts trait made him too eager to find explanations for his discoveries. He eventually realised that his first ideas were almost certainly wrong.

CONCLUSION

One important benefit of individual self-awareness is the opportunity to disguise some personality characteristics and assessment headings, for example high ambition, high emotion, pronounced ways of interacting and pronounced ways of relating. By this means, the disadvantages which may sometimes come from some personality characteristics and assessment headings can be reduced. However, there are other personality characteristics and assessment headings which cannot be effectively disguised for any period of time. Examples are the different lifestyles associated with the pronounced facts and possibilities traits as influenced by high or low sociability.

Good career decisions are another very important benefit from self-awareness. Since individuals' personality profiles vary so much from each other, people are likely to succeed in very different circumstances. If people choose careers or opportunities which suit their personality profiles, then good outcomes are more likely. For example, a person with low sociability and a pronounced facts trait performs well in individual tasks which consist of detailed observation, careful analysis and the assessment of information. We have already seen instances of this, for example in the scientific research of Marie Curie. However, this person risks doing badly when working with others in situations which are subject to frequent, sudden and unforeseeable change. A person with high sociability and a pronounced possibilities trait thrives when working with others in situations which demand teamwork and imaginative insights. Albert Einstein demonstrated the value of these ways of working. Equally, this person risks doing badly when working alone in situations which demand considerable detailed planning.

Individuals are liable to make errors because of their personality characteristics and assessment headings. For this reason, everyone's work gains from thoughtful contributions by others. At work, we cooperate together to improve our performance. This aspect is explored in Chapter 23.

KEY POINTS

SELF-AWARENESS OF PERSONALITY is people's understanding of their own personality profiles and life experiences.

People with HIGH SELF-AWARENESS have considerable insight into their personalities and life experiences.

People with LOW SELF-AWARENESS have little insight into their personalities and life experiences.

YOUR NOTES (OPTIONAL AT YOUR OWN RISK)

How self-aware are you?

What evidence are you using?

Do you know anyone personally or by reputation who has high self-awareness?

What evidence are you using?

Do you know anyone personally or by reputation who has low self-awareness?

What evidence are you using?

Do you need to disguise any of your personality characteristics and assessment headings? If so, which ones?

What evidence are you using?

With regard to your personality profile, in which work situations could you be expected to perform well and in which work situations could you be expected to perform badly?

What evidence are you using?

FURTHER NOTES

CHAPTER 22

Job specification using the personality profile

Successful organisations need employees who perform at their best. People can only maximise their contributions if they are in the right jobs. In particular, their personalities must match the jobs' requirements. The best appointments can only be made if we understand the candidates' personalities and know the jobs' personality requirements. So far, we have learned how to assess personality using the personality profile and life experiences. Now, we learn how to establish a job's personality requirements using the personality profile. We need to establish the minimum personality characteristics and assessment headings which are necessary for competent performance in a particular job. We describe this process as preparing a 'job specification'.

A JOB SPECIFICATION identifies the minimum personality characteristics and assessment headings needed for competent performance in that job.

A job specification is prepared from a job description, which lists the job's responsibilities and performance levels.

Good appointments maintain or improve performance, while bad appointments harm performance and are costly to correct. Furthermore, mistakes made in appointing senior people can seriously damage an organisation. For example, the appointment of a chairperson or chief executive who lacks at least a high organiser social role is likely to be disastrous. As we have already seen with Henry Ford, senior managers who lack a high or very high organiser social role are ineffective, because they feel threatened by employees who have at least a high organiser social role. In no time at all, the new, weak chairperson or chief executive will drive the competent managers out of the organisation. They replace competent managers with incompetent ones, who are low or absent in the organiser role, and can, therefore, be more easily controlled. For any organisation, disaster soon follows.

There are, of course, other issues which are important when making appointments besides the job specification and candidates' personality profiles and life experiences. For example, certain kinds of experience are essential for some jobs. Other careers require professional or other qualifications. Some jobs demand expert skills. In this chapter, we largely ignore these specialist requirements.

At present, organisations use many different words to describe an employee's personality and the personality requirements of a job. However, in the workplace, there are significant advantages in having generally accepted descriptions of personality so that this important information can be exchanged between people using words which everybody understands. For example, we could say of some colleagues that they are excitable, very frank, impulsive, talkative, intuitive and highly critical of the organisation's traditions or we could say the same thing using other words. However, it is much clearer and more accurate if we all use the same words with agreed meanings. We should say of

these people that they are, for example, high in sociability
(talkative), high in emotion (excitable), pronounced
possibilities (impulsive and intuitive), pronounced
independent (highly critical of tradition) and pronounced
own-feelings (very frank). It is not enough to have words
which are generally understood. We also need a shared
framework. Fortunately, the personality profile provides the
framework both for understanding people at work and for
preparing job specifications.

The preparation of a job specification for each job in an
organisation would be a time-consuming task. Fortunately,
we can simplify the procedure. We first create job
specifications which give the minimum personality
characteristics and assessment headings for the occupations in
an organisation, for example finance executives and sales
executives. We then add to these occupational job
specifications the additional personality characteristics and
assessment headings which are essential in a particular job.
We illustrate this process by starting with job specifications
for occupations.

JOB SPECIFICATIONS FOR AN ORGANISATION'S OCCUPATIONS

An occupational job specification for an organisation lists the
minimum personality characteristics and assessment
headings required for competent performance in that
occupation.

**An OCCUPATIONAL JOB SPECIFICATION for an
organisation lists the minimum personality
characteristics and assessment headings required for
competent performance in that occupation.**

We illustrate the preparation of an occupational job specification using two typical business occupations, the first in finance and the second in sales. Finance and sales jobs are very different in most commercial organisations. At the risk of some oversimplification of the issues, we establish the typical minimum requirements in terms of personality characteristics and assessment headings for both occupations in a commercial enterprise.

Example one – finance executives

Finance executives are generally responsible for collecting, processing, preparing and interpreting financial transactions and information. They also have to know and apply correctly, consistently and fairly many accounting, taxation and organisational rules. Additionally, they play an important part in assessing the financial consequences of management proposals. Finally, they play an essential role in planning and controlling the organisation's finances. Most finance executives need to work on their own, although they also have significant contact with their finance staff and other colleagues throughout the organisation. From this broad job description, we can see that the finance executives' tasks involve working on their own, using information and planning. It follows that finance executives generally need a sociability assessment heading of above average or lower and a primary facts trait. The mostly planned lifestyles, which flow from an above average or lower sociability assessment heading and a primary facts trait, suit the finance executives' work pattern. Finance executives often have significant tasks which consist of weekly, monthly and annual routines. This is normally the case, but there are always exceptions. In a less routine environment, finance executives may need broadly equal facts and possibilities traits. Finance executives are sometimes labelled, unfairly or otherwise, as boring. Perhaps, it is the relative lack of sociability, routine lifestyle and interest in facts, which gives finance people their boring image.

Organisations benefit from a careful assessment of their financial information. Calmness, real or assumed, is often desirable in finance people. Everyone needs ambition if they are to succeed in their profession. There seems to be no reason for finance people to have any particular primary traits within the ways of interacting, ways of relating or social interests dimensions. Some pessimism can be seen as an advantage in finance, because the finance department may need to challenge the optimism of the sales department. We shall see soon why sales executives tend to be optimists. Finance executives have to be high or very high cost-benefit calculators in order to give sound financial advice on the use of resources. Average or above communicator, educator and organiser social roles are likely to be useful at more senior levels. At least high intelligence is essential. We now summarise this occupational information in an occupational job specification for finance executives based on the personality profile. This occupational job specification lists the typical minimum personality characteristics and assessment headings needed by a finance executive for competent performance in a commercial enterprise (see Table 22.1).

Example two – sales executives

Sales executives are well-known for being talkative and lively, which is to be expected as they have to spend lots of time with customers. Good personal relationships with customers are essential to successful selling. Moreover, effective sales executives are always finding different ways of making sales. They also have to take advantage immediately of any opportunities. From this description, we

Table 22.1 Occupational job specification for finance executives in a commercial enterprise

PERSONALITY CHARACTERISTICS	ASSESSMENT HEADINGS
A) DISPOSITIONS	
1) Sociability	Above average or lower
2) Emotion	Average or lower (although higher emotion can be effectively disguised)
3) Ambition	Above average or higher
B) DIMENSIONS	
1) Facts / possibilities	Primary facts (broadly equal facts and possibilities may be appropriate in some circumstances)
5) Optimistic / pessimistic	Primary pessimistic (too much pessimism may be unhelpful)
C) SOCIAL ROLES	
2) Cost-benefit calculator	High or above
D) INTELLIGENCE SPAN	High or above

can see that the sales executive's job involves working with others, variety and spontaneity. Consequently, sales people generally have high or very high sociability and a primary possibilities trait. The resulting varied lifestyle with its enjoyment of new situations is suited to the frequent travel and meetings which are often an essential part of selling.

Sales executives also need ambition if they are to succeed in their profession. As with finance people, there seems no reason for sales people to have any particular primary traits within the ways of interacting, ways of relating or social interests dimensions. However, optimism seems essential to most careers in sales, especially if the selling often involves rejections. Otherwise, the repeated disappointments are too discouraging and, in the end, completely demoralising for non-optimists. The finance executives' slight pessimism is needed in most businesses to offset this necessary optimism required in sales. High emotion is often desirable in selling. The self-confidence of an emotional optimist convinces many customers. Anyone who sells has to be a good communicator. If a sales executive is involved in pricing negotiations, then at least an average or higher cost-benefit social role would be necessary, depending on the amount of responsibility given to the executive. Average or above educator and organiser social roles are likely to be useful at more senior levels. High intelligence is likewise essential. We now summarise this occupational information in an occupational job specification for sales executives based on the personality profile. This occupational job specification lists the typical minimum personality characteristics and assessment headings needed by a sales executive for competent performance in a commercial enterprise (see Table 22.2).

A comparison of example one (finance executives) and example two (sales executives) occupational job specifications in a commercial enterprise

We can now compare the occupational job specifications for finance and sales executives on a combined personality profile (see Table 22.3). The number of differences is striking. We can no longer be surprised if the finance and sales departments sometimes become upset with each other.

Table 22.2 Occupational job specification for sales executives in a commercial enterprise

PERSONALITY CHARACTERISTICS	ASSESSMENT HEADINGS
A) DISPOSITIONS	
1) Sociability	High or above
2) Emotion	High or above
3) Ambition	Above average or higher
B) DIMENSIONS	
1) Facts / possibilities	Primary possibilities
5) Optimistic / pessimistic	Primary optimistic (too much optimism may be unhelpful)
C) SOCIAL ROLES	
1) Communicator	High or above
2) Cost-benefit calculator	Average or higher, in some cases
D) INTELLIGENCE SPAN	High or above

At the beginning of this section, we acknowledged the risk of some oversimplification of the issues with regard to the typical minimum requirements in terms of personality characteristics and assessment headings for finance and sales executives in a commercial enterprise. For example, there are many different kinds of selling. Some sales to business customers require patience, detailed knowledge, little travel and a planned approach. This kind of selling is appropriate to a person with a primary facts trait. John D Rockefeller, although he had a very pronounced facts trait, was effective

Table 22.3 Occupational job specifications for finance and sales executives in a commercial enterprise

PERSONALITY CHARACTERISTICS	ASSESSMENT HEADINGS	
	FINANCE	SALES
A) DISPOSITIONS		
1) Sociability	Above average or lower	High or above
2) Emotion	Average or lower (although higher emotion can be effectively disguised)	High or above
3) Ambition	Above average or higher	Above average or higher
B) DIMENSIONS		
1) Facts / possibilities	Primary facts (broadly equal facts and possibilities may be appropriate in some circumstances)	Primary possibilities
5) Optimistic / pessimistic	Primary pessimistic (too much pessimism may be unhelpful)	Primary optimistic (too much optimism may be unhelpful)
C) SOCIAL ROLES		
1) Communicator		High or above
2) Cost-benefit calculator	High or above	Average or higher, in some cases
D) INTELLIGENCE SPAN	High or above	High or above

at selling to merchants because of his above average sociability, very high emotion, very high ambition, very pronounced optimistic trait, very high intelligence and good manners (high self-awareness).

JOB SPECIFICATIONS FOR PARTICULAR JOBS WITHIN AN ORGANISATION

So far, we have established two occupational job specifications for a commercial organisation. The next task is to use these to produce job specifications for particular jobs. Many factors influence the additional personality characteristics and assessment headings which may be needed for each job specification within an organisation. There are too many factors for a comprehensive description in this chapter. Nevertheless, we look at examples of how an organisation's culture, management needs or the individual relationships within an organisation can affect a job specification.

Example one – an organisation's culture

An organisation's culture describes the attitudes and values which people have to accept at work. It is often revealed by an organisation's traditions and in the senior executives who succeed in the organisation. There are many different organisational cultures, which have many origins, for example the nature of the business, its ownership and the influence of individuals, particularly founders. If employees have personality characteristics and assessment headings which conflict significantly with a company's culture, they are unlikely to be effective in their work. Accordingly, it is essential to recruit employees whose personalities are suited to the organisation's culture. For example, a particular organisation may demand that management teams meet socially outside work in order to create a spirit of togetherness and commitment. Any executives who have low or very low sociability would dislike attending the organisation's social events or, for them, the even worse outcome of having to take holidays with colleagues from work. They would make very unsuitable employees for this organisation. Another example of a culture clash is employees with a pronounced or very pronounced independent trait in an organisation that is a large, inflexible bureaucracy. They are very likely to be frustrated by the organisation's many rules and regulations.

An organisation's decisions on the kinds of personality characteristics and assessment headings that are essential in all employees have to be entered on every job specification. These choices can have important commercial consequences. An organisation's policy that employees should partly combine their work and their social lives means that all employees should desirably be average or higher in their sociability. Consequently, candidates with below average or lower sociability will not normally be appointed. Inevitably, this leads to some uniformity in the personalities of employees. Since employees with below average or lower sociability are not found in this company, there will be no one to solve the problems which need people with these assessment headings. This could mean restricting the commercial opportunities that are appropriate for this organisation to, for example, parts of the service sector.

Example two – management needs

Many jobs have specific management requirements which are part of an individual executive's responsibilities. For example, a particular finance executive's responsibilities may include challenging the organisation's traditions and practices. In order to carry out this management responsibility, the finance executive needs high ambition, a pronounced independent trait and very high intelligence. These personality characteristics and assessment headings, which are in addition to those typically required for finance executives, must be entered onto the job specification.

If the finance executive is also going to do general finance work in a small commercial organisation, the job description will include a wide variety of tasks. Consequently, the job specification will need to list flexible personality characteristics as well as high ambition, a pronounced independent trait and very high intelligence (see Table 22.4). Nevertheless, in all appointment decisions, common sense is essential. A job specification is only a guide. For example, even though the organisation is looking for a finance candidate with flexible personality characteristics, one additional pronounced trait may still be acceptable for general finance work.

We now prepare a job specification for a sales executive who is also required to keep in close touch with worldwide market trends. This senior, specialised job is in the head office of a large international company. The sales executive needs sensitivity to others, an interest in the world at large and a desire for new experiences. Therefore, the job specification includes a pronounced others'-feelings trait, a pronounced wide-interests trait and a high accumulator social role. All these personality characteristics and assessment headings assist in discovering significant new market trends from customers and competitors (see Table 22.5). As before, common sense is essential. A job specification is only a guide.

Example three – personal relationships

Personal relationships within an organisation may also influence the personality characteristics and assessment headings required for particular jobs. Two people who have to work closely together have to be sufficiently compatible,

Table 22.4 Job specification for a finance executive who has to challenge the organisation's traditions and practices and do general finance work in a small commercial organisation

PERSONALITY CHARACTERISTICS	ASSESSMENT HEADINGS
A) DISPOSITIONS	
1) Sociability	Above average or lower
2) Emotion	Average or lower (although higher emotion can be effectively disguised)
3) Ambition	High
B) DIMENSIONS	
1) Facts / possibilities	Primary facts (broadly equal facts and possibilities may be appro-priate in some circumstances)
2) Group / independent	Pronounced independent
5) Optimistic / pessimistic	Primary pessimistic (too much pessimism may be unhelpful)
C) SOCIAL ROLES	
2) Cost-benefit calculator	High or above
D) INTELLIGENCE SPAN	Very high

because, otherwise, the outcome can be highly damaging. For example, an organisation wants to recruit a senior executive to work closely with an existing senior executive who has very pronounced group and others'-feelings traits. The executive already employed by the organisation believes in

Table 22.5 Job specification for a sales executive who has to keep in close touch with worldwide market trends in a large international company's head office

PERSONALITY CHARACTERISTICS	ASSESSMENT HEADINGS
A) DISPOSITIONS	
1) Sociability	High or above
2) Emotion	High or above
3) Ambition	Above average or higher
B) DIMENSIONS	
1) Facts / possibilities	Primary possibilities
3) Own-feelings / others'-feelings	Pronounced others'-feelings
4) Wide-interests / narrow-interests	Pronounced wide-interests
5) Optimistic / pessimistic	Primary optimistic (too much optimism may be unhelpful)
C) SOCIAL ROLES	
1) Communicator	High or above
2) Cost-benefit calculator	Average or higher, in some cases
7) Accumulator	High
D) INTELLIGENCE SPAN	High or above

harmony and wants everyone to cooperate together. In most circumstances, it would be a mistake to recruit an executive to work closely with him who has very pronounced independent and own-feelings traits. The new executive would follow his own agenda and publicly and bluntly criticise his staff. These two senior executives would have difficulties working successfully together. Consequently, with regard to the ways of interacting and the ways of relating dimensions, the job specification for the new executive should probably require broadly equal traits or primary group and others'-feelings traits.

JOB SPECIFICATIONS USED FOR RECRUITMENT, SELECTION AND PROMOTION

Job specifications should not be kept secret. Their publication helps internal and external candidates as well as the organisation to make better decisions by ensuring candidates' personalities match the needs of the job and organisation. An internal appointment based on an employee's personality profile and a job specification can often be made with confidence because of the knowledge and self-knowledge of both the employee and the organisation. Sometimes, internal appointments are not possible, especially for smaller organisations or for senior positions. External recruitment is a time-consuming, difficult and expensive process. The principal problem is to understand complex individuals in a few hours or days, particularly if they have sufficient self-awareness to disguise their personality profiles. The personality profile and the job specification have a crucial role to play in sound recruitment decisions. If a job has been fully defined by the job description, job specification, job knowledge, qualifications and experience, there is a clear and agreed understanding of what constitutes a suitable candidate.

In making appointments, a job specification can prevent managers from being too easily impressed by people like themselves. They may be tempted to recruit or promote a person with a pronounced possibilities trait and a pronounced group trait for no other reason than they have a pronounced possibilities trait and a pronounced group trait. Equally, managers may be too easily impressed by candidates who have different talents to their own. A manager may be a below average communicator and appoint a wholly unsuitable candidate for no other reason than the candidate is high in the communicator social role. The job specification will prevent these mistakes by making managers concentrate on the personality characteristics and assessment headings required for the job.

The choice of assessment method often reflects the recruiting manager's personality profile rather than the requirements of the job specification. Executives who have low sociability and a primary facts trait are much more comfortable with one-to-one discussions in which the candidate's previous history is explored in detail. Candidates who have low sociability and a primary facts trait are likely to do well in individual interviews of this kind. However, this is little guide to a good candidate if the job specification requires high sociability and a pronounced possibilities trait. Candidates who have high sociability and a pronounced possibilities trait are much more likely to do well in a panel interview in which the candidate is invited to explore relevant case studies. The recruitment process has to match the job specification. Otherwise, the wrong candidate may be appointed.

Assessment time is short for both the external candidates and the organisation. The amount of assessment time should clearly reflect the importance of the decision. A properly prepared job specification allows both the candidate and the organisation to concentrate immediately on the important personality issues when making an appointment.

CONCLUSION

The appointment of the best person for a particular job is a very difficult management task. We need all the help we can find. Only the best appointments produce the best results. In many organisations, too many costly mistakes are made. A very significant amount of human resources and money are wasted. The job specification based on the personality profile is an essential management tool for improving performance.

KEY POINTS

A JOB SPECIFICATION identifies the minimum personality characteristics and assessment headings needed for competent performance in that job.
An OCCUPATIONAL JOB SPECIFICATION for an organisation lists the minimum personality characteristics and assessment headings required for competent performance in that occupation.

YOUR NOTES (OPTIONAL AT YOUR OWN RISK)

With regard to the same organisation, prepare occupational job specifications for two occupations with which you are familiar.

Compare the two occupational job specifications.

With regard to one of the previous occupations, prepare another job specification for a specific vacancy which requires additional personality characteristics and assessment headings.

Describe the culture of the organisation in which you work. For example, are the organisation's values in favour of high or low sociability; group or independent attitudes; or own-feelings or others'-feelings responses?

What evidence are you using?

How has your employer's culture affected your recruitment decisions?

What evidence are you using?

Describe a recruitment or promotion in which individual relationships have affected the choice of candidate.

Describe one of your good appointments and one of your bad appointments. What lessons can be learned in terms of a job specification and the candidate's personality profile, life experiences and self-awareness?

FURTHER NOTES

CHAPTER 23

Effective decision making units using the personality profile

Rapid technological and economic development, globalisation and climate change provide ever greater challenges to governments, organisations and businesses worldwide. Everywhere, individuals have to cooperate with each other to take decisions of great complexity and exceptional difficulty. These decisions need to be of the highest quality. Our future depends on them. We have to find ways to maximise the chances of success. The personality profile makes an important contribution to the organisation of effective, cooperative decision making at work.

As we have already seen in Chapter 21, some individuals can reveal a lack of flexibility in their decision making. For example, they solve problems using pronounced or very pronounced facts or possibilities traits. However, these one-sided approaches can be used to advantage. People with a variety of personality characteristics and assessment headings can work together to take better decisions. We first look at a short case study, which illustrates the benefits of cooperative decision making.

During the First World War, Winston Churchill was

blamed, rightly or wrongly, for setbacks. It is, perhaps, one of the highest tributes to Churchill's greatness that he very largely avoided similar mistakes during the Second World War. His wartime triumphs in the Second World War were not only due to his many talents but also to his self-awareness and self-restraint. Alan Brooke was Churchill's military Chief of Staff for the last four years of the Second World War. Churchill's choice of Brooke was no accident. Churchill and Brooke had some very different personality characteristics and assessment headings. For example, Churchill had a very pronounced possibilities trait and a low cost-benefit calculator social role, while Brooke had a pronounced facts trait and a high cost-benefit calculator social role. Their cooperation together proved highly productive. Churchill supplied the oratory and vision, while Brooke provided the sound judgement for decisions about military action and the attention to military detail and planning.

When two highly emotional, ambitious people with very different ways of thinking work closely together, there is always a risk of serious and angry disagreements arising from their conflicting ways of thinking and different lifestyles. In fact, Churchill and Brooke had many furious arguments. In ordinary circumstances, the partnership between Churchill and Brooke would have collapsed. What overcame all their personal difficulties was their shared determination to win the war. Churchill knew that he lacked the skills to organise and direct the British military war effort, while Brooke greatly admired Churchill's extraordinary talents.

At this stage, we need to introduce some important concepts with regard to effective, cooperative decision making. A 'decision making unit' is a number of people working together to take decisions. We generally refer to a decision making unit as a 'unit'.

A DECISION MAKING UNIT consists of individuals who together solve problems, reach conclusions, take actions and review progress.

Individuals' personality profiles are 'complementary', when, as members of a decision making unit, they have together the necessary personality characteristics and assessment headings for effective, cooperative decision making.

Individuals have COMPLEMENTARY PERSONALITY PROFILES when, as members of a decision making unit, they have together the necessary personality characteristics and assessment headings for effective, cooperative decision making.

Unit members have 'competent' personality profiles, when they have all the necessary personality characteristics and assessment headings to complete successfully their individual tasks. In other words, the unit members' personality characteristics and assessment headings satisfy their job specifications.

COMPETENT PERSONALITY PROFILES enable unit members to carry out successfully their individual tasks. The unit members' personality characteristics and assessment headings satisfy their job specifications.

We continue to assume the truth of the hunter-gatherer theory of personality explained in Chapter 18. The most effective unit for complex decision making is one which has the same features as a hunter-gatherer extended family. Consequently, individuals who cooperate effectively together to take complex decisions:

- Belong to a unit with between approximately six and ten members
- Possess a complementary set of competent individual personality profiles

A hunter-gatherer extended family had approximately twelve to twenty active adults. For complex decisions that were largely limited to one sex, for example those relating to gathering or hunting, the maximum number of people who would effectively cooperate would be half the total adults. Consequently, complex decisions would be made by units with approximately six to ten members. A similar observation about the size of cooperating units, for example in team sports, has been made many times and certainly agrees with all the evidence. Depending on the present-day context, individuals who cooperate together to make complex decisions generally form units of approximately six to ten members. Many executive committees that manage companies have approximately this number of members.

The personality characteristics and assessment headings of a unit's members strongly influence its decision making. For example, if members with a primary facts trait are in a majority, then thinking with facts is likely to be used more often than thinking by imagining possibilities. We now examine how each of the eighteen personality characteristics contributes to effective unit decision making. In other words, we identify the personality characteristics and assessment headings which are required of a unit's members for them to have complementary personality profiles. As always, we follow the order of the personality profile and start with the dispositions.

THE DISPOSITIONS AND ASSESSMENT HEADINGS REQUIRED FOR COMPLEMENTARY PERSONALITY PROFILES

Sociability

There is a close connection between sociability and cooperation in decision making. A person with high or very high sociability enjoys sharing thoughts and experiences with other people. Individuals who cooperate together to make decisions have to share their thoughts and experiences. Accordingly, the sociability disposition plays an essential part in cooperative unit decision making. Moreover, a majority of the cooperating individuals need to be of average or higher sociability in order to enable sufficient social contact between members. However, people with below average or lower sociability bring their own resources to decision making. Consequently, complementary personality profiles consist of a majority who have average or higher sociability and a minority who have below average or lower sociability. A few people with high or very high sociability are useful in order to supply a personal link between everyone who is cooperating together.

Emotion

Similar arguments which were used about sociability apply to emotion. In order to have the passion to succeed, a majority of the cooperating individuals in the unit should be of average or higher emotion. One or two individuals of high or very high emotion might be needed to inspire the others. We need the passion of the majority to drive the unit forward. Nevertheless, a minority of people with below average or lower emotion is necessary to avoid the dangers of excessive enthusiasm. One person who is low or very low in emotion is very useful in a crisis.

Ambition

If there are complex and difficult decisions which have to be taken, everyone in the unit should be of at least high ambition. This ensures that these complex and difficult tasks have the best chance to be completed successfully. However, there is a real danger that the unit will be over-ambitious and attempt to achieve the impossible. This can be avoided by subjecting the unit's objectives to an effective, independent, external review by experts.

Curiosity

At least one member with very high curiosity is necessary if the task's successful completion requires the continual asking of questions and finding of answers. Too many individuals with high or very high curiosity will harm a unit's performance, because there will be insufficient people to carry out the essential day-to-day tasks.

Uncertainty

The thrill and exhilaration of the tension that comes from unpredictability is unlikely to be part of complex decision making. Consequently, there is little need in a unit for individuals who are high or very high in uncertainty.

Summary

A unit for taking complex, difficult decisions should have a majority of members who are of average or higher sociability. There also has to be a majority who are of average or higher emotion. All members need high or very high ambition, but their objectives must be subject to effective, independent, external review by experts. One or two members with a high or very high curiosity disposition may be required for certain tasks, but, in normal circumstances, no one with an above average or higher uncertainty disposition is necessary. These conclusions are summarised in Table 23.1.

Table 23.1 The dispositions and assessment headings needed by a unit taking complex decisions for the members to have complementary personality profiles

DISPOSITION	PROPORTION OF DISPOSITIONS IN THE AVERAGE OR HIGHER ASSESSMENT HEADINGS REQUIRED BY A UNIT
Sociability	A majority who are average or higher
Emotion	A majority who are average or higher
Ambition	All high or very high, but their objectives should be subject to an effective, independent, external review to establish whether the unit's objectives are over-ambitious
Curiosity	One or two high or very high, if required by the task
Uncertainty	None in normal circumstances

THE DIMENSIONS AND ASSESSMENT HEADINGS REQUIRED FOR COMPLEMENTARY PERSONALITY PROFILES

Ways of thinking

Knowledge of the facts is essential to cooperative decision making. Moreover, complex decision making often requires careful consideration over long periods of time, which necessitates the routine and planning of a facts lifestyle. Consequently, in normal circumstances, at least half of the unit should have a primary facts trait. Nevertheless, the insights of unit members with a primary possibilities trait are essential as an influential minority. The unit needs the contributions from at least one member who is pronounced or very pronounced facts and one member who is pronounced or very pronounced possibilities. These individuals can concentrate on the analysis of facts or the assessment of alternatives.

Ways of interacting

Loyalty to the unit is of great importance. Consequently, at least half of the unit's members should have a primary group trait. However, loyalty to the unit is insufficient on its own. The contributions of a minority with a primary independent trait are necessary, for example, to criticise a mistaken unit consensus. The unit needs the contributions from at least one member who is pronounced or very pronounced group and one member who is pronounced or very pronounced independent. These members supply the most powerful arguments for and against the unit's consensus.

Ways of relating

The ways of relating primary traits within the unit should be similar in number. Individuals with a primary own-feelings trait supply the toughness, frankness and bluntness to deal with difficult decisions, especially concerning people. Individuals with a primary others'-feelings trait provide the sympathy and compassion which helps to bring the unit together. Since the unit requires a full range of contributions to its decision making, there should be one or two unit members with a pronounced or very pronounced own-feelings trait and one or two members with a pronounced or very pronounced others'-feelings trait.

Social interests

The proportion of the social interests primary traits depends very much on the nature of the decisions. If the decision affects the community at large, then at least half of the members should have a primary wide-interests trait. However, if the decision is concerned entirely with a business problem, then primary wide-interests traits may be mostly unnecessary.

Attitudes to the future
One or two members with a primary optimistic trait are necessary to emphasise the opportunities, as well as a member with a primary pessimistic trait to warn of the dangers.

Summary
A unit for taking complex, difficult decisions should have at least half the members with a primary facts trait and a significant minority with a primary possibilities trait. Similar proportions apply to the ways of interacting. At least half should have a primary group trait and a significant minority should have a primary independent trait. The own-feelings primary traits and others'-feelings primary traits should be similar in number. The proportion of wide-interests and narrow-interests primary traits depends on the nature of the task. One or two members with a primary optimistic trait and a member with a primary pessimistic trait are also required. These conclusions are summarised in Table 23.2.

THE SOCIAL ROLES AND ASSESSMENT HEADINGS REQUIRED FOR COMPLEMENTARY PERSONALITY PROFILES

Communicators
The communicator social role is not a major contributor to complex decision making. If information has to be

Table 23.2 The dimensions and assessment headings needed
by a unit taking complex decisions for the members to have
complementary personality profiles

DIMENSION	PROPORTION OF PRIMARY TRAITS REQUIRED BY A UNIT
Ways of thinking	At least half with a primary facts trait and a significant minority with a primary possibilities trait
Ways of interacting	At least half with a primary group trait and a significant minority with a primary independent trait
Ways of relating	A similar number of primary own-feelings traits and primary others'-feelings traits
Social interests	Depends on the task
Attitudes to the future	One or two members with a primary optimistic trait and a member with a primary pessimistic trait

communicated, then one or more members with a high or
very high communicator social role could be very useful.

Cost-benefit calculators

This social role is essential in complex decision making.
Decisions have to be sensible in terms of their short-term and
long-term advantages and disadvantages. Only high or very
high cost-benefit calculators are good at this kind of decision.
Consequently, at least several high or very high cost-benefit
calculators are necessary.

Educators

One or two members with at least a high educator social role could be useful in a task where people's knowledge and skills may need to be improved during the task. Otherwise, educators are not required.

Innovators

In a complex task that can gain from new ideas, a high or very high innovator has an essential part to play. Innovation is time consuming, and new ideas are difficult to assess and use. Moreover, only one or two new ideas can be assessed at any one time. Consequently, for each area which can gain from innovation, for example marketing or engineering, only one member with a high or very high innovator social role seems appropriate.

Lifelong learners

This social role only contributes to a task which offers opportunities for individuals to learn new ideas and skills.

Organisers

Every unit needs a member with at least a high or very high organiser social role, who manages the unit. This individual coordinates the unit and identifies the unit's consensus. The unit may need to be divided into smaller units of more than three members for specific tasks. Each of these smaller units also requires a member with at least an above average organiser social role. The members of these smaller units also need complementary and competent personality profiles for their delegated tasks.

Accumulators

This social role is only useful, if the collection and retention of experiences is helpful to successfully completing the task.

Summary

Only the cost-benefit calculator social role and organiser social role are essential in the high or very high assessment headings for taking complex decisions. The numbers depend on the task. The necessity for the high or very high assessment headings in other social roles also depends on the task. It seems very likely for complex tasks in the industrial world that an innovator with very high intelligence for each area which can gain from innovation is nearly always required. Educators, lifelong learners and accumulators are only necessary in some tasks. The communicator is only needed if the unit's aims and achievements have to be broadcast to a wider audience. These conclusions are summarised in Table 23.3.

THE INTELLIGENCE SPAN AND ASSESSMENT HEADINGS REQUIRED FOR COMPLEMENTARY PERSONALITY PROFILES

In order to complete successfully a complex task, high intelligence is essential for all members. One or more members, for example an innovator, need to be of very high intelligence.

AN EXAMPLE OF A UNIT WITH COMPETENT AND COMPLEMENTARY PERSONALITY PROFILES

We have established the personality characteristics and assessment headings required by a unit which has to take effective, cooperative, complex decisions. In other words, we have identified the requirements for the unit's complementary personality profiles. However, these

Table 23.3 The social roles and assessment headings needed by a unit taking complex decisions for the members to have complementary personality profiles

SOCIAL ROLES	NUMBER OF SOCIAL ROLES REQUIRED IN THE HIGH OR VERY HIGH ASSESSMENT HEADINGS
Communicators	Possibly one or more, depending on the unit's need to communicate information
Cost-benefit calculators	Several are essential
Educators	Possibly one or more, depending on the task
Innovators	One is essential for each area which can gain from innovation
Lifelong learners	Possibly one or more, depending on the task
Organisers	One is essential
Accumulators	Possibly one or more, depending on the task

personality characteristics and assessment headings can only be present in individual unit members. We describe a unit in which members' competent personality profiles are also complementary. The unit is the executive committee of a fictitious international company in the high technology sector. This company is a successful business in consumer electronics, which is neither dominated by a family nor by a founder. A period of intense competition has necessitated important changes in company culture and organisation.

The executive committee manages the company. The seven members of the company's executive committee are the:

- Chairperson
- Chief executive
- Finance director
- Human resources director
- Marketing and sales director
- Production director
- Research director

The long term is important to this business as are relations with investors, customers, employees and governments. We now describe a realistic set of competent and complementary individual personality profiles for the members of the executive committee. The curiosity disposition is identified only where a high or very high assessment heading is required. The uncertainty disposition has been ignored, because it is irrelevant to this example. The social roles and intelligence span are identified only where a high or very high assessment heading is required.

NOTE

For reasons of simplicity, all the executive committee members are men, but any or all of the members could be women. Accordingly, the conclusions apply equally to women and men.

Chairperson

The function of the chairperson is to ensure that the executive committee efficiently reaches a consensus on the way forward. In performing this duty, the chairperson has to make certain that the committee successfully makes complex decisions, takes actions and reviews performance. The chairperson also takes the lead with investor relations. A personality profile is given in Table 23.4.

From his personality profile, we know the chairperson works really well with his colleagues. He is calm when faced with a crisis and, as part of his calmness, is prepared to delegate. He is ambitious. He pays attention to the facts. His high sociability and his more facts than possibilities lifestyle mean he is able to plan ahead but has some real flexibility. The company is of first importance to him and comes before personal friendships. However, he is approachable and generally sympathetic. He places emphasis on opportunities. His handling of presentations to investors and employees is convincing and inspiring. Moreover, he is very good at assessing the short-term and long-term advantages and disadvantages of proposals put before the committee. He is distinguished in appearance with an impressive personal presence and natural authority. He enjoys learning something new. His latest venture is to master a few words of a foreign language in order to impress some important suppliers. He has been in this industry for many years and is one of its best-known executives.

He does not, however, dominate his colleagues intellectually. Difficult ideas have to be explained fully to him. This is partly, but only partly, pretence. He has learned that a visible humility means his colleagues are also prepared to admit their limitations and lack of knowledge. The outcome is that everyone eventually understands the issues discussed at executive committee meetings and is prepared to comment on

Table 23.4 Chairperson's personality profile

PERSONALITY CHARACTERISTICS	ASSESSMENT HEADINGS
A) DISPOSITIONS	
1) Sociability	High
2) Emotion	Low
3) Ambition	Very high
4) Curiosity	
5) Uncertainty	
B) DIMENSIONS	
1) Facts / possibilities	More facts than possibilities
2) Group / independent	Pronounced group
3) Own-feelings / others'-feelings	More others'-feelings than own-feelings
4) Wide-interests / narrow-interests	More wide-interests than narrow-interests
5) Optimistic / pessimistic	More optimistic than pessimistic
C) SOCIAL ROLES	
1) Communicator	High
2) Cost-benefit calculator	High
3) Educator	
4) Innovator	
5) Lifelong learner	High
6) Organiser	Very high
7) Accumulator	
D) INTELLIGENCE SPAN	High

them. His loyalty to the company means that he sometimes stops some executive committee members following their personal objectives. His way of ensuring that all committee members work to company objectives gives rise to some resentment from those members who find their freedom restricted.

Chief executive

The chairperson thinks very highly of the hardworking, energetic and young chief executive, who makes things happen. The chief executive, who trained as an engineer, is responsible for carrying out the board's decisions with regard to the management of the company. A personality profile is given in Table 23.5.

As expected from his personality profile, the chief executive mixes his business and social life. Any success in business is an excuse for a celebration paid for by the company. His passionate ambition inspires nearly everyone in the company. His resulting excesses are very largely forgiven because of his self-awareness, humour and ability to criticise himself. He believes in his sudden insights. In his view, it is the way the best engineers work. His high sociability and pronounced possibilities lifestyle mean that he enjoys variety but can cope with some routine. He is determined to transform the company by abandoning its outdated customs and inappropriate traditions. His own objectives are very important to him, and he is prepared to consider better job offers from competitors. His blunt, tough comments cause some unhappiness. He is not really worried by other people's feelings. In his view, the company and its employees have to be prepared to face up to some harsh and unpleasant truths.

He has an immediate and very good understanding of the financial and investment side of the business. When asked about his most important function in the company, he replies

Table 23.5 Chief executive's personality profile

PERSONALITY CHARACTERISTICS	ASSESSMENT HEADINGS
A) DISPOSITIONS	
1) Sociability	High
2) Emotion	Very high
3) Ambition	Very high
4) Curiosity	
5) Uncertainty	
B) DIMENSIONS	
1) Facts / possibilities	Pronounced possibilities
2) Group / independent	Pronounced independent
3) Own-feelings / others'-feelings	Pronounced own-feelings
4) Wide-interests / narrow-interests	Broadly equal
5) Optimistic / pessimistic	Broadly equal
C) SOCIAL ROLES	
1) Communicator	
2) Cost-benefit calculator	High
3) Educator	High
4) Innovator	
5) Lifelong learner	
6) Organiser	Very high
7) Accumulator	
D) INTELLIGENCE SPAN	Very high

'teacher'. In his view, he has to teach everyone in the company about the reality of business in today's global market. He has no difficulty in establishing a personal ascendancy over his people. The chief executive is totally committed to judging people and their ideas on merit. Nevertheless, he is somewhat in awe of the effortless way the chairperson performs his job. He admits his reliance on the chairperson's support and worries what will happen when the chairperson retires.

Finance director

The finance director is responsible for the company's financial affairs and administration, which need a considerable financial and regulatory knowledge. Since he is highly organised and has made himself very well informed about the company products, markets and technology, he has assumed responsibility for administering the company's planning function. A personality profile is given in Table 23.6.

Consistent with his personality profile, the finance director is rather unsociable. He only attends company social functions when his absence would be noticed. He is known for his astonishing ability to spot the weaknesses in any argument. Moreover, he is exceptionally good at assessing the short-term and long-term advantages and disadvantages of ideas put before the committee. The other committee members have found it advisable to check their ideas with him before presenting them to the executive committee. Some of them become a little impatient with the time he takes to respond to their ideas. His low sociability and pronounced facts lifestyle mean he enjoys the routine of head office. He is convinced that the best decisions are based on understanding all the facts. However, he readily agrees that he lacks the creativity of some of his colleagues. His refusal to believe sales forecasts no longer surprises anyone.

Table 23.6 Finance director's personality profile

PERSONALITY CHARACTERISTICS	ASSESSMENT HEADINGS
A) DISPOSITIONS	
1) Sociability	Low
2) Emotion	Average
3) Ambition	High
4) Curiosity	
5) Uncertainty	
B) DIMENSIONS	
1) Facts / possibilities	Pronounced facts
2) Group / independent	More group than independent
3) Own-feelings / others'-feelings	Broadly equal
4) Wide-interests / narrow-interests	Broadly equal
5) Optimistic / pessimistic	More pessimistic than optimistic
C) SOCIAL ROLES	
1) Communicator	
2) Cost-benefit calculator	Very high
3) Educator	
4) Innovator	
5) Lifelong learner	
6) Organiser	
7) Accumulator	
D) INTELLIGENCE SPAN	Very high

The enthusiasm of the sales people has no effect on him. He has a remarkable sixth sense as to whether ideas are financially viable.

Human resources director

The human resources director plays a major role in all staff recruitment and promotion. Employees have the right to discuss with him any issue or problem arising from work. However, the human resources director makes few contributions outside his department. A personality profile is given in Table 23.7.

As we might expect from his personality profile, the human resources director thoroughly enjoys being in the company of other people. He is always present at the chief executive's celebrations of success (parties would be a better word). The human resources executive is much admired for promoting excellent working relationships and solving disputes of all kinds within the company. No one sees him as any kind of threat. He is very rarely wrong in his assessment of people. He tells people to trust his judgement, which they have learned to do. His pronounced possibilities lifestyle is one of variety and change but somewhat restricted by his high sociability. Although he has worked for several companies, he is regarded as very loyal to this company. His sensitivity to others is widely admired, and his sympathetic comments have helped solve many disputes. He happily puts himself out for other people, and this has made him very popular. He sometimes upsets the chief executive with his reluctance to make criticisms of people or agree to the dismissal of inadequate employees, whom he always seeks to retrain.

Marketing and sales director

The marketing and sales director is responsible for finding

Table 23.7 Human resources director's personality profile

PERSONALITY CHARACTERISTICS	ASSESSMENT HEADINGS
A) DISPOSITIONS	
1) Sociability	High
2) Emotion	Average
3) Ambition	High
4) Curiosity	
5) Uncertainty	
B) DIMENSIONS	
1) Facts / possibilities	Pronounced possibilities
2) Group / independent	Pronounced group
3) Own-feelings / others'-feelings	Pronounced others'-feelings
4) Wide-interests / narrow-interests	Broadly equal
5) Optimistic / pessimistic	Broadly equal
C) SOCIAL ROLES	
1) Communicator	
2) Cost-benefit calculator	
3) Educator	
4) Innovator	
5) Lifelong learner	
6) Organiser	
7) Accumulator	
D) INTELLIGENCE SPAN	High

and developing markets and products. The day-to-day management of the sales force has been delegated to his well-liked and equally enthusiastic, if somewhat impulsive deputy. The marketing and sales director's personality profile is given in Table 23.8.

Consistent with his personality profile, the self-confident marketing and sales director is another frequent guest at the chief executive's parties. He is always investigating changes in the market and trying to find out about the next revolution in the marketplace before it happens. Over the years, his genuine interest in other people has enabled him to build up a large number of useful contacts in the industry. He is often the first to introduce the company to the latest ideas about which he shows a passionate enthusiasm. One of the chairperson's many talents is keeping the unsociable, slightly pessimistic finance director and the sociable, optimistic marketing and sales director on good terms. The marketing and sales director's greatest skill is in discovering original ways for the company to create its own unique selling point from new market trends. Some of his ideas are clever adaptations of successes he has previously seen, heard or read about. The depth of his marketing knowledge amazes his colleagues.

Production director

The company has production units and suppliers worldwide. The production director spends much of his time managing the supply chain. New product launches take very careful planning. He turns the company's ideas and plans into saleable products. A personality profile is given in Table 23.9.

As expected from his personality profile, the production director manages his part of the business by meetings and committees. While he does not often openly lose his temper,

Table 23.8 Marketing and sales director's personality profile

PERSONALITY CHARACTERISTICS	ASSESSMENT HEADINGS
A) DISPOSITIONS	
1) Sociability	High
2) Emotion	High
3) Ambition	High
4) Curiosity	High
5) Uncertainty	
B) DIMENSIONS	
1) Facts / possibilities	More facts than possibilities
2) Group / independent	Broadly equal
3) Own-feelings / others'-feelings	Pronounced others'-feelings
4) Wide-interests / narrow-interests	Pronounced wide-interests
5) Optimistic / pessimistic	Pronounced optimistic
C) SOCIAL ROLES	
1) Communicator	
2) Cost-benefit calculator	
3) Educator	
4) Innovator	High
5) Lifelong learner	
6) Organiser	
7) Accumulator	High
D) INTELLIGENCE SPAN	High

Table 23.9 Production director's personality profile

PERSONALITY CHARACTERISTICS	ASSESSMENT HEADINGS
A) DISPOSITIONS	
1) Sociability	High
2) Emotion	High
3) Ambition	High
4) Curiosity	
5) Uncertainty	
B) DIMENSIONS	
1) Facts / possibilities	Pronounced facts
2) Group / independent	Pronounced group
3) Own-feelings / others'-feelings	Pronounced own-feelings
4) Wide-interests / narrow-interests	Broadly equal
5) Optimistic / pessimistic	Broadly equal
C) SOCIAL ROLES	
1) Communicator	
2) Cost-benefit calculator	High
3) Educator	
4) Innovator	
5) Lifelong learner	
6) Organiser	High
7) Accumulator	
D) INTELLIGENCE SPAN	High

he demands high standards and anyone who lets him down is soon aware of his displeasure. He is full of praise for those who do a good job for the company. He insists that his staff must plan for every realistic eventuality. He checks all the important details himself. His pronounced facts trait leads to a planned lifestyle, but his high sociability means he has some flexibility. He is passionately loyal to the company, its values and objectives. He is widely respected for the way he puts the company's interests before his own. If there is an unpleasant job that needs to be done, he is the first to volunteer. His comments are often blunt. He is prepared to upset people to make his views clear. He is very good at assessing the short-term and long-term advantages and disadvantages of proposals. He is a forceful person whom people naturally follow. His one difficulty, which requires the chairperson's attention from time to time, is his dislike of the chief executive's changes to some of the company's customs and traditions.

Research director

The research director is responsible for developing new products in a rapidly changing high technology market. A personality profile is given in Table 23.10.

No one disputes the brilliance of the research director's new ideas, which have been a significant factor in the company's success. As we might expect from his personality profile, he is always asking questions and looking for answers. He personally carries out the important tests and experiments. He becomes very excited about a new project but is soon likely to lose interest once its correctness has been proved. His work is somewhat spontaneous and chaotic, and some of his ideas have proved totally impractical. He insists on following his own interests rather than company objectives. Fortunately, he

Table 23.10 Research director's personality profile

PERSONALITY CHARACTERISTICS	ASSESSMENT HEADINGS
A) DISPOSITIONS	
1) Sociability	Low
2) Emotion	High
3) Ambition	High
4) Curiosity	Very high
5) Uncertainty	
B) DIMENSIONS	
1) Facts / possibilities	Pronounced possibilities
2) Group / independent	Pronounced independent
3) Own-feelings / others'-feelings	Broadly equal
4) Wide-interests / narrow-interests	Broadly equal
5) Optimistic / pessimistic	Broadly equal
C) SOCIAL ROLES	
1) Communicator	
2) Cost-benefit calculator	
3) Educator	
4) Innovator	Very high
5) Lifelong learner	
6) Organiser	
7) Accumulator	
D) INTELLIGENCE SPAN	Very high

deeply admires the chairperson, who uses his considerable influence to redirect the research director's efforts to company goals. The organisational problems in the research department (it was becoming increasingly chaotic) were solved when the chairperson insisted on appointing a suitable deputy with a facts lifestyle. After some initial conflict, which took the best efforts of the chairperson and human resources director to sort out, the research director and his deputy successfully coexist with their largely separate areas of responsibility.

The calculation of the executive committee's personality characteristics and assessment headings

In order to establish that the executive committee members have complementary personality profiles, we need to calculate the executive committee's personality characteristics and assessment headings. In Table 23.11, the personality characteristics and assessment headings of the seven committee members are added together to arrive at the executive committee totals, which are in the right hand column. In a number of cases, the high assessment heading for dispositions includes some very high examples. For some of the dispositions and dimensions, the total is less than seven, although this is the membership of the executive committee. The reason is that for dispositions and dimensions the average and broadly equal assessment headings are omitted from the total. For example, as regards emotion, the total is less than seven because the committee members with the average assessment headings (the finance director and the human resources director) are excluded. All social roles which are identified have high or very high assessment headings. All the committee members have high or very high intelligence.

We now show that the executive committee members'

Table 23.11 The executive committee's personality characteristics and assessment headings

PERSONALITY CHARACTERISTICS AND ASSESSMENT HEADINGS	Chairperson	Chief executive	Finance	Human resources	Marketing/ sales	Production	Research	TOTAL
A) DISPOSITIONS								
High sociability	✓	✓		✓	✓	✓		5
Low sociability			✓				✓	2
High emotion		✓			✓	✓	✓	4
Low emotion	✓							1
High ambition	✓	✓	✓	✓	✓	✓	✓	7
High curiosity					✓		✓	2
B) DIMENSIONS (PRIMARY TRAITS)								
Facts	✓		✓		✓	✓		4
Possibilities		✓		✓			✓	3
Group	✓		✓	✓		✓		4
Independent		✓					✓	2
Own-feelings		✓				✓		2
Others'-feelings	✓			✓	✓			3
Wide-interests	✓				✓			2
Optimistic	✓				✓			2
Pessimistic			✓					1
C) SOCIAL ROLES								
Communicator	✓							1
Cost-benefit calculator	✓	✓	✓			✓		4
Educator		✓						1
Innovator					✓		✓	2
Lifelong learner	✓							1
Organiser	✓	✓				✓		3
Accumulator					✓			1
D) INTELLIGENCE SPAN	✓	✓	✓	✓	✓	✓	✓	7

personality characteristics and assessment headings satisfy the requirements for complementary personality profiles. These requirements for each personality characteristic (see Tables 23.1 to 23.3) are given in brackets after each heading. We follow the order of the personality profile.

Sociability

(Requirement: a majority who are average or higher)
The executive committee has five members with high sociability and two members with low sociability. The majority with high sociability supply the internal social relationships which bind the committee together. However, there are two committee members who can work effectively by themselves.

Emotion

(Requirement: a majority who are average or higher)
The members with high emotion outnumber those with low emotion by four to one. This ensures the committee has the passion to succeed. However, the highly influential chairperson has low emotion. Consequently, he will not panic in a crisis and will be able to guide the committee through difficult situations.

Ambition

(Requirement: all high or very high)
Every member's high or very high ambition unites the committee and contributes to its unity of purpose. The approval of the unit's objectives by independent, external experts could avoid the danger of excessive ambition.

Curiosity

(Requirement: one or two high or very high, if required by the task)
The research director's curiosity disposition is very high and

the marketing and sales director's curiosity disposition is high. One or two other members with above average curiosity about the business would be useful.

Uncertainty
(Requirement: none in normal circumstances)
A high or very high uncertainty disposition does not appear and has no relevance to this business.

Ways of thinking
(Requirement: at least half with a primary facts trait and a significant minority with a primary possibilities trait)
The primary facts trait is in a majority, which means that the facts trait (and, therefore, reasoning based on information) guides the decision making process. However, the three members with a primary possibilities trait are highly influential, and their views contribute very significantly to all decisions.

Ways of interacting
(Requirement: at least half with a primary group trait and a significant minority with a primary independent trait)
The primary group traits outnumber the primary independent traits by four to two. If we assume a consultative decision making process, then the committee's objectives and values have priority over committee members' individual objectives and values. However, there are enough members with a primary independent trait to challenge a committee consensus.

Ways of relating
(Requirement: a similar number of primary own-feelings traits and primary others'-feelings traits)
There are two members with primary own-feelings traits

and three with primary others'-feelings traits. Accordingly, in arriving at a committee decision, some members largely ignore the feelings of others, while other members are strongly influenced by other people's feelings. Both points of view can be presented for the committee's assessment. In this way, the committee is able to reach an appropriate decision.

Social interests
(Requirement: depends on the task)
Only the chairperson and the marketing and sales director deal significantly with the outside world and have primary wide-interests traits.

Attitudes to the future
(Requirement: one or two members with a primary optimistic trait and a member with a primary pessimistic trait)
There are two primary optimistic traits and one primary pessimistic trait. This is sufficient to present each alternative viewpoint (optimism and pessimism) to the committee without causing wider conflict between members.

Communicators
(Requirement: possibly one or more high or very high, depending on the unit's need to communicate information)
The chairperson has a high communicator social role and explains the executive committee's decisions to internal and external audiences.

Cost-benefit calculators
(Requirement: several high or very high are essential)
There are three high and one very high cost-benefit calculators.

Educators
(Requirement: possibly one or more high or very high,
depending on the task)
The chief executive has a high educator social role.

Innovators
(Requirement: one high or very high is essential for each
area which can gain from innovation)
The marketing and sales director has a high innovator social
role and the research director a very high innovator social
role.

Lifelong learners
(Requirement: possibly one or more high or very high,
depending on the task)
The chairperson has a high lifelong learner social role.

Organisers
(Requirement: one high or very high is essential)
The chairperson and chief executive are very high in the
organiser social role, while the production director is high in
the organiser social role.

Accumulators
(Requirement: possibly one or more high or very high,
depending on the task)
The marketing and sales director has a high accumulator
social role.

Intelligence span
(Requirement: high intelligence is essential for all members.
One or more members, for example an innovator, need to be
of very high intelligence)
All the committee members have at least high intelligence,

which is essential for this committee. In fact, both the finance director and research director are of very high intelligence.

Conclusion

The preceding analysis reveals that the executive committee members have complementary personality profiles. Together, the executive committee members have all the necessary personality characteristics and assessment headings to perform successfully the executive committee's functions. Moreover, each member of the committee has a competent personality profile. Individual committee members have the appropriate personality profile with which to complete successfully their tasks. If sub-committees are used for specific tasks, the members of these smaller units also need complementary and competent personality profiles for their delegated tasks.

UNIT PERSONALITY CHARACTERISTICS AND ASSESSMENT HEADINGS CHART

We can represent the unit members' personality characteristics and assessment headings by four diagrams (see Figs. 23.1 to 23.4). We call these four diagrams a 'unit personality characteristics and assessment headings chart'.

A UNIT PERSONALITY CHARACTERISTICS AND ASSESSMENT HEADINGS CHART represents the unit members' personality characteristics and assessment headings by four diagrams.

In Figs. 23.1 to 23.4, the personality characteristics and assessment headings are taken from the executive committee example (see Table 23.11).

A) Dispositions

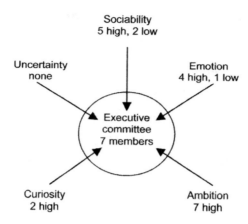

Fig. 23.1 The unit's number of high and low assessment headings for dispositions (high includes very high)

B) Dimensions (primary traits)

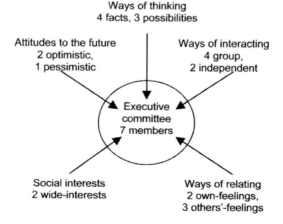

Fig. 23.2 The unit's number of primary traits in each dimension

C) Social roles

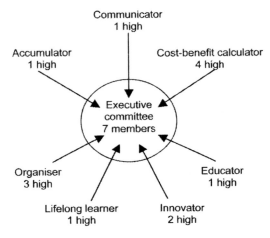

Fig. 23.3 The unit's number of high assessment headings for social roles (high includes very high)

D) Intelligence span

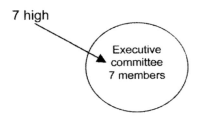

Fig. 23.4 The unit's number of high (includes very high) assessment headings for intelligence span

UNIT MEMBERSHIP

Flexible personality characteristics

Unit members with flexible personality characteristics can sometimes be very useful. In particular, members who can use both traits of a dimension are able to adjust their contributions according to the changing requirements of the company. For example, if tough decisions are necessary regarding employees, a member who is broadly equal in the ways of relating can adopt an own-feelings point of view. Members with flexible personality characteristics who are self-aware are especially able to alter their contribution to suit the needs of the moment.

Unit members with similar personality characteristics and assessment headings

The selection of unit members with similar personality characteristics and assessment headings for cooperative decision making on the grounds that they work well together is a serious mistake. On the contrary, people with similar personality characteristics and assessment headings often upset each other. Moreover, units consisting of members with similar personality characteristics and assessment headings lack the variety of attitudes, points of view and talents to solve complex problems. For example, a unit consisting entirely of people with low sociability will fail to form sufficient internal social relationships and, for that reason, will be ineffective. A unit of members with pronounced or very pronounced facts traits may be good at planning but will lack imagination and fail to respond immediately to crises. It will also be unable to take advantage of unexpected opportunities. A unit of members with pronounced or very pronounced possibilities traits may cope well with crises but will disregard facts, be ineffective at planning and find decision making difficult where they lack experience. A unit of those with a pronounced or very pronounced group trait will be too anxious to achieve a consensus and lack self-criticism. A unit of those with a pronounced or very pronounced independent trait will fail to agree common objectives. The list can be continued (see Table 23.12).

Table 23.12 Some weaknesses of decision making units with members having the same pronounced or very pronounced trait

PRONOUNCED OR VERY PRONOUNCED TRAIT	EXAMPLES OF UNIT'S DECISION MAKING WEAKNESSES
Facts	Lack imagination and fail to respond immediately to crises
Possibilities	Disregard facts, ineffective at planning and find decision making difficult where they lack experience
Group	Too anxious to achieve a consensus and lack self-criticism
Independent	Fail to agree common objectives
Own-feelings	Ignore the feelings of other people
Others'-feelings	Pay too much attention to the feelings of other people
Wide-interests	Ignore problems within the unit
Narrow-interests	Pay insufficient attention to the consequences for the wider community
Optimistic	Assume good outcomes
Pessimistic	Assume bad outcomes

CONCLUSION

R Meredith Belbin has carried out very important and highly innovative research into effective management teams in action. His exceptionally valuable conclusions from many years' practical studies of teamwork are consistent with the contents of this chapter. Many businesses are managed by executive committees which have some similarities to the committee described in the example. Nevertheless, the complementary and competent personality profiles described in the example are only one alternative among many others which could be equally effective. Executive committees necessarily differ, because each member is unique. Moreover, the requirements of different industries affect the membership of executive committees. Nevertheless, the starting point is always the unit members' individual job specifications, which supply the minimum personality characteristics and assessment headings for competent performance in that job. Appropriate personality characteristics and assessment headings are then added to each member's job specification in a way which creates complementary personality profiles for the unit.

KEY POINTS

A DECISION MAKING UNIT consists of individuals who together solve problems, reach conclusions, take actions and review progress.

Individuals have COMPLEMENTARY PERSONALITY PROFILES when, as members of a decision making unit, they have together the necessary personality characteristics and assessment headings for effective, cooperative decision making.

COMPETENT PERSONALITY PROFILES enable unit members to carry out successfully their individual tasks. The unit members' personality characteristics and assessment headings satisfy their job specifications.

A UNIT PERSONALITY CHARACTERISTICS AND ASSESSMENT HEADINGS CHART represents the unit members' personality characteristics and assessment headings by four diagrams.

Effective decision making units have:

- Six to ten members
- Members with complementary and competent personality profiles

YOUR NOTES (OPTIONAL AT YOUR OWN RISK)

In view of your personality profile, what kind of work in a decision making unit would be most suitable for you?

Have you observed an effective decision making unit? Why were the individuals in the unit able to cooperate effectively together?

Have you observed an ineffective decision making unit? Why were the individuals in the unit unable to cooperate effectively together?

Prepare a unit personality characteristics and assessment headings chart for a decision making unit with which you are familiar.

Examine the personality profiles of the two individuals in Table 23.13. Explain why these two individuals may have initially chosen to cooperate together in an area of common interest. Also explain why you might expect that these two people would be unable to cooperate together successfully for any period of time. A suggested answer is at the end of this section.

Table 23.13 Personality profiles of two individuals

PERSONALITY CHARACTERISTICS	FIRST	SECOND
A) DISPOSITIONS		
1) Sociability	Below average	Low
2) Emotion	Very high	Very high
3) Ambition	Very high	Very high
4) Curiosity	Very high	Very high
5) Uncertainty	–	–
B) DIMENSIONS		
1) Facts / possibilities	V. P. possibilities	V. P. facts
2) Group / independent	P. independent	V. P. independent
3) Own-feelings / others'-feelings	P. own-feelings	V. P. own-feelings
4) Wide-interests / narrow-interests	P. narrow-interests	P. narrow-interests
5) Optimistic / pessimistic	Broadly equal	P. optimistic
C) SOCIAL ROLES		
1) Communicator	High	High
2) Cost-benefit calculator	–	Average
3) Educator	High	High
4) Innovator	Very high	Very high
5) Lifelong learner	–	–
6) Organiser	High	Absent
7) Accumulator	–	High
D) INTELLIGENCE SPAN	Very high	High

Note: V. = Very; P. = Pronounced

Suggested answer

The two individuals may initially be interested in each other's ideas because:

- They share very high curiosity and a very high innovator social role.
- Their very different ways of thinking may inspire each other, especially if they are working on the same problems.

These two individuals would be unable to cooperate together for any period of time because:

- They have a pronounced or very pronounced independent trait. They would be interested in their own objectives and values rather than those of the other person.
- They have a pronounced or very pronounced own-feelings trait. They would take little account of each other's feelings and this could lead to conflicts.
- As a result of the preceding two points, they would, in time, have little interest in each other's original ideas, which come from their very high innovator social roles.
- Their very high individual (independent trait) ambition would also lead to conflict, which would be made more intense by their very high emotion.
- They have below average or low sociability and would, therefore, work alone.
- Their very conflicting lifestyles (routine and spontaneous), which arise from their very different ways of thinking, would lead to disagreements.

Carl Jung has some similarities to the first individual, and Sigmund Freud has some similarities to the second individual (see Chapter 17, example number two and Chapter 17, exercise number three). After initial cooperation, the two men had major disagreements.

FURTHER NOTES

CHAPTER 24

The evidence

So far, the evidence for the personality theory proposed in this work is largely based on individuals, although Chapter 23 is consistent with the practical research of R Meredith Belbin into effective teamwork. This evidence is insufficient on its own to prove the theory is true. Fortunately, research has been carried out into the personality of millions of people over many years. The outcome of this comprehensive research is that there are four main sources of compelling evidence in favour of the personality characteristics. These are:

- Carl Jung's theory of personality types
- Raymond B Cattell's (1905–98) language research into the description of personality (the sixteen personality factors and the related 'big five' personality factors)
- The Gallup Organization's research into its thirty-four personality strengths
- Medical diagnostic criteria used for assessing certain children's behaviour

Towards the end of the chapter, the evidence in favour of the principle of autonomy is also discussed.

CARL JUNG'S CONTRIBUTION

Carl Jung was an innovative and important researcher into personality. Nevertheless, as he acknowledged, his ideas were incomplete in that they classified only a small minority of people into eight personality types. Moreover, his explanation of his ideas was often obscure and confusing. Nevertheless, Jung's theory is still widely used. Jung largely developed his theory of personality to make sense of his experiences with patients. Jung's personality theory can be explained as being about people's attitudes to their external environment, to objects and to each other. In his view, the fundamental attitude was with regard to the environment. The other two attitudes (to objects and to each other) affected the focus of the fundamental attitude (to the external environment).

Jung saw people's attitude to the external environment as two contrasting personality types. The first personality type looked outwards to the external environment, while the second contrasting personality type looked inwards away from the external environment to the internal environment of the mind. If we were to select a combination of personality characteristics and assessment headings that looked outwards to the external environment, we would probably select high or very high sociability, a pronounced or very pronounced group trait, a pronounced or very pronounced wide-interests trait and a pronounced or very pronounced optimistic trait. If we were to select a combination of personality characteristics and assessment headings that looked inwards to the internal environment of the mind, we would probably select low or very low sociability, a pronounced or very pronounced independent trait, a pronounced or very pronounced narrow-interests trait and a pronounced or very pronounced pessimistic trait. Jung made these choices. To describe these contrasting aspects of personality, he introduced into psychology the ideas of the extravert (the personality that looks outwards) and the introvert (the personality that looks inwards).

Jung also observed that people can have contrasting attitudes to objects. They can either know the details about objects (facts) or imagine the uses to which objects can be put (possibilities). Consequently, if we were to select the personality characteristic that described people's attitudes to objects, we would select the ways of thinking (the facts and possibilities traits). Jung also realised that people can have contrasting attitudes to each other. They can base their decisions either on their own feelings or on their perceptions of other people's feelings. If we were to select the personality characteristic that described these attitudes to each other, we would select the ways of relating (the own-feelings and others'-feelings traits). Again, we would be, in effect, following Jung.

The main source of Jung's ideas was his twenty years' experience as a doctor treating mental illness. He was much influenced in his thinking by Friedrich Schiller (1759–1805) and William James (1842–1910). With regards to people's attitudes to objects, Jung realised that Sigmund Freud's very pronounced facts trait contrasted greatly with his own very pronounced possibilities trait. This comparison of Freud's very pronounced facts trait with his own very pronounced possibilities trait suggested to Jung people's contrasting attitudes to objects (the ways of thinking dimension). Jung's concept of people's attitudes to each other was largely taken from William James, who had earlier identified tough-minded people and tender-minded people (in effect, the ways of relating dimension).

We can now summarise Jung's ideas using the theory presented in this book. The basis of Jung's personality theory was to divide personality into three distinct aspects, each aspect containing two contrasting features of personality. We can explain in our concepts Jung's three distinct aspects of personality as consisting of:

1. A disposition (sociability) plus a bundle of three dimensions (ways of interacting, social interests and attitudes to the future)
2. A dimension (ways of thinking)
3. A further dimension (ways of relating)

Table 24.1 summarises Jung's personality theory using personality characteristics and assessment headings.

Table 24.1 Jung's personality theory summarised using personality characteristics and assessment headings

ASPECTS OF PERSONALITY	THE CONTRASTING FEATURES OF JUNG'S THREE ASPECTS SUMMARISED USING PERSONALITY CHARACTERISTICS AND ASSESSMENT HEADINGS	
First	High sociability, pronounced group, pronounced wide-interests and pronounced opti-mistic (extravert)	Low sociability, pro-nounced independent, pronounced narrow-interests and pronounced pessimistic (introvert)
Second	Pronounced facts	Pronounced possibilities
Third	Pronounced own-feelings	Pronounced others'-feelings

Note: the high and low assessment headings also include very high and very low, and the pronounced assessment headings also include very pronounced

Jung's personality theory suffers from some fundamental weaknesses. The first is incompleteness, which he acknowledged. He also very unhelpfully combined together the sociability disposition and a bundle of three dimensions in his distinction between extravert and introvert. Our previous examples from famous or well-known people have already shown that the principle of autonomy applies to all dispositions and dimensions. In other words, the disposition and dimensions which Jung included together under the extravert and introvert concepts have no necessary connection with each other. They are simply present in some individuals.

The weakness of Jung's theory is clear if we compare the relevant parts of Winston Churchill's and John D Rockefeller's personality profiles with Jung's extravert personality type. Some of Churchill's and Rockefeller's personality characteristics and assessment headings have similarities to those of Jung's extravert. However, their personality characteristics and assessment headings do not fully satisfy Jung's extravert definition. Churchill had a pronounced independent trait instead of the extravert's pronounced or very pronounced group trait. Rockefeller had a pronounced narrow-interests trait rather than the extravert's pronounced or very pronounced wide-interests trait (see Table 24.2). It is a basic weakness in Jung's theory that Churchill and Rockefeller are outside his system. Accordingly, as Jung admitted, his theory only applied to a small number of individuals.

From his extravert and introvert distinction and his two additional aspects (equivalent to the ways of thinking and ways of relating), Jung created eight personality types. Using his and our concepts, we can identify the eight types as:

Table 24.2 A comparison of Jung's extravert type with the relevant personality characteristics and assessment headings of Winston Churchill and John D Rockefeller

JUNG'S EXTRAVERT TYPE	CHURCHILL	ROCKEFELLER
High or very high sociability	High sociability	Above average sociability
Pronounced or very pronounced group	Pronounced independent	Very pronounced group
Pronounced or very pronounced wide-interests	Very pronounced wide-interests	Pronounced narrow-interests
Pronounced or very pronounced optimistic	Pronounced optimistic	Very pronounced optimistic

1. Extravert, pronounced or very pronounced facts and own-feelings traits
2. Extravert, pronounced or very pronounced facts and others'-feelings traits
3. Extravert, pronounced or very pronounced possibilities and own-feelings traits
4. Extravert, pronounced or very pronounced possibilities and others'-feelings traits
5. Introvert, pronounced or very pronounced facts and own-feelings traits
6. Introvert, pronounced or very pronounced facts and others'-feelings traits
7. Introvert, pronounced or very pronounced possibilities and own-feelings traits

8. Introvert, pronounced or very pronounced possibilities and others'-feelings traits

Jung's concepts and explanations were difficult to understand. Nevertheless, his contribution was influential and important. His ideas, which have been used by millions of people, are impressive evidence for the sociability disposition and the five dimensions.

RAYMOND B CATTELL'S CONTRIBUTION

Cattell was a tireless researcher into personality. His ambition was to identify the key features of personality. His method was to examine the ordinary usage of the English language with regard to personality. The plausible argument was that descriptions of personality found in ordinary language would identify the main aspects of personality. His work was important, because it revealed the aspects of personality described by everyday language. His research into language produced sixteen personality 'factors'. Each factor consisted of two contrasting aspects of personality.

There are, however, some very serious weaknesses in using everyday language in personality research. The language we use in day-to-day conversations about personality is inexact. In particular, the same word can be used to describe different personality characteristics. For example, we could describe people as 'conscientious', which could mean they have either a primary facts trait (a planned lifestyle) or a primary group trait (do their duty) or both. Again, we could describe people as 'active', which could mean they have high sociability, high uncertainty, a primary optimistic trait or a primary wide-interests trait or any combination of these four personality characteristics and assessment headings. In order to avoid this difficulty, the eighteen personality characteristics used in this book to describe personality have been defined precisely. Finally, personality researchers using ordinary language have to combine many words together in order to arrive at a manageable number of personality factors. These words often have different meanings in different situations.

There are further difficulties with using ordinary language. Some of the words used to describe personality are specific to particular cultures. Furthermore, ordinary language confuses personality characteristics with reactions to life experiences and the results of self-awareness. Finally, social situations are also relevant to many descriptions of personality. For example, whether a person is deferential, cooperative, submissive or obedient can be the result of their circumstances or life experiences.

Nevertheless, research using ordinary language has proved useful in identifying many aspects of personality. Accordingly, the theory of personality proposed in this work needs to account simply and easily for the results from this language research. In fact, the hunter-gatherer theory of personality successfully meets this challenge. For example, four of Cattell's sixteen factors are, in effect, the four dispositions of sociability, emotion, ambition and uncertainty. Six more factors can be related to four of the five dimensions. The dimension missing from Cattell is the social interests dimension. Two more of Cattell's factors are connected to the innovator and organiser social roles. Another factor is equivalent to a primary facts trait and the intelligence span. In this way, thirteen of Cattell's sixteen factors can be matched to eleven of the personality characteristics. The remaining three of Cattell's personality factors can be matched to a suitable combination of dispositions, dimensions and the intelligence span.

Cattell's sixteen personality factors can be combined together into just five factors. Personality researchers agree that these five personality factors capture much of the information included in Cattell's original sixteen factors. Moreover, the existence of these five factors has been repeatedly proved by comprehensive research over many decades. These five factors are known by several names, for example the big five personality traits or five factor model. We shall call these five factors the 'big five factors'. As is the case with Cattell's sixteen factors, there is no theoretical basis to the big five factors. They also suffer from all the weaknesses of using everyday language in personality research. Additionally, the words used to describe four of the big five factors can be seen as making judgements about people. The big five factors are also in error because they conflict with the principle of autonomy. The big five factors are:

- Extraversion
- Openness to experience
- Conscientiousness
- Agreeableness
- Neuroticism

In identifying the big five factors, researchers are incorrectly dividing the personality characteristics into five groups based on five themes of personality. Words with similar meanings define each theme. Thus, the extraversion theme is 'positive' emotions, for example happiness, enthusiasm and excitement. However, there is no common origin in personality characteristics or life experiences to 'positive' emotions. For example, above average or higher sociability, above average or higher uncertainty, a primary wide-interests trait and a primary optimistic trait can give rise to different kinds of 'positive' emotions. Many different kinds of life experiences, the effect of which varies according to personality, can also give rise to 'positive' emotions. Consequently, there are many different types of extraverts who are found with many different life experiences.

The big five personality factors and their associated themes are:

- Extraversion – 'positive' (pleasant) emotion (for example happiness, enthusiasm and excitement)
- Openness to experience – questioning, creative and original
- Conscientiousness – take planned, sensible decisions
- Agreeableness – cooperative and sympathetic
- Neuroticism – 'negative' (unpleasant) emotion (for example anxiety, apprehension and anger)

The big five personality factors and their associated themes can be broadly matched to dispositions, traits and social roles in a straightforward manner:

- Extraversion – 'positive' (pleasant) emotion (for example happiness, enthusiasm and excitement) – high sociability, high uncertainty, pronounced wide-interests and pronounced optimistic
- Openness to experience – questioning, creative and original – high curiosity, pronounced possibilities and high innovator social role
- Conscientiousness – take planned, sensible decisions – pronounced facts and high cost-benefit calculator social role
- Agreeableness – cooperative and sympathetic – pronounced group and pronounced others'-feelings
- Neuroticism – 'negative' (unpleasant) emotion (for

example anxiety, apprehension and anger) – high emotion, pronounced pessimistic, negative life experiences and low self-worth

The high and low assessment headings also include very high, very low and absent, while the pronounced assessment headings also include very pronounced.

The big five personality factors, their associated themes and their approximate equivalents in dispositions, traits and social roles are summarised in Table 24.3. However, the explanation of the big five personality factors in terms of personality characteristics can only be approximate because of the weaknesses in the big five methodology. In some cases, the reconciliation between the personality characteristics and assessment headings and the big five factors is a matter of judgement about which reasonable people may differ. The big five personality factors can be matched to four of the dispositions (ambition is excluded), the five dimensions and two of the social roles (cost-benefit calculator and innovator).

The big five definition and Jung's definition of extravert are both similar in terms of personality characteristics and assessment headings. However, the big five definition includes a high uncertainty disposition but excludes a pronounced group trait, while Jung's definition excludes a high uncertainty disposition but includes a pronounced group trait (see Table 24.4). Consequently, a big five extravert seeks excitement from unpredictable situations, while Jung's extravert looks outwards towards the community. However, both types of extravert enjoy the company of others, take an interest in society and are cheerful. Winston Churchill satisfies the big five definition of an extravert. Both definitions of an extravert suffer from the same weakness in that they contradict the principle of autonomy. Accordingly, the combination of dispositions, traits and assessment

Table 24.3 The big five factors and their associated themes matched to personality characteristics and assessment headings

BIG FIVE PERSONALITY FACTOR	BIG FIVE PERSONALITY THEME	APPROXIMATE EQUIVALENT IN PERSONALITY CHARACTERISTICS AND ASSESSMENT HEADINGS
Extraversion	'Positive' (pleasant) emotion (for example happiness, enthusiasm and excitement)	High sociability, high uncertainty, pronounced wide-interests and pronounced optimistic
Openness to experience	Questioning, creative and original	High curiosity, pronounced possibilities and high innovator
Conscientiousness	Take planned, sensible decisions	Pronounced facts and high cost-benefit calculator
Agreeableness	Cooperative and sympathetic	Pronounced group and pronounced others'-feelings
Neuroticism	'Negative' (unpleasant) emotion (for example anxiety, apprehension and anger)	High emotion, pronounced pessimistic, negative life experiences and low self-worth

Note: the high and low assessment headings also include very high, very low and absent, while the pronounced assessment headings also include very pronounced

Table 24.4 A comparison of the big five definition of extravert with Jung's definition of extravert in terms of personality characteristics and assessment headings

BIG FIVE DEFINITION OF EXTRAVERT	JUNG'S DEFINITION OF EXTRAVERT
High sociability	High sociability
High uncertainty	–
–	Pronounced group
Pronounced wide-interests	Pronounced wide-interests
Pronounced optimistic	Pronounced optimistic

NOTE ON NEUROTICISM

Some people because of their personality profiles or circumstances have more difficulty than others in coping with life in an industrial society. Accordingly, they experience more negative life experiences and have lower feelings of self-worth than average. These 'negative' emotions are increased by high or very high emotion and a pronounced or very pronounced pessimistic trait. These people are described by the neuroticism factor. For example, women are more disadvantaged than men in an industrial society and are, therefore, more likely than men to be described by the neuroticism factor. However, a person can have high or very high emotion and a pronounced or very pronounced pessimistic trait and yet lack 'negative' emotion because of their positive life experiences, for example Charles Darwin and J R R Tolkien.

headings in the big five extraversion factor means, as supporters of the big five personality factors readily admit, that many 'extraverts' cannot be fitted into the big five definition.

In fact, the big five personality factors consist of ten contrasting aspects of personality. Thus, the contrasting aspect to extraversion ('positive' emotion) is introversion (absence of 'positive' emotion). The contrasting personality characteristics in the big five factor of extraversion, using dispositions, traits and assessment headings, is from high sociability, high uncertainty, pronounced wide-interests and pronounced optimistic to low sociability, low uncertainty, pronounced narrow-interests and pronounced pessimistic (see Table 24.5).

Some further supporting evidence to the conclusions of the hunter-gatherer personality theory is also found in the work of H J Eysenck (1916–97), although Eysenck's work is inconsistent with the principle of autonomy. Eysenck's research identified three components to personality, which can be matched to four of the big five factors in a straightforward manner. Two of Eysenck's components of personality are, in effect, the extraversion and neuroticism factors of the big five. Eysenck's third component of personality is largely the contrasting aspect to a combination of the conscientiousness and agreeableness factors. The big five openness to experience factor is missing from Eysenck's components.

The hunter-gatherer personality theory explains in a straightforward manner both Cattell's sixteen factors and the big five personality factors. The sixteen and big five personality factors can be matched to the personality characteristics and assessment headings, which is powerful evidence for the truth of the hunter-gatherer theory of personality.

Table 24.5 The contrasting aspects of the big five personality factors explained by personality characteristics and assessment headings

THE BIG FIVE PERSONALITY FACTORS	THE CONTRASTING ASPECTS OF THE BIG FIVE PERSONALITY FACTORS EXPRESSED IN TERMS OF PERSONALITY CHARACTERISTICS AND ASSESSMENT HEADINGS	
	From:	To:
Extraversion	High sociability, high uncertainty, pronounced wide-interests and pronounced optimistic	Low sociability, low uncertainty, pro-nounced narrow-interests and pronounced pessimistic
Openness to experience	High curiosity, pronounced possibilities and high innovator	Low curiosity, pronounced facts and low innovator
Conscientiousness	Pronounced facts and high cost-benefit calculator	Pronounced possibilities and low cost-benefit calculator
Agreeableness (see Chapter 11)	Pronounced group and pronounced others'-feelings	Pronounced independent and pronounced own-feelings
Neuroticism	High emotion, pronounced pessimistic, negative life experiences and low self-worth	Low emotion, pronounced optimistic, positive life experiences and high self-worth

Note: the high and low assessment headings also include very high, very low and absent, while the pronounced assessment headings also include very pronounced

THE GALLUP ORGANIZATION'S CONTRIBUTION

During the last thirty years, The Gallup Organization has carried out very important research into personality, based on over two million interviews. Their exceptionally valuable research was carried out worldwide and covered both sexes. The Gallup Organization's innovative research identifies the thirty-four most common aspects of personality (strengths) found in successful people. The Gallup Organization's thirty-four strengths are consistent with sixteen of the eighteen personality characteristics. The Gallup Organization's research is important evidence in favour of the hunter-gatherer theory of personality.

EVIDENCE FROM CHILDREN'S MEDICAL DIAGNOSTIC CRITERIA

Medical diagnostic criteria for children identify four personality types. These four personality types are thought to be universal among children worldwide. Boys are estimated to outnumber girls in these personality types by very approximately four to one. Hunter-gatherer personality theory explains these four childhood personality types in a straightforward manner. However, children's personalities are highly variable. Although a child's personality may come broadly within one of the four types identified by medical criteria, each child is unique. Each child represents its own combination of dispositions, dimensions, social roles, intelligence span, assessment headings and life experiences.

Personality type number one
The first personality type is described medically in highly unfavourable words as inattentive, careless, lacking

persistence, disorganised and easily distracted. This is consistent with children whose personality characteristics and assessment headings include below average or lower sociability and a very pronounced possibilities trait.

Personality type number two

The second personality type is described medically in highly unfavourable words as undisciplined, impulsive, fidgety, overactive, noisy and talkative. This is consistent with children whose personality characteristics and assessment headings include above average or higher sociability and a very pronounced possibilities trait.

Personality type number three

The third personality type covers approximately half the children included in types one and two. They are described medically in highly unfavourable words as short-tempered, argumentative, provocative, defiant, angry, resentful, easily provoked and vindictive. This is consistent with children whose personality characteristics and assessment headings include very high emotion and a very pronounced possibilities trait. In some cases, the defiance and resentment may result from a frustrated pronounced or very pronounced group trait or unachieved ambitions, as in the case of Adolf Hitler. Equally, the defiance may arise from a pronounced or very pronounced independent trait or a pronounced or very pronounced own-feelings trait. Much would depend on a child's life experiences. For example, with regard to the own-feelings trait, this defiance may be expressed as unkindness to others in response to negative life experiences, for example being deceived by companions.

Personality type number four

The fourth personality type is described medically in highly unfavourable words as socially isolated, lacking spontaneity, lacking empathy, highly stereotyped, excessively routine in lifestyle and mannerisms, and preoccupied with isolated facts. This is consistent with children whose personality characteristics and assessment headings are very low sociability, very pronounced facts and very pronounced own-feelings. The addition of a very pronounced independent trait and a very pronounced narrow-interests trait may reinforce the effects of the other personality characteristics and assessment headings.

Boy / girl ratio

The larger number of boys compared to girls in all these four childhood personality types may be explained by the ways of relating dimension. Research has consistently shown that more males than females have a primary own-feelings trait and more females than males have a primary others'-feelings trait. The increased frequency of a primary others'-feelings trait in females is plausibly explained by their function in childrearing. The girls' more frequent primary others'-feelings trait would tend to make them more willing to respect the wishes of other children and adults. Accordingly, girls would be, on average, more obedient and less obviously disruptive than boys. Consequently, girls would tend to be excluded from these four types. The ease with which the theory of personality proposed in this book explains these four medical diagnostic criteria is further strong evidence in the theory's favour.

THE EVIDENCE IN FAVOUR OF THE PRINCIPLE OF AUTONOMY

The most important evidence in favour of the principle of autonomy is Cattell's language research. His analysis of ordinary language revealed no words which describe individuals who have the same combination of personality characteristics and assessment headings. Therefore, enough individuals do not have the same combination of personality characteristics and assessment headings for a word describing them to have been created within ordinary language. The same conclusion also follows from The Gallup Organization's research. Furthermore, researchers who wish to describe individuals with the same combination of personality characteristics and assessment headings have been forced to invent their own words to describe these personality types, for example Jung's extravert and introvert. Consequently, at this level of detail, there are no combinations of personality characteristics and assessment headings which appear to occur much more frequently than suggested by the operation of chance. Otherwise, there would be names for them within ordinary language. Accordingly, the principle of autonomy seems to be substantially true. Naturally, the principle of autonomy can be tested to a higher level of accuracy by further specific research.

CONCLUSION

The very large amount of evidence from Jung, Cattell (the sixteen personality factors), the big five factors, The Gallup Organization and medical diagnostic criteria provides a highly compelling case for the theory of personality proposed in this work. The highly specific predictions about personality which follow from the hunter-gatherer theory of personality are consistent with all of this research into many millions of individuals over several generations. Moreover, all these predictions from hunter-gatherer personality theory, including the existence of dispositions, dimensions, social roles and intelligence span, can be rigorously investigated and tested by further research.

The philosopher of science, Karl Popper (1902–94), argued convincingly that a scientific theory is different from other kinds of explanation because of its refutability. The very detailed predictions that can be made from the hunter-gatherer theory of personality meet this scientific criterion of refutability. The hunter-gatherer theory of personality has successfully explained many famous, complex and very different individuals. It has also explained the results of research into many millions of people. So far, this theory of personality has successfully overcome all these severe tests.

CHAPTER 25

Conclusion

People's personalities consist of eighteen personality characteristics, which are the five dispositions, five dimensions, seven social roles and intelligence span. By the use of seven assessment headings with these eighteen characteristics, we can prepare a personality profile to describe each individual's personality. We gain an even better understanding by also considering a person's life experiences and self-awareness. These are large claims but ones which you can now judge for yourself from your own knowledge and experience.

We all benefit from an improved insight into our own personalities. We need to understand the situations in which we are likely to do well and those in which we are likely to make mistakes. We have to know when we should seek advice and when we should cooperate with other people. Our decisions and choices are expressions of our personalities. Accordingly, in order to take a major decision sensibly, each of us needs to be self-aware of our own personality profile and life experiences. This is an essential first step in making the right choices.

Another benefit of the personality profile is in our

relationships with other people. We work better with colleagues, customers and suppliers if we understand their personalities. The fact that other people behave differently from us does not mean they are being deliberately difficult or foolish. More often than not, they are revealing that they do not share some or all of our personality characteristics and assessment headings. A sound understanding of other people's personalities provides important opportunities, for example we can identify the tasks that our colleagues can do really well.

We have seen how the personality profile is a unique and comprehensive assessment system for employee recruitment, selection and promotion. The accurate assessment of personality and the correct job specification are essential to the successful matching of people and career opportunities, as well as a vital aid to career choice. Personality assessment is already widely used in business and government and is uncontroversial. The personality profile represents a major breakthrough in the assessment of personality.

The personality of individuals with the most influence in an organisation is of great importance. Their personalities need to be understood by themselves and by others. For example, the senior people in an organisation need a self-awareness of the limitations which arise out of their personality characteristics and assessment headings. As we have seen, there are significant risks attached to some personality characteristics and assessment headings. For example, executives with pronounced or very pronounced possibilities traits can supply inspiring aims. However, they may take decisions of great importance while being very largely ignorant of the relevant facts. In these circumstances, there is the danger of making significant mistakes. Executives who have a pronounced or very pronounced facts trait may reach decisions after a careful study of all the information.

However, they are inflexible and unable to change their plans quickly. For this reason, sudden crises may be handled badly. They may also miss the likelihood of something new altering the situation. Again, this may lead to significant mistakes.

The personality profile is an essential tool for the creation of well-managed, correctly staffed and effective decision making units. These units offer very important opportunities for improved work performance and results. The selection of members with complementary and competent personality profiles ensures these units have the personality resources needed to take the best decisions.

Perhaps to our surprise, we now know that we have the personalities of hunter-gatherers who lived in close-knit, economically-interdependent extended families. The extraordinary variety and complexity of our personalities is a consequence of the instability of nature. In the past, the world's climate has changed dramatically in a few decades. Our powers of reasoning and the variety of our personalities give us the adaptability to cope with this sudden change. With the help of this adaptability, we have, so far, overcome the challenges of intense environmental variability and succeeded in occupying the whole world. Today, we still face many challenges, but the remarkable variety of our personalities is one of our greatest resources.

Glossary

ACCUMULATORS collect and retain experiences.

The AMBITION DISPOSITION describes the strength of people's determination to achieve something.

ASSESSMENT HEADINGS, PERSONALITY see PERSONALITY ASSESSMENT HEADINGS

The ATTITUDES TO THE FUTURE DIMENSION describes an individual's expectations with regard to forthcoming events.

AUTONOMY, PRINCIPLE OF see PRINCIPLE OF AUTONOMY

BROADLY EQUAL TRAITS within a dimension have approximately the same influence on an individual's personality.

BUNDLE, PERSONALITY see PERSONALITY BUNDLE

CHARACTERISTICS, PERSONALITY see PERSONALITY CHARACTERISTICS

CHECKLIST, PERSONALITY see PERSONALITY CHECKLIST

COMBINATION, PERSONALITY TRAIT see PERSONALITY TRAIT COMBINATION

COMMUNICATORS express or transmit information, ideas or emotion to individuals and communities.

COMMUNITIES are any kind of organisation to which people belong.

COMPETENT PERSONALITY PROFILES enable unit members to carry out successfully their individual tasks. The unit members' personality characteristics and assessment headings satisfy their job specifications.

Individuals have COMPLEMENTARY PERSONALITY PROFILES when, as members of a decision making unit, they have together the necessary personality characteristics and assessment headings for effective, cooperative decision making.

COST-BENEFIT CALCULATORS assess whether the benefit achieved from a future course of action is worth the cost.

The CURIOSITY DISPOSITION describes the strength of people's determination to learn and understand more by asking questions and seeking answers.

A DECISION MAKING UNIT consists of individuals who together solve problems, reach conclusions, take actions and review progress.

DIMENSIONS, PERSONALITY see PERSONALITY DIMENSIONS

DISPOSITIONS, PERSONALITY see PERSONALITY DISPOSITIONS

EDUCATORS assist people in gaining the knowledge and skills which improve their understanding and performance.

The EMOTION DISPOSITION describes the strength of people's reactions in response to either other people or events.

FACTS LIFESTYLE, VERY PRONOUNCED see VERY PRONOUNCED FACTS LIFESTYLE

The FACTS TRAIT describes solving problems and making decisions by using information.

FLEXIBLE PERSONALITY CHARACTERISTICS describe individuals who have average, above average or below average assessment headings for most of their dispositions and broadly equal or more than assessment headings for most of their traits.

The GROUP TRAIT describes a person's interaction with communities which is based on the communities' objectives and values.

People with HIGH SELF-AWARENESS have considerable insight into their personalities and life experiences.

HIGH SELF-WORTH describes individuals' satisfaction with their achievements.

The HUNTER-GATHERER PERSONALITY HYPOTHESIS states that people have the highly varied, complex personality profiles of reasoning, social, nomadic, tool-using, omnivorous hunter-gatherers adapted to intense environmental variability.

The INDEPENDENT TRAIT describes a person's interaction with communities which is based on that person's own objectives and values.

INNOVATORS solve problems or make decisions through the application of original ideas.

The INTELLIGENCE SPAN is a measure of people's ability to solve problems and take decisions.

INTERACTING, WAYS OF see WAYS OF INTERACTING

A JOB SPECIFICATION identifies the minimum personality characteristics and assessment headings needed for competent performance in that job.

LIFE EXPERIENCES are the significant events in an individual's personal history.

LIFE EXPERIENCES, NEGATIVE see NEGATIVE LIFE EXPERIENCES

LIFE EXPERIENCES, POSITIVE see POSITIVE LIFE EXPERIENCES

LIFELONG LEARNERS acquire additional skills and knowledge on a continuing basis.

LIFESTYLE, VERY HIGH SOCIABILITY see VERY HIGH SOCIABILITY LIFESTYLE

LIFESTYLE, VERY LOW SOCIABILITY see VERY LOW SOCIABILITY LIFESTYLE

LIFESTYLE, VERY PRONOUNCED FACTS see VERY PRONOUNCED FACTS LIFESTYLE

LIFESTYLE, VERY PRONOUNCED POSSIBILITIES see VERY PRONOUNCED POSSIBILITIES LIFESTYLE

LIFESTYLES are some people's usual ways of behaving which also reveal their personality.

People with LOW SELF-AWARENESS have little insight into their personalities and life experiences.

LOW SELF-WORTH describes individuals' dissatisfaction with their achievements.

The NARROW-INTERESTS TRAIT describes a person's interest in events and issues which affect them directly.

NEGATIVE LIFE EXPERIENCES decrease a person's feelings of wellbeing.

An OCCUPATIONAL JOB SPECIFICATION for an organisation lists the minimum personality characteristics and assessment headings required for competent performance in that occupation.

The OPTIMISTIC TRAIT describes the attitudes of a person who expects good outcomes.

ORGANISERS, with their natural dignity and authority, bring about cooperation between individuals and between communities.

The OTHERS'-FEELINGS TRAIT describes a person's relationships with other individuals in which that person's perceptions of other individuals' needs and feelings take priority.

The OWN-FEELINGS TRAIT describes a person's relationship with other individuals in which that person's own needs and feelings take priority.

PERSONALITY is a description of a person's character which reveals both similarities and differences to other individuals.

PERSONALITY ASSESSMENT HEADINGS are used to describe an individual's location on each of the eighteen personality characteristics.

A PERSONALITY BUNDLE is two or more personality dimensions considered together.

The PERSONALITY CHARACTERISTICS are the eighteen principal features of our personality and consist of the five dispositions, five dimensions, seven social roles and intelligence span. Each personality characteristic is a scale, which measures, for example, intensity, influence or ability.

PERSONALITY CHARACTERISTICS, FLEXIBLE see FLEXIBLE PERSONALITY CHARACTERISTICS

PERSONALITY CHARACTERISTICS, WELL-DEFINED see WELL-DEFINED PERSONALITY CHARACTERISTICS

The PERSONALITY CHECKLIST is a list of the eighteen personality characteristics.

PERSONALITY DIMENSIONS are descriptions of those parts of personality which consist of two conflicting aspects.

PERSONALITY DISPOSITIONS are five universal characteristics of personality and consist of sociability, emotion, ambition, curiosity and uncertainty.

The PERSONALITY PROFILE is a list of the eighteen personality characteristics with an assessment heading attached to each personality characteristic.

A PERSONALITY PROFILE CHART represents an individual's personality profile by seven diagrams.

PERSONALITY PROFILES, COMPETENT see COMPETENT PERSONALITY PROFILES

PERSONALITY PROFILES, COMPLEMENTARY see COMPLEMENTARY PERSONALITY PROFILES

A PERSONALITY TRAIT COMBINATION is two or more traits from different dimensions considered together.

PERSONALITY TRAITS are the two conflicting aspects within each personality dimension.

The PESSIMISTIC TRAIT describes the attitudes of a person who expects bad outcomes.

POSITIVE LIFE EXPERIENCES increase a person's feelings of wellbeing.

POSSIBILITIES LIFESTYLE, VERY PRONOUNCED see VERY PRONOUNCED POSSIBILITIES LIFESTYLE

The POSSIBILITIES TRAIT describes solving problems and making decisions by imagining and assessing alternative outcomes.

A PRIMARY TRAIT of a dimension is the trait of that dimension which has the greater influence on an individual's personality.

The PRINCIPLE OF AUTONOMY applies to dispositions, dimensions, social roles and the intelligence span. There is no consistent, predictable relationship connecting dispositions, dimensions, social roles and the intelligence span to each other. In other words, the dispositions, dimensions, social roles and the intelligence span are all independent of each other.

PROFILE CHART, PERSONALITY see PERSONALITY PROFILE CHART

PROFILE, PERSONALITY see PERSONALITY PROFILE

RELATING, WAYS OF see WAYS OF RELATING

A SECONDARY TRAIT of a dimension is the trait of that dimension which has the lesser influence on an individual's personality.

SELF-AWARENESS OF PERSONALITY is people's understanding of their own personality profiles and life experiences.

SELF-AWARENESS, HIGH see HIGH SELF-AWARENESS

SELF-AWARENESS, LOW see LOW SELF-AWARENESS

SELF-WORTH is people's assessment of their own achievements.

SELF-WORTH, HIGH see HIGH SELF-WORTH

SELF-WORTH, LOW see LOW SELF-WORTH

The SOCIABILITY DISPOSITION describes the extent to which people spend their time associating with companions.

SOCIAL ATTITUDES describe the combined effect of a person's ways of interacting dimension and ways of relating dimension.

The SOCIAL INTERESTS DIMENSION describes the scope of an individual's concerns about society.

SOCIAL ROLES are specific functions undertaken by those

community members who have the relevant resources.

SPAN, INTELLIGENCE see INTELLIGENCE SPAN

SPECIFICATION, JOB see JOB SPECIFICATION and OCCUPATIONAL JOB SPECIFICATION

THINKING, WAYS OF see WAYS OF THINKING

TRAIT, PRIMARY see PRIMARY TRAIT

TRAIT, SECONDARY see SECONDARY TRAIT

TRAIT COMBINATION, PERSONALITY see PERSONALITY TRAIT COMBINATION

TRAITS, BROADLY EQUAL see BROADLY EQUAL TRAITS

TRAITS, PERSONALITY see PERSONALITY TRAITS

The UNCERTAINTY DISPOSITION describes the intensity of people's enjoyment which derives from the tension of unpredictable outcomes.

A UNIT PERSONALITY CHARACTERISTICS AND ASSESSMENT HEADINGS CHART represents the unit members' personality characteristics and assessment headings by four diagrams.

A VERY HIGH SOCIABILITY LIFESTYLE is one of working and relaxing with others through social contact.

A VERY LOW SOCIABILITY LIFESTYLE is one of working and relaxing by oneself.

A VERY PRONOUNCED FACTS LIFESTYLE is very planned and routine.

A VERY PRONOUNCED POSSIBILITIES LIFESTYLE is very spontaneous and varied.

The WAYS OF INTERACTING DIMENSION describes people's attitudes towards their communities.

The WAYS OF RELATING DIMENSION describes people's priorities with regard to their dealings with other individuals.

The WAYS OF THINKING DIMENSION describes how individuals solve problems and make decisions.

WELL-DEFINED PERSONALITY CHARACTERISTICS describe individuals who have high, very high, low or very low assessment headings for most of their dispositions and pronounced or very pronounced assessment headings for most of their traits.

The WIDE-INTERESTS TRAIT describes a person's interest in events and issues which affect society as a whole.

Further reading

Alanbrooke, Field Marshal Lord., 2002. *War Diaries 1939 – 1945*. London: Phoenix Press.

Bair, D., 2004. *Jung: a biography*. London: Little, Brown.

Baldwin, N., 2001. *Edison: Inventing the Century*. Chicago: The University of Chicago Press.

Belbin, R. M., 1993. *Team Roles at Work*. Oxford: Elsevier Butterworth-Heinemann.

Belbin, R. M., 2004. *Management Teams: Why They Succeed or Fail*. 2nd ed. Oxford: Elsevier Butterworth-Heinemann.

Best, G., 2002. *Churchill a study in greatness*. London: Penguin Books.

Boswell, J., 1893. *Life of Johnson*. London: MacMillan and Co., Limited.

Brian, D., 1996. *Einstein: A Life*. New York: John Wiley & Sons, Inc.

Buckingham, M., Clifton, D. O., 2005. *Now, Discover Your Strengths: How to develop your talents and those of the people you manage*. London: Pocket Books.

Bullock, A., 1991. *Hitler and Stalin: Parallel Lives*. London: HarperCollins Publishers.

Bullock, A., 1962. *Hitler: a study in tyranny*. London: Penguin Books Ltd.

Calaprice, A., Lipscombe, T., 2005. *Albert Einstein: a biography*. Westport, CT: Greenwood Press.

Carpenter, H., Tolkien, C., 1981. *Letters of J. R. R. Tolkien.* London: George Allen & Unwin Ltd.

Carpenter, H., 1978. *J. R. R. Tolkien: A biography.* London: George Allen & Unwin Ltd.

Chaplin, C., 2003. *My Autobiography.* London: Penguin Books Ltd.

Chernow, R., 2004 *Titan: The Life of John D. Rockefeller, Sr.* 2nd ed. New York: Vintage Books.

Churchill, W. S., 1959. *My Early Life: A Roving Commission.* London: Fontana Books.

Darwin, C., 1929. *Autobiography of Charles Darwin.* Cambridge: Icon Books Ltd.

Desmond, A., Moore, J., 1992. *Darwin.* London: Penguin Books.

Ellis, J. J., 1998. *American Sphinx: The Character of Thomas Jefferson.* New York: Vintage Books.

Franklin, B., 1996. *The Autobiography of Benjamin Franklin.* Mineola, NY: Dover Thrift Editions.

Goldsmith, B., 2005. *Obsessive Genius: The Inner World of Marie Curie.* London: Phoenix.

Hayman, R., 2002. *A Life of Jung.* London: Bloomsbury Publishing Plc.

Isaacson, W., 2004. *Benjamin Franklin: An American Life.* New York: Simon & Schuster Paperbacks.

Jenkins, R., 2002. *Churchill.* London: Pan Macmillan Ltd.

Jones, E., 1964. *The Life and Work of Sigmund Freud.* London: Penguin Books.

Jung, C. G., Storr, A., 1998. *The Essential Jung.* 2nd ed. London: Fontana Press.

Jung, C. G., Jaffé, A., 1995. *Memories, Dreams, Reflections.* London: Fontana Press.

Lacey, R., 1986. *Ford: the men and the machine.* London: William Heinemann Ltd.

O'Brian, P., 2003. *Picasso: A Biography.* London:

HarperCollinsPublishers.

Renshaw, P., 2004. *Franklin D. Roosevelt.* Harlow: Pearson Education Limited.

Robinson, D., 1985. *Chaplin: His Life and Art.* London: William Collins Sons and Co. Ltd.

Service, R., 2005. *Stalin: A Biography.* London: Pan Books.

Solomon, M., 1996. *Mozart: a life.* New York: Harper Perennial.

Speer, A., 1971. *Inside the Third Reich.* London: Sphere Books Limited.

Westfall, R. S., 1994. *The Life of Isaac Newton.* Cambridge: Press Syndicate of the University of Cambridge.

Wheen, F., 2000. *Karl Marx.* London: Fourth Estate Limited.

Index